1,000,000 Books

are available to read at

Forgotten Books

www.ForgottenBooks.com

Read online
Download PDF
Purchase in print

ISBN 978-1-330-28369-1
PIBN 10012898

This book is a reproduction of an important historical work. Forgotten Books uses state-of-the-art technology to digitally reconstruct the work, preserving the original format whilst repairing imperfections present in the aged copy. In rare cases, an imperfection in the original, such as a blemish or missing page, may be replicated in our edition. We do, however, repair the vast majority of imperfections successfully; any imperfections that remain are intentionally left to preserve the state of such historical works.

Forgotten Books is a registered trademark of FB &c Ltd.
Copyright © 2018 FB &c Ltd.
FB &c Ltd, Dalton House, 60 Windsor Avenue, London, SW19 2RR.
Company number 08720141. Registered in England and Wales.

For support please visit www.forgottenbooks.com

1 MONTH OF
FREE
READING

at
www.ForgottenBooks.com

By purchasing this book you are eligible for one month membership to ForgottenBooks.com, giving you unlimited access to our entire collection of over 1,000,000 titles via our web site and mobile apps.

To claim your free month visit:
www.forgottenbooks.com/free12898

* Offer is valid for 45 days from date of purchase. Terms and conditions apply.

English
Français
Deutsche
Italiano
Español
Português

www.forgottenbooks.com

Mythology Photography **Fiction**
Fishing Christianity **Art** Cooking
Essays Buddhism Freemasonry
Medicine **Biology** Music **Ancient Egypt** Evolution Carpentry Physics
Dance Geology **Mathematics** Fitness
Shakespeare **Folklore** Yoga Marketing
Confidence Immortality Biographies
Poetry **Psychology** Witchcraft
Electronics Chemistry History **Law**
Accounting **Philosophy** Anthropology
Alchemy Drama Quantum Mechanics
Atheism Sexual Health **Ancient History**
Entrepreneurship Languages Sport
Paleontology Needlework Islam
Metaphysics Investment Archaeology
Parenting Statistics Criminology
Motivational

JAMES CHALLEN & SON, Publishers, Philadelphia,
No. 25 South Sixth Street.

HOW TO ENJOY LIFE;
OR,
PHYSICAL AND MENTAL HYGIENE.
BY WILLIAM M. CORNELL, M. D.

FELLOW OF THE MASSACHUSETTS MEDICAL SOCIETY, PERMANENT MEMBER OF THE AMERICAN MEDICAL ASSOCIATION, PROFESSOR OF PHYSIOLOGY AND HYGIENE, MEMBER OF THE PENNSYLVANIA HISTORICAL SOCIETY, CORRESPONDING MEMBER OF THE NEW ENGLAND HISTORIC-GENEALOGICAL SOCIETY, ETC.

This work explains the reciprocal action of the body and mind, and shows how much human *happiness* depends upon their nice adjustment and the knowledge of their agency. The author is well known as a lecturer on Physiology and Hygiene and the treatment of Nervous Diseases, and having devoted years of study to this department, is enabled to present a popular treatise of great value and interest to every student, Professional man, and in fact to every family. It embodies the principles and facts contained in his able work, "Clerical Health," which was universally commended by the Press.

Flexible Cover, 75 *cents; Cloth,* $1.00.

Books in Press.

LIFE OF ROBERT RAIKES, Founder of Sunday Schools. By Dr. W. M. Cornell.

THE SABBATH MADE FOR MAN. By Dr. W. M. Cornell.

OBSERVATIONS ON EPILEPSY AND NERVOUS DISEASES. By Dr. W. M. Cornell.

INHALATION IN DISEASES OF THE AIR-PASSAGES AND LUNGS. By Dr. W. M. Cornell.

CONSUMPTION PREVENTED AND TREATED. By Dr. W. M. Cornell.

PREMATURE OLD AGE. By Rev. Hubbard Winslow, D. D. And **PHYSICAL EDUCATION.** By Walter Channing, M. D. Edited by Dr. W. M. Cornell, with a Treatise on the Laws of Health.

HOW TO ENJOY LIFE;

OR,

PHYSICAL AND MENTAL HYGIENE.

HOW TO ENJOY LIFE:

OR,

PHYSICAL AND MENTAL HYGIENE.

BY

WILLIAM M. CORNELL, M.D.

PHILADELPHIA:
JAMES CHALLEN & SON.
NEW YORK: SHELDON & CO. BOSTON: CROSBY, NICHOLS,
LEE & CO. CINCINNATI: RICKEY, MALLORY & CO.
CHICAGO: S. C. GRIGGS & CO.
1860.

PUBLIC
HEALTH
LIBRARY

Entered, according to Act of Congress, in the year 1860, by

WILLIAM M. CORNELL,

in the Clerk's Office of the District Court of the United States for the Eastern District of Pennsylvania.

STEREOTYPED BY J. FAGAN. . . . . PRINTED BY I. ASHMEAD.

TO

REV. EBENEZER BURGESS, D.D.,

OF DEDHAM, MASSACHUSETTS,

WHO FIRST

ADVISED ME TO WRITE UPON THESE SUBJECTS;

AND WHO

KINDLY AIDED IN ITS PUBLICATION,

THIS WORK

IS

𝔥umbly and gratefully 𝔦nscribed

BY

THE AUTHOR.

CONTENTS.

CHAPTER I.

Ill Health of Students and Clergymen — Necessity of Medical and Hygienic Knowledge — Wonderful Formation of the Human Body—Design Manifested—Beauty of the Human Countenance — The Mind united to the Body — God's Natural and Moral Laws—Violations of them justly punished—Harmony between God's Government of Nature and of Men — A Christian Duty to preserve Health — Value of Health to a Professional Man — Culture of the Mind at the expense of the Body .... PAGE 21-31

CHAPTER II.

Loss of Health — Study under Improper Stimulants and at Improper Times—Relaxation necessary—Cicero—Not Study soon after Eating, nor late at Night — Clergyman's Sore Throat — Ascribed to Various Causes—Disease of the Throat only Symptomatic — Its Real Cause — The Symptoms — Where seated — Local Treatment of Little Use — The Sick often in Error as to their Disease 32-44

CHAPTER III.

Travelling for Health — Vanity from Travel — Injury from Travelling — Agriculture Better — Fashionable Watering Places — Periodical Dissipation — Pleasures of Home — Taking Children to Hotels and Places of Fashionable Resort — Absence of Clergymen — Objections to sending Consumptive Patients abroad —The North should be preferred to the South—Old Treatment for Consumption — New Better — Good Advice and some Medicine often Useful — Mutual Confidence and Respect necessary to Success in any Profession 45-61

CHAPTER IV.

Mental Excitement—Its Effect on the Body—Blanches the Hair—The Miser—Vain Ambition—Fastidious Hearers—Meddlesome Parishioners—A City Call—Hope and Disappointment—Failure of Success—Trouble in the Parish—Dismission—Variety of Preaching—Anxiety for his Family—Poverty—The Apostle Paul—A True and a False Ambition............ 62–77

CHAPTER V.

The word Nervous — Nervous Diseases Numerous — The People imitate the Minister—Mesmerism—Spiritualism—A Suspicious Temper—Faith a Good Medicine — Eating too much — Evils produced by a Nervous Clergyman upon his Family — Remedy for Nervous Diseases—Illustration in an Accommodating Clergyman—*How* the Nerves Act—Action of the Mind on the Body—Cause of Traits of Character—Some Never Change—Others Always — Dr. Abernethy's Prescription — Value of Health — Causes which Destroy Peace—Small Salaries—Pay by Orders—Life made up of Little Things—Much that is Pleasant in the Life of a Good Clergyman................................ 78–103

CHAPTER VI.

Locality Important to Usefulness — Frequent Removals — Cause originated with the Clergy — The People soon learned it — Sleepy Hearers—Advertising Ministers—No Excuse—Ministerial Tones — Sermons too Nice — President Wayland — Archbishop Usher 104–114

CHAPTER VII.

Enjoyment of Life dependent on Speech — The Voice — Where formed — Power of Habit in Speaking — Its Sounds — Much Culture required to make an Orator—Power and Beauty of the Human Voice — Aphonia — Clergyman's Sore Throat — Treatment—Written Sermons—Supposed Ignorance of the Clergy on the Common Affairs of Life—The Literary Lady 115–125

CONTENTS. ix

CHAPTER VIII.

Misery or Happiness from the Feet — The Feet — Their Proper Use and Management—The Anatomy of the Foot—The Turks and their Feet—Boots and Shoes—Cotton and Woollen Stockings—Sympathy between the Feet and other Organs 126-132

CHAPTER IX.

Insanity the Child of Civilization and Education—Clergymen and all Students should be acquainted with Diseased Minds—Their Special Charge over the Sick — Mather and Burroughs — Insanity Hereditary—Many are Insane on one Thing—The True Cause of Millerism and Spiritualism — Men have supposed themselves Beasts, Dogs, Cats, Wolves—Cruden—Cunning of the Insane in Concealing their Malady — Improved Treatment of the Insane — Their Love of Freedom — One Case — How to prevent Insanity and escape Mental Decay — Combine Study with Amusement — The Poet and the Philosopher — Religious Excitement sometimes causes Insanity — Cause of Fatuity in Old Age—Why called Lunacy—Insanity usually comes on Gradually — Incipient Symptoms of Insanity — Drs. Parker and Gilman 133-158

CHAPTER X.

Our System of Education — The Body should receive Attention First — No Necessity for Early Mental Pressure — Meaning of Education—The kind of Schools for Little Children—Physical Training to keep pace with Mental — Moral and Religious Instruction—A Parent's Opinion—No Study out of School—Rewards for Intellectual Superiority Condemned — For Moral Conduct Approved 159-180

CHAPTER XI.

Value of Opium as a Medicine—Injury by its Habitual Use—Its Effects—Difficulty of breaking off its Use—Ministers, Lawyers, and Ladies use it — Use of it in England — De Quincey, the Opium Eater 181 189

CHAPTER XII.

The Skin — Scarf — True — Pigment — Capillaries — Perspiratory Tubes — Of the Skin — Sympathy between, and other Organs — Hygienic Uses of Water — The Cold, Plunge, Shower, Sponge, Bath — Caution in using the Cold Bath — Quotation from Dr. J. C. Warren — The Warm Bath — Mr. Wilson — Dr. Combe — Whitefield's Remarks — Water the best drink — The Feet and Water 190–218

CHAPTER XIII.

The Poets on Sleep — A Source of Enjoyment — Sleep a Mystery — A Means of preserving Health — Want of Sleep a cause of Disease and of Insanity — When, where, and how long should we sleep — Napoleon — John Wesley on Sleep — Curiosities of Sleep 219–238

CHAPTER XIV.

The Ear — Importance of Hearing — Curious Formation of the Ear — Transmission of Sound — Difference of the External Ear in Man and other Animals — Deafness Hereditary — Propagation of Sound — Injury from tinkering the Ear — Hearing by the Teeth 239–245

CHAPTER XV.

The Eye — Beauty — Design — Education of — Rules for Preserving the Sight — Effects of Darkness — Spectacles — Importance of Vision — Waywardness of the Blind — Bad effect of Tobacco on the Eye — Of Reading in Cars — Of Quack Oculists 246–257

CHAPTER XVI.

Amusements — Man superior to other Animals — The Hand — Speech — Laughter — Fun — Individuality of Countenance — Reading Countenances on the Street — Enjoyments from the Imagination — Natural and Artificial Appetites — The true province of Body and Mind — Skating — Ball — Billiards — Bagatelle ... 258–270

CONTENTS.

CHAPTER XVII.

The Passions Defined — Effect on the System — Love Letters — Nelson's—Napoleon's—Difference between Man and Woman a chief source of Happiness—Love—Choice of a Wife—Importance of Good Health in a Wife—Paul a Widower—Sir James Mackintosh's Wife 271–282

CHAPTER XVIII.

Ventilation—Effect of Air on the Blood—Scrofula—Impure Air in Church — Beds — Food, Animal and Vegetable — Hot Bread and Butter—Fruit—Homœopathic Diet—Bad Cooking—Quantity of Food in Winter and Summer for the Laboring and the Sedentary 283–297

CHAPTER XIX.

Biblical Rules relating to Health—Bible designed for all—Blood the Life — Hygiene of the Bible — Bread — Fish — Shell-fish — Swine's Flesh — Mosaic Ritual of Health, founded in Nature —Daniel and his Companions—Prescribed Care for the Sick—Cleanliness—Hebrew Law of Marriage—Hereditary Diseases — The proper use of Stimulants 298–308

CHAPTER XX.

Longevity — Instances of Longevity among Philosophers, Physicians, and Clergymen — Greatest among active men, Farmers, Soldiers, Hunters—Religion, a Companion of Longevity—The body must die, the spirit live 309–316

CHAPTER XXI.

Sympathy in the Human Body—Spare Diet—Cornaro—Brandy and Rheumatism — Cases in Point 317–322

CHAPTER XXII.

Tobacco—Neatness a Gain—The Deacon and the Merchant—Tobacco ruins Health; defiles everything — Its Expense — The Theological Student 323–328

CHAPTER XXIII.

Extract from an English writer — Health promoted by Conversation — English Dinners productive of Health — "Take me on Leather" — Clergymen should understand something about the Business of Life — Example of Paul; of the Great Teacher—A Successful Minister 329–335

CHAPTER XXIV.

Historical Sketch of the Union of Theology and Medicine — The Jewish Priests made Doctors—Luke and the Apostles follow the example of Christ, their Master — Medical Books written by Clergymen before the sailing of the "Mayflower" — Clerical Missionary Physicians — John Wesley's Primitive Physic. 336–343

CHAPTER XXV.

Health of Clergymen's Wives — The Health of a Clergyman's Wife depends much on her Husband — More Clergymen's Wives die than Clergymen — Anxiety, Care, and Cruel Treatment on the part of Parishioners, often a cause — Reflections on this great evil — Want of proper Education a cause — Conclusion with an Eastern Tale 344–360

INTRODUCTION.

Without health no man can be happy, find earthly enjoyment, or properly perform the duties of life. The valetudinarian is uncomfortable to himself, and annoying to those around him. Health of body and mind is the mainspring of action — the wheel that puts all the machinery of the world in motion. It is generally considered to be the special boon of heaven. To some extent, this is true, as one man inherits from his parents a much better constitution than another. But experience has proved, that far more is depending upon proper care, than on original stamina, as to health and enjoyment. One of the greatest evils which young people have to struggle with is, not *knowing how to take proper care of themselves*. They do a thousand things to their injury, which they would not, did they know how to manage themselves. On these points they need instruction, and a text-book on this subject seems as necessary as one upon Grammar, or History, or Natural Philosophy. The diffusion of so much knowledge among the young as shall enable them to preserve their health of both body and mind, is their only road to safety, happiness, and usefulness. Take the young *Lady*. She desires *beauty*. She is anxious to look and appear well. To attain this end, she expends much upon dress and cosmetics. But no artificial adornments or lotions can bestow upon her anything that will approximate to the glow, and hue, and *beauty* of health. How vast the contrast between the paint of art and the ruddy countenance and delightful blush of health! The former we detest, while the latter calls forth our highest admiration. Health was personified in the mythology of the ancients by the goddess HYGEIA. They pointed out for her abode places remarkable for sylvan beauty — the mountain side, the shady grove, the undulating hill and dale, with the musical ripple of the meandering brook; and all gently fanned by the Western zephyr, or Southern breeze. No bloody sacrifices smoked upon her altar, — but Oriental fragrance perfumed her atmosphere—the flowers of nature strewed her path—the music of the shepherd's pipe and of rustic maidens celebrated her festivals. She, indeed, had temples reared to her in the cities; but her most favored resort was in the gymnasium and the palestra. Here she trained her youth to elegance of person, strength of body, and purity of morals. The rules of Hygeia guide to the best code of laws — to civil, literary and popular freedom — to pure and elastic minds. The old Greek poet, Ariphron, of Sycion, has a beautiful little poem, which conveys our ideas of the *blessings* of health. It will bear the following translation:

> "Hygeia! most revered of the blest,
> With thee I'd live of all my life the rest;
> Be thou to me a willing fellow-guest.
> If aught there be in riches, of delight,
> Or, what is godlike most to human sight,
> In kingly rule, or in the stolen rite
> Of love, which we to gain with toil have striven;
> If any other joy to men by heaven,
> Or breathing space from strife be ever given,
> Through thee they flourish all, Hygeia blest!
> Through thee are graced with a Spring-like zest;
> Nor any man, deprived of thee, is blest."

In introducing, at the present time, to the public a book upon the reciprocal agency of matter and mind, as found in the compound species, the human race, we cannot but feel that, however imperfect the work, the *subject* is one of momentous importance. As the work is now very much enlarged, improved (as the writer believes), and rendered more general in its application, and more vitally connected with *Human Enjoyment*, it may claim the perusal of all classes in the community. Still, in this *Introduction*, it may not be inappropriate to present to the reader a few of the favorable notices of the press, of that portion of it which was first published under the title of "Sketches on Clerical Health;" especially, as many of the points herein referred to, are illustrated by reference to the *Clergy*, as fitting representatives of the literary classes.

The Rev. Professor F. D. Huntington, D. D., in the *Monthly Religious Magazine*, of which he was then editor, said: "There is great ingenuity and good sense in this compact and interesting treatise. Dr. Cornell has made a faithful and conscientious study of his subject, bringing to it a large observation and shrewd faculties. Of the questions treated in it belonging to medical science we cannot competently judge; but it is a saddening thought what miseries there are in the bodies and families of ministers, and what disasters to parishes and to the Church at large, which this practical advice might forestall or remove. We have been surprised at the number of important details which the author has found room to bring to profitable notice within so small a space. A part of the counsel is as much needed by laymen and parishioners as by the clergy. And any one who wishes to make his pastor a cheap and useful present, can hardly make a better selection." The *Boston Journal* said: "In this pamphlet-volume, which can be carried in the pocket, have been collected a series of very sensible articles upon physiological subjects, designed especially for the perusal and benefit of clergymen, but many of which are applicable to every professional man. The subjects treated upon are numerous, including the voice, the eye, use of tobacco, longevity, use of water, mental excitement, &c. It is a work of practical value, and is forcibly written." The *Christian Register* remarked: "This series of articles will be found full of wise and interesting suggestions for students, clergymen, and also the laity, for all are concerned in the welfare of 'Saints and their Bodies,' directly or indirectly." The *Happy Home* contained the following: "There is more common sense in this series of articles on the health of clergymen, than we have ever seen compressed into a volume of five times its size. Every clergyman should read it. Their people, too, will find many valuable hints in it. The last article is on clergymen's wives, and is well worth the price of the work." The *Boston Traveller* said: "We commend to our readers especially, the chapters on Travelling for Health, and the one upon Opium." The *Presbyterian Banner* had the following: "Dr. Cornell is a sprightly and vigorous writer. He has had much experience, and been a close observer. His book may be read with very great advantage." The *Boston Daily Transcript* said: "We advise all our readers to procure a copy, especially, if they are going on a journey, as it can be carried in the pocket and will beguile a leisure moment." The *Philadelphia Christian Observer* said: "It is a book for the times." Rev. Samuel Findley, editor of the *Educator*, Pittsburg, Pa., says: "An excellent book, on a most important subject, written in a racy flowing style, by one who proves himself to be master of his theme. Full of instructive thoughts, and hygienic suggestions, enforced by illustrative facts and appropriate anecdotes, the reader's attention is kept awake and active, and he moves rapidly from page to page with an interest such as holds enchained the reader of an interesting narrative or a thrilling novel. We like such a book on such a theme, and wish we could induce every clergyman in the land to read it. In his enumeration of the causes of ill health in clergymen, he abounds in well-directed sallies of witty sarcasm, at which we are compelled to make free use of our risible functions, sometimes at the expense of the clergymen, and sometimes of the congregation. It ought to have a place in every minister's and teacher's library."

Among many private letters of commendation, the following may be selected; the first from Rev. Joseph H. Jones, D. D., of Philadelphia, who has written an excellent book treating upon some of the same subjects: "I have read your work on 'Clerical Health' with *uncommon* interest and edification. It evinces much reading and a judicious selection of facts which you have arranged with skill and effect. On the subject of *pork*, some will think that you *Judaize* — especially those of your readers who are fond of it. Your last chapter in relation to minister's *wives* is worthy of being published as a tract, and should be put into every family of Christendom. The truths you have published will have a value while ministers so live as to *need* your *counsels* and deserve your *admonition*." The second is from Professor John D. Philbrick, Superintendent of the Boston Public Schools: "I have read your 'Clerical Health' with pleasure as well as profit. It is a book calculated to do much good. It contains many excellent suggestions respecting the *preservation of health*, which would be found useful not only to the clergy, but to teachers, parents, and the laity generally. Hygiene is too much neglected among us: I am grateful to you for this effort to instruct the community upon this important subject, and I most cheerfully commend your book as one which deserves a wide circulation."

Physical and mental hygiene is intimately connected with our highest interest and purest enjoyment. It forms a part of the will and government of God, which cannot be set aside or violated with impunity. The will of God as revealed to man is found engraved upon his *works*, as well as in *his written word:* and the laws of the former are as obligatory as the commands and precepts of the latter; and never will Christianity become practically what its Divine author intended, in its fullest beauty, perfection and enjoyment, as characterized in Him, our great Exemplar, while here on earth, till *those laws which govern the body, in connection with the mind, are correctly understood and obeyed.* We take this high position; and here we verily believe the clergy have been much at fault in not teaching and preaching these laws, and practising in accordance with them. This is the reason why the writer has chosen to illustrate so large a portion of physical and mental hygiene by clerical examples. If they will study the *natural laws* of God more, they will find fewer "mysterious Providences," and see more clearly "his Eternal Power and Godhead" in His works; and the people, understanding that no atonement has been made, or will be, for a violated natural law of God, but that the penalty must be paid, will be careful to live in harmony with the Divine economy

HOW TO ENJOY LIFE:

OR,

PHYSICAL AND MENTAL HYGIENE.

CHAPTER I.

Ill Health of Students and Clergymen — Necessity of Medical and Hygienic Knowledge — Wonderful Formation of the Human Body — Design Manifested — Beauty of the Human Countenance — the Mind united to the Body — God's Natural and Moral Laws — Violations of them justly punished — Harmony between God's Government of Nature and of men — A Christian Duty to preserve Health — Value of Health to a Professional Man — Culture of the Mind at the expense of the Body.

For a number of years past there has been such sad havoc among students, ministers, and all classes of sedentary men, that some remarks upon this subject may be useful, as tending to the *preservation* of health and the way to happiness. We shall treat it, not as a common, only, but also as a *religious* duty. No man can injure his health, knowingly, without violating that command which says, "Thou shalt not kill." The spirit of this command requires us to do all in our power "to preserve our own lives, and the lives of others." This subject is referred to, in the sacred writings, in such passages as the following: "Beloved, I wish above all things that thou mayest prosper and be in health, even as thy soul prospereth;" and Paul, in one of his letters to his beloved son, Timothy, says, "Drink no longer water, but use a little wine for thy stomach's sake and thine often infirmities." There was nothing in which the Saviour, himself, manifested his benevolent feeling, and put forth the efforts of his power, in a more conspicuous manner, than in regard to the life and health of mankind. When he sent out his disciples to preach the Gospel, he enjoined upon them this precept, "As ye go, heal the sick." Indeed, this principle, put in practice, has always been of great service in opening a door of usefulness to ministers. *Dr. Parker* has been instrumental in bringing many of the heathen to love the truth, by his medical knowledge and surgical skill. *Dr. Grant*, armed with his cataract needle, found his way where no mere herald of the cross could have had access. Every observant Christian knows, that the surest way to gain religious access to the *minds* of men, both in heathen and nominally Christian lands, is to do good to their *bodies*. This is the way to be happy. It is in being in a condition of body and mind to do good to others, that human happiness chiefly consists. In this way, the "Hill of Zion yields," &c.

The Psalmist said, "I am fearfully and wonderfully

made." The sacred Scriptures abound with expressions setting forth the wonderful workmanship of the Creator in the organization of our complex being. Job says, " Thou hast clothed me with skin and flesh, and hast fenced me with bones and sinews." And again, "There is a spirit in man, and the inspiration of the Almighty giveth him understanding."

In writing upon health, as connected with both these, physical and mental, or upon body and mind, and their reciprocal agency, it seems appropriate to speak, in the first place, of man's physical organization, or the human body.

It is not our purpose to speak, at length, either of the anatomy or physiology of the body, or of the structure or faculties and functions of the mental powers: but rather, to give a brief sketch of the wonderful combination of elements brought together in our bodies.

That all the organs were designed to discharge peculiar functions, no one can doubt. If there be design in a watch, there is design in the construction of an eye: and if there is design in the construction of an eye, there is design in the construction of every organ in the human body.

Galen, that wonderful man, whose opinions influenced the medical world for thirteen hundred years with unbounded sway, was converted from atheism by the dissection of a human body. Nor shall we deem such an event singular, if we consider, for a moment, how wisely and wonderfully it is made.

Look at the elements wrought into this animal economy; at its structure and functions. What variety of parts! How unlike! How singular its structure! How diverse its functions! Here are bones and blood, solids and fluids: here the opaque muscle, and the transparent humor; the brilliant, adorning, vegetating hair; the keenly sensitive nerve; the more than curious digestive apparatus; the breathing lungs and beating heart. How various the organs designed for multifarious uses! In health they discharge all their functions well.

Here, are gathered into one frame, "compacted by that which every joint supplieth," harmonized, and stowed side by side, the most different, contrary, and conflicting elements — oil and water, acid and alkali, solid and fluid, vegetable and animal, iron and oxygen. In this organism, all these, and more, not only tolerate each other, but harmonize and co-operate together for the general good. Each is indispensable to its fellow, and one cannot say to the other, "*I* have no need of thee." Such are the elements, not heterogeneously commingled, but wisely arranged in this body.

Mr. Blair, speaking of the *beauty* of the human countenance, says: " Nothing can bear comparison with it." But this comeliness is all derived from the *skin*, that delicate covering, so admirably united and made to co-operate with the nerves and mind so as to convey *expression*.

We may add, no tints of the rainbow, Deity's emblem of security to man,—no ethereal blue, or lily white, or pink, or violet,—no diamond, emerald, crystal, topaz, can bear comparison with, or scarcely approximate to it. As the last and crowning act of the Creator's work, man outshines all others.

Can we admire the man himself, and not be led to reverential and adoring views of the Great Architect?

To man's organism is united an indefinable, thinking agent, which moves at pleasure, but in an unknown way, the whole animal machine. This is the crowning excellency, the glory of our frame. This raises man above all other animals, and allies him to spiritual beings of a higher order.

In view of this animal organism, united to this intellectual agent, and both conspiring to form the man, one may be allowed to say,

> "'T was from thy hand, my God, I came,
> A work of such a curious frame:
> In me thy fearful wonders shine,
> And such proclaim thy skill divine.

> "At last, to show my Maker's name,
> God stamped his image on my frame;
> And, in some unknown moment, joined
> The finished members to the mind."

In speaking of health and happiness, it will be necessary to keep in view this great fact, — that man is a *compound* being; of a material body, and an immaterial mind. This, we shall do in these sketches. As the whole machinery of the body moves on without friction, in health, so when this is the case with both body and mind, the whole *compound* man is in a proper frame not for action only, but also for *happiness*. No one can be happy, or enjoy life, who has not "a sound mind in a healthy body." Here is the great secret of earthly bliss.

"Order is Heaven's first law."

Every thing, and every being in the universe of God act in accordance with laws. Thus, the solar and planetary systems act in accordance with the laws of gravitation; the growth and decay of plants, with the laws of vegetation; and of animals, with the laws of animation.

Doctor Carpenter, in his great work on Physiology, has well said, "The so-called Laws of Nature are nothing else than general expressions of the condition under which certain assemblages of phenomena occur. In no case can natural phenomena be correctly said to be *governed* by laws; since the laws themselves are nothing else than manifestations of the will of the governing power. But they may be said to take place *according to* certain laws; these laws being framed by man, as expressions and descriptions of the slight glimpses he possesses of the *plan* according to which the Creator sees fit to operate in the natural world. Thus understood, the use of the term law can be in no way supposed to imply that the Deity stands in any other relation to the phenomena of the universe, than as their direct and constantly operating cause."

God has a system, both of natural and moral laws, in accordance with which, he requires man to act. If he violate a moral law of his nature, he is guilty, and exposed to punishment. If he refuse to obey, or to act in accordance with the natural laws of his being, injury, suffering, or death must follow.

It is a natural law that fire shall burn, and, if we disregard this law, and thrust our hand into the fire, it will be burned. The same may be said of any other natural law which we transgress. The legitimate penalty is inflicted.

We may think it cruel, or barbarous, and inveigh against our Maker, or the instrument through which we are made to suffer; but the *Author* of nature does not change his course of procedure, or alter his plan. We surfeit, and he punishes us with headache, fever, or gout. We continue to live in luxury many days, and he ends our life with apoplexy. The same is the case with the mind. We overtask its powers, and it is weakened or destroyed.

All this is but nature, or rather, God, working habitually, and in accordance with his plan, "formed of old, or ever the foundations of the earth were laid." The very finger of God may be as clearly seen in disease, following imprudence and excess, as is ever the hand of justice in plying the scourge to the culprit's back. Such suffering, in consequence of refusing to live in accordance with God's natural government, is even more conspicuous than would be the suffering of an individual by the hand of human justice; because *this* might be but a single case, standing out in bold relief,—whereas, God's messengers of disease, or suffering, are sure, and always come in accordance with fixed laws.

The machinery of our being, when properly worked, is designed to promote health, and to prolong life, till it wears out by the natural friction inseparable from all creatures and all things. But, if overworked, it is certain to induce disease, decay, and premature death: and, we may add, it was just as much *designed* that this should be the case, as it is certain to occur.

Our complaints and murmurs do not move the Deity to lay aside his constituted order of things, or to suspend the laws of nature, or to desist from the infliction of bodily pains and penalties, as a consequence of transgression. Nor will the infliction of those ills cease, because we infringe upon nature's laws *ignorantly*. Arsenic will as certainly produce its poisonous effects, if we take it in innocent ignorance of its deleterious qualities, as it will, if swallowed by design, to destroy life; and, in the great laboratory of nature, catarrh, fever, palsy, gout, apoplexy, and other diseases will continue to afflict human beings, whether they ignorantly infringe nature's laws, or knowingly disobey them.

Nature does not step aside for us from her grand movement of order. She acts certainly and always in harmony with her laws, and no law is more sure than that "man will reap, as he sows." Would we have all our powers of mind and body move on in successful and quiet operation, we must obey.

Where disobedience has not greatly prevailed in the parent, or his ancestors, the infant, ordinarily, comes into being with all the powers of a man, in miniature, for a vigorous mind in a healthy body. But, in order that he may possess both these, on his arrival at manhood, and they have their proper and natural development, he must be placed under the due observance of all the laws designed to give "*sana mens in sano corpore*," — "a sound mind in a healthy body."

It is a Christian duty to use all possible means to establish and preserve health. — "Thou shalt not kill," is a Divine command, forbidding every thing that has a tendency to shorten life. It is always a wrong wish to desire death "before our time;" and equally a sin-ful act to do any thing to hasten that event. Our Saviour often did much to restore health and to preserve life; but did nothing to destroy that rich boon of heaven.

The health of every one is of vast moment to himself. But, there are many reasons why the health of a *professional* man seems to be, and really *is*, more valuable than that of some others. It is no disparagement to any, that the health of *Washington* was of more value than that of one of his contemporaries; the health of Paul, than that of Nero; or the health of such men as Whitefield, and Fuller, and Robert Hall, and Dwight, and Chalmers, more precious than that of many others. The friends of David, when he was about to jeopard his life, reasoned conclusively, when they said, "Thou art worth ten thousand of us,' though the expression is hyperbolical. We often witness an exhibition of this truth in the failure of the health of the *young* student. Learning is comparatively of but little value without health. Who has not seen the young man, the idol of his mother, the hope of his father, and the consolation of a beloved sister, toil on, through the academy, and the college, and sink just at the time, when his course of study was completed? To save *such*, with others, is the object of these remarks. Friends had toiled, affection had long sown with diligence, and the laurel wreath of academic honors had been twined around his brow; but all to no purpose. He fell at the hour of conquest.

The mind was cultivated; every intellectual faculty improved; every mental power fully developed; but the body, the house in which all these powers dwelt, was neglected. Its foundation was undermined, its pillars sapped, and its final fall prematurely hastened, by the very course pursued to rear its superstructure. A knowledge of those laws, and a compliance with them, which the Creator has ordained for the formation of a firm constitution, and the preservation of health, might have enabled him still to have lived to be both useful and happy, to solace friends and bless the world.

To approach still nearer the subject of *clerical*, or *professional Health of the students:* Who has not seen a more finished picture than the above? We mean *religion in the heart*, superadded to all intellectual and moral endowments. He had passed the seminary with honor, and holy hands had been laid upon him. He had become Heaven's commissioned herald to lost men, and a pastor to "feed the flock of God." He had graced the pulpit, and hundreds of listening, weeping, repenting hearers had hung upon the eloquence of his lips. But the sword was too sharp for the scabbard — the intellect too keen and energetic for the corporeal powers.

CHAPTER II.

Loss of Health — Study under Improper Stimulants and at Improper Times — Relaxation necessary — Cicero — Not Study soon after Eating, nor late at Night — Clergyman's Sore Throat — Ascribed to Various Causes — Disease of the Throat only Symptomatic — Its Real Cause — The Symptoms — Where Seated — Local Treatment of Little Use — The Sick often in Error as to their Disease.

WHAT are some of the principal causes of the loss of Clerical, Professional, and Students' Health? These are not all of one kind; nor, do they all spring from the same source.

The first cause of the loss *among Students' health*, which we shall name, is, *study at unseasonable hours and under the excitement of stimulants.*

We need not here speak of the intimate and reciprocal influence which exists between the mind and body. This is too well known to require repetition. Nor do we apprehend that health is often lost *by too much study*. The health of *German* students is rarely affected by study; though, on an average, they study quite as diligently, and more hours of the twenty-four than we do. But, they take good care of the *house* for the sake of the *tenant* which inhabits it: and *they carefully observe intervals and hours of relaxation.*

These are as necessary to health, as food and drink. Cicero, who was feeble in his youth, before he learned the means of preserving health, or travelled from Rome to Greece, to strengthen his physical powers, in the Gymnasium of the latter, in his oration for the poet Archias, has the following passage, which gives us a clue to the manner in which he relaxed his mind: "You will, doubtless ask, Gracchus, the reason of my being so delighted with this man? It is because he furnishes me with what relieves my mind and charms my ears, after the fatigue and noise of the forum. Do you imagine that I could possibly plead, every day, on such a variety of subjects, if my mind were not cultivated with *science?* Or, that it could bear being stretched to such a degree, if it were not sometimes unbent by *amusement.*" By *science*, this great man, undoubtedly, meant that fund of knowledge, which he had treasured up for the discharge of the duties of his professional life; and by *amusement*, those poetic effusions, which such men as Archias sent forth. We have here, the secret of Cicero's accomplishing so much, and verifying his prediction in another place, that, "he was writing for the latest posterity."

It is no time to study soon after eating. This will be fully shown when we come to speak of the process of digestion. It is sufficient to say, at present, that the mind requires rest, while the digestive apparatus is discharging its peculiar functions. There are many clergymen who spend the week, till near its close, in other duties; and, as late as Friday, betake themselves to study to prepare for the Sabbath. They feel that their "full tale of brick" must be rendered, "straw" or "no straw." Hence the intellect is overtasked, while the physical man is neglected.

In the midst of his study, the minister is called to dinner, swallows it in hot haste, scarcely aware whether he is eating or writing; and, as though the hand of necessity were upon him, without allowing a moment for the repose of his physical man, hastens back to the study. The hour for supper arrives, and the same course is repeated. Amidst the ringing of the door-bell, and numerous interruptions, which serve only to perplex, night has overtaken him, and the sermons are not finished. The labor grows upon his hands. The subject is cumulative. He cannot curtail, criticise, and trim. In a word, he *must* make a *long* sermon, because he has not time to make a *short* one.

The study is continued to a late hour of the night. Now, no man can think intensely, without the flow of more blood to the brain, than takes place at other times. By keeping up this determination of blood to the brain, for hours, this great central organ becomes *congested*. An excess of excitability obtains in it, and, it is not possible that so important an organ, the acknowledged seat of the superiority of man over the whole animated world; the residence of consciousness; the throne of intellect; of reason, memory, judgment; the fountain from which every passion, and every feeling, and every manifestation of human intellect flow; can be thus affected, thus *abused*, without the whole system's participating in the injury.

While these operations are going on in the brain; while too much of the vital fluid is collected there, the rest of the system is proportionally deprived of *its* due share; hence, from want of this natural stimulus, the liver, the great wheel of all the digestive apparatus, with the whole alimentary canal, becomes torpid, and a long train of nervous, dyspeptic, and hypochondriacal complaints is the result. To hasten on, and perpetuate this abnormal state of things, unfortunately and strangely, the physical appetite is often in an inverse ratio to the intellectual; and, with the love of study, there is frequently associated great debility of the digestive organs. The weary brain can no more sleep, than the overstrained muscle can be quiet. But of *sleep*, we may speak hereafter.

The case is similar with all students, and the case of the clergyman is selected only as a specimen of the whole class of studious men and women.

The sensation, thus induced, affects every part of the body, and frequently the poor sufferer imagines that he is laboring under incurable disease. When such an idea has taken possession of the mind, it is not easily dislodged from the imagination. Argument only deepens the impression. Happiness has fled.

There is no remedy for this state of things but for the professional man to do his work "in season," and for the wife to scour out the *lamp*, and allow no more oil to be put into it.

Night-study ruins many constitutions, by keeping up a chaos of impressions upon the brain, during the succeeding sleep, if that can be called sleep, which is constantly interrupted by incoherent dreams and half-waking trains of thought. The brain must have rest, or perpetually overloading it with blood will destroy its energy.

Another excitement, under which study is improper, is that produced by *narcotics* or *stimulants*. We say, narcotics *or* stimulants, because most of these are the same, the first effect being to stimulate or excite; the second, to render the system sedative, or narcotized.

The effects of all the narcotic poisons on the animal economy are analogous; some being more rapid in their operation than others; some causing convulsions; some dilating, and others contracting, the pupil of the eye. Their *first* effect (and alcohol is included among them) is to *excite* nervous energy. They pour fresh oil into nature's exhausted lamp; sharpen mental energy, and dissipate sorrow. The "Wise-man" perfectly understood the principle of their operation, when he said, "Give strong drink to him that is ready to perish, and wine to him that is of a heavy heart. Let him drink and forget his poverty, and remember his sorrow no more." Under their influence, the mind acts powerfully. Wit unfurls her proudest banner. Fancy and imagination, fully aroused, luxuriate with unfettered license; and the poet and the orator pour forth their sublimest strains, and utter their grandest conceptions; visions of unearthly joy light up the countenance.

But all this soon gives place to stupor, and failure of both mind and body. The statesman, who never spoke till he had warmed his powers of eloquence; and the poet, who would never sing, till he had drunk of the intoxicating cup; and the minister who would neither write nor preach, till he had taken his pill of opium, or his potation of wine or brandy; and who then spoke with the power of a Cicero, or sung with the muse of Orpheus, or preached with the eloquence of Apollos; all found that this was so much detracted from the real powers of life; and rued the day when they drank of the poisoned chalice, or tasted the Circæan cup, by the contents of which, reason was floated from the capital; the powers of intellect swamped, and the health of the body and energy of the mind prostrated.

4

It may appear to some that the student's health is never injured by such means. *It is.* Even strong tea or coffee (though these are comparatively innocent), taken with but little food, may unnaturally excite any man of nervous temperament; and he ought never to study under such influence. The stimulus, alone, without study, is quite enough. But, as I shall speak of some of the narcotics again, I will say no more of them in this place.

No one should attempt to study when the body is fatigued, or when the mind is perplexed. All such attempts should then be out of the question. It is not injurious only, but impracticable, and destructive to enjoyment.

Such are some of the *times*, at which, and *influences*, under which, no man ought to study, if he would preserve health, and enjoy life.

Clergymen, of course, are liable to all the diseases that other men are. But every class and profession of men are peculiarly liable to some one disease more than to others. "The Clergyman's Sore Throat" is a term which has been applied to men of their profession, as peculiarly descriptive of a disease to which they are subject. Not, however, because this disease is confined to them; for it is not. Others are, also, subject to it; such as singers, lawyers, merchants, shoe-makers, and teachers. Almost the only classes who are free from it are farmers and sailors; and, it is occasionally, met with even in these.

I have heard many reasons given for the great prevalence of this disease among clergymen; such as "wearing high cravats;" frequently "using cold water, while preaching;" "speaking in damp, underground vestries;" "and speaking too much and too loud."

Now, some of these *may* have contributed to the development of this disease; but in my opinion, it is not often to be ascribed to any one cause alone, but to several causes combined. Many who are subject to it, have some *humor* in the "blood," which Moses, one of the best physiologists who ever lived, has informed us, "is the life of the flesh." This humor, (call it by what name you please,) locates itself, or is deposited, by this ever-circulating fluid, the blood, upon any organ, or apparatus of the body which is much used, and consequently, often filled with blood. The vessels of the throat are thus filled, when we speak long and loud, in the same manner as we have formerly said, the brain is, when we think long and intensely.

In this respect, long and loud speaking does tend to develop disease of the throat.

Clergymen might learn a profitable lesson by hearing such men as Doctors Jacob Bigelow, and John Ware, of Boston, or, Doctors Wood and Mitchell, of Philadelphia, lecture. In neither of these men, all eminent instructors in medical science, and whose lectures are never wanting in thought, would they ever witness anything like that general excitement and loudness of voice which most pulpit orators consider so indispensable to give effect to their preaching.

But there is a remote cause, back of any immediately exciting one, which lays a foundation for the disease now under consideration. In fact, the trouble in the throat is not often the real disease of the sufferer; but only one of the many phases, by which, the disease manifests itself. The disease, itself, is some fault of the digestive organs. They do not perform their proper functions well. Indeed, there are but few cases of *consumption*, in which the difficulty does not primarily commence in the organs of digestion; and hence, in this disease physicians, generally, since they have addressed their remedies to these organs, and pursued the *sustaining*, rather than the *depleting* course, have found their patients oftener recover, or live longer, even when they at last die. A defect in digestion soon causes a diseased, or depraved state of the whole system, and makes consumption just what the celebrated Dr. Rush called it, "a disease all over."

The liver and its secretions first become disordered; and this arises, partially, from want of out-of-door exercise; partially, from eating unsuitable food, or suitable food at improper times, and in undue quantity; but more especially, from anxiety and perplexity of mind.

For the want of that gentle out-of-door exercise, which throws the blood to the extremities, the hands and feet become cold; and from a want of circulation in the extremities, the blood is retained in the large vessels in the viscera, till they become *congested*. Soon after the ordinary exercise of speaking, the throat begins to suffer. The mucous follicles and the glands become irritated. Often, the first trouble is *high up* in the throat, and the sensation, immediately after speaking, is of something there, which must be swallowed, or, as though *the throat had been scraped*. Sometimes the trouble is *lower down*, in the larynx, or on the vocal chords, where the voice is formed, and then, a degree of roughness of the voice, and of hoarseness upon speaking, is perceptible. Sometimes, the whole tube, called the *trachea*, is in a congested, irritated, or ulcerated condition; and, sometimes, the difficulty is still lower in the bronchial tubes, after they bifurcate, or leave the trachea to go to each lung. When this last is the case, there is usually some cough and expectoration.

I have said above, that anxiety and perplexity of mind are the remote and most common cause of this disease. This statement, I trust, I shall fully verify before I conclude the subject. Suffice it to say, at present, that the ancients considered disease of the liver, or *biliousness* (to use a common phrase) as synonymous with *choleric* or *wrathy*. Now, I do not mean to say, or imply, that clergymen are more *choleric* than other men. But this is meant, to wit, that the peculiar trials of these men, at the present day, do give rise to a train of emotions and perceptions in the mind, which seriously interfere with the proper secretions of the body, and thus lay a foundation for diseased digestion and nervousness, which are an almost certain prelude to the sore throats of clergymen.

Though in this disease, local or topical applications may often prove serviceable, in conjunction with other medical treatment, yet the patient had better do nothing than to rely on these alone. I have known persons go the whole round of this *burning* with caustic (as they call it), and other acrid and astringent applications, and still grow worse. Sometimes, a patient of this description presents himself, who has been so completely saturated with *nitrate of silver*, that his skin has taken on that peculiar *tinge*, which is neither that of the white, black, nor red man, but a combination of the dirty color of all of them, ("a mark" as indelible as that "set upon Cain") and, without receiving any benefit, or removal of the disease. While a little good advice, as to the proper management of the mind, in avoiding excitement and anxiety; and of the body, as to air, exercise, and diet; with, perhaps, a very little medicine addressed to the digestive organs, would have set all right, and soon have given to the poor sufferer renewed health and vigor. In these remarks, I would not be understood, as not sufficiently appreciating *topical applications*, or *inhalations* of appropriate medicinal substances into the "Air Passages." All that is intimated, is, that they do not reach the whole case. The real origin of the difficulty lies still deeper, and one might as well expect to revivify the tree whose roots and trunk were diseased, by lopping off a few of the dead and dying twigs, as to remove this disease by any mere local or topical treatment. If it were a mere local trouble, caused by speaking alone, and confined to the throat, such treatment might be sufficient; but as it is not, some other remedy is demanded. The influence of the mind upon the body is often clearly seen in this disease, as also in many other diseases.

Perhaps, there is no one thing in which the sick are more deceived than in regard to the origin or character of their disease. A young man, a student, of slender frame, very nervous, with tremors, and unable to apply himself to study, recently called for medical advice. His first inquiry was, "What was the matter with him? Why was he so nervous, timid, and trembling? Why could he not apply his mind to study, as formerly?"

The symptoms indicated an excessive use of alcohol,

or of some narcotic poison. But he said, he used no spirits, and took no opium. To the question, Do you use tobacco? he answered, "Yes." When asked how much, he said, "A great deal;" and to the inquiry *how* he used it, he answered, "Both by chewing and smoking." Here was developed the whole cause of his disease. The excessive use of this narcotic, acting upon a youthful and naturally delicate frame, conjoined with his sedentary habits, had produced the whole difficulty. Yet, he never once thought that this narcotic poison was the cause of his trouble.

There are a multitude of students in this same condition, especially, *Medical Students*. A gentleman estimated that five hogsheads of tobacco-juice were spit in one winter upon the floor of the Jefferson Medical College, in Philadelphia.

A clergyman called one day, and said, "he had some difficulty about the throat, and did not know but he was threatened with consumption." He was told, he was in more danger of dying of apoplexy. He was "thick set," fleshy, short-necked, and every way formed for apoplexy; and within a month from that time, he did die in an apoplectic fit. Such cases verify the above remark, that many persons mistake altogether the true origin of their disease.

CHAPTER III.

Travelling for health — Vanity from Travel — Injury from Travelling — Agriculture Better — Fashionable Watering Places — Periodical Dissipation — Pleasures of Home — Taking children to Hotels and Places of Fashionable Resort — Absence of Clergymen — Objections to sending Consumptive Patients Abroad — The North should be preferred to the South — Old Treatment for Consumption — New Better — Good Advice and some Medicine often Useful — Mutual Confidence and Respect necessary to Success in any Profession.

It is well for a man, who has the means to take his family with him, to go abroad. It enlarges his views and elevates his mind. It shows him more of the wonders of Divine power, and of the works of men. Such a one, visiting different portions of the world, returns home a wiser and a better man, and better satisfied with his own sphere of usefulness.

But no one ought to travel abroad till he is a man; till his habits of life are established, and he prepared to profit by seeing the world. Most of the young professional men, like half-fledged butterflies, are rendered vain, not to say insolent, by visiting foreign climes too early. They can scarcely speak, without lugging in something that *they saw;* or, somebody, with whom they dined, "across the water." We have often been disgusted with such professional, mushroom pride of accidence. Had it devolved on *them* to furnish the means, they would have resembled *Pollok's* man in more respects than one, —

<blockquote>
——— "Who never had a dozen thoughts in all his life,
And never changed their course — lived, where
His father lived; and died, where he died."
</blockquote>

We have, sometimes, seen half a dozen such, as to thought and judgment, moored high and dry, by a single remark of some wise old physician or clergyman, who possessed more brains than an army of such migratory birds.

There is no one cause for which professional men oftener travel abroad than to regain lost health. Now, we affirm, without hesitation, that, in nine cases out of ten, health is more often injured, than benefited by such journeys. Our reasons for this opinion will appear in the sequel.

Dr. Armstrong, one of the most shrewd, intelligent, and popular physicians of England, has left the following testimony, as the result of his contemplation and experience, of sending invalids from home with the hope of regaining health in foreign climes.

"With regard to climate, I thought favorably of a change some time ago; but so many appalling facts have come to my knowledge, that I have been induced to change my mind. If consumption be threatened, the patient has the best chance at home. To remove the invalid from his friends is to wrench him from all the affections which have held him from the time of his birth; and no man can bear this, without receiving a shock, which may be exceedingly injurious. Besides which, the fatigue of travelling, the risk of cold, the worry and bustle of inns, the diet, which becomes in some measure dependent upon chance on the road, the danger of damp beds, and the necessity of changing the abode at different seasons of the year, must all be taken into the account. They more than counterbalance the good which might arise from a less variable climate; and many persons who have left this country in a state of threatened consumption, have returned with confirmed phthisis. If an individual of a delicate constitution, with a slight cough and slow pulse, should pass to a warmer climate, he can scarcely ever return with safety to this. Medical men have been too much accustomed quietly to take up with errors of men who lived in times of darkness and ignorance; and, the age in which we live is remarkable for the fortitude with which some individuals have thrown off this cumbrous load, and have dared to think and act for themselves. This independence of mind has led to very beneficial results in the improvement of professional knowledge."

Many around us can bear testimony to the truthfulness of the above remarks. They have sent their invalid friends abroad, with the hope that a change of climate would prove beneficial to their health. But this hope has been more frequently disappointed than realized, and they have either died in foreign lands, or returned just in season to expire in the arms of their friends. Often they would have lived longer, and much more comfortably, had they remained at home.

It is very customary now for a parish to allow their minister to be absent a number of months, for the benefit of his health; and to furnish him with the means for travelling abroad. We commend such for their kindness and liberality. It manifests a good feeling towards their minister, and shows that, after having received of him "spiritual blessings," they are willing he should partake of their "carnal things."

We would suggest a different course both for the parish and for the enfeebled minister. One which we believe, would better improve his health and more "abound to the riches of their liberality." It is to furnish him with land for tillage, and with the implements of husbandry. It need not be a fifteen thousand, or even a six thousand dollars farm, such as the papers inform us have been supplied to two of the pastors in Brooklyn in New York. A very small farm, or even a garden, would be sufficient. There let the minister, worn down by the cares, labor, and anxiety attendant upon professional duty, breathe the pure air of heaven and exercise his bodily powers. Let him lay hold of the hoe, the axe, the plough, the scythe and the rake, and take gentle, daily exercise. Let him not fear the loss of a delicate hand, or a lily-like face, or a slender arm. In "the labor of his hands" let him rejoice, and in "the sweat of his face, let him eat bread." Thus will he soon find that even the curse denounced on our first parents, embodies one of our richest earthly blessings. Professional men, and others also, are too much afraid of labor. How few of them can say, "these hands have ministered to my necessities."

Agriculture and horticulture are among the best means to restore declining health and rejuvenate the exhausted and jaded mind. The benefit of such employment has been sung by poets and praised by philosophers from early ages. Reference is here had to clergymen as specimens of studious men. To all *Professional* men, lawyers, teachers, students, these remarks are equally applicable.

Any sedentary invalid, who will resort to this Heaven-ordained means of health of body and peace of mind, will soon understand why the old clergymen of this country had a long ministry, and a green old age. We have the reason in the following lines, —

"By *toil*, our long-lived fathers earned their food;
Toil strung their nerves, and purified their blood."

This more redounds to the health and happiness of an invalid, than travel; and he can have it without the exposure, fretting, expense, loss of society, bad food, uncomfortable beds, stinted sleeping rooms, and a thousand other perplexities and annoyances which necessarily beset the path of the traveller. But, it is the *fashion* to travel. We know it is, and "there's the rub." Fashion is a wonderful creature. She has access to all places, and operates throughout all time. She renders the wasp-formed female beautiful; and the greasy-mustached beau fascinating. She gives a club-foot to the Chinese damsel, and a long tail to her brother; a flat nose and a bandy leg to the African, and imposes many uncouth and inconvenient forms of dress upon the community.

In our own country there is much travel, ostensibly for health, where, we unhesitatingly pronounce that, the injury far surpasses the gain. Inexorable *Fashion* says, we must go from our home in dog-days; and in obedience to her mandate, there is a rush from all our cities and towns, from the metropolis down to the smallest village, to the places where this "goddess" specially presides. This is the season, when our climate renders the quiet and comfort of home the most healthful and necessary. The best protection, at such a season, can be found at home. But, *de gustibus non disputandum est*, we must allow those who please, (and who do not?) to exchange the large, airy, brick-walled rooms of the town, and the cool mattress, and fine linen, for the narrow, wooden, sun-burnt chamber, the heating cotton, greasy feathers, and dirty sheets of a country Inn, or a pent-up village boarding house. We once knew a gentleman, who, after a cab-ride of three hours, around one of these fashionable resorts, to find accommodations, at last, compelled to take up with such quarters for himself and family, as he would have scorned for his servant, or his dog, at home. But who could live through a hot summer without visiting Nahant, Newport, Saratoga, Niagara, or Cape May? It is not against visiting these places that we would speak; and towards those who *need* an occasional plum to sweeten the acidity of their domestic circle; or who want,

"That first sure symptom of a mind in health;
Rest at heart, and pleasure felt at home,"

we would not be so ungracious as to deny them the boon of absence. It is certain, however, that if life is not enjoyed at home, it will not be anywhere. If you would be happy, make home "Sweet home," indeed. The chief blessing of life consists in having a good home.

But we protest against taking the hottest season to make these *periodical* visits, with the expectation of thereby promoting *health*. At this season, the organs of digestion are the least able to discharge their function. They sympathize with all the other parts of the body; and, like them, require rest: and, is this the time to leave the frugal, wholesome fare at home, and rush to the gathering places where every board groans with its life-killing feasts; and, where the luxuries provided, and the exciting presence and example of hundreds of mouths, eager to gratify the appetite, at the expense of the stomach, render it next to impossible to obey the laws of health. Where, besides, this poor pack-horse, this groaning organ, is teased with mineral waters, wines, bitters, pills, tobacco-juice, and tobacco fumes, taken throatwise and lungwise, to ease itself of its cumbersome burdens.

Would it not be wise for all studious persons, before they run such a risk, to ask themselves, "who is sufficient for these things?" and to pray, "lead us not into temptation?"

Nothing is more delusive than the impression usually present with persons visiting such places, that they are growing better, because, as they suppose, they are gaining flesh. Under the spasmodic action of this paraphernalia of stimulants, it cannot be denied that there is often an appearance of more flesh. But it is diseased, not sound, healthy flesh — *mere bloat,* — like self-righteousness, the more a man has of it, the poorer he is. He vainly thinks he is on the high road to health; whereas, he is fast hastening to the grave. For every pound of such flesh, nature will be revenged, and the day of retribution will surely follow.

Hence it is, that many persons, soon after a return from such fashionable gathering places, have an attack of dyspepsia, biliousness, sick-headache, pulmonary affection, or cutaneous eruption. Like the morning dew, their ill-gotten flesh soon vanishes, and, as was the case with "Pharoah's lean kine, it would not be known that they had eaten" such fat things, but for their greater emaciation than when they left home. These abuses, occurring *periodically*, undermine the best constitution. More sudden deaths occur at such places of public resort, than in the safer place of a cheerful home. Such visitors may rest assured that, in nine cases out of ten, they will be injured rather than benefited by such sojourns.

Taking *children* to such places is the consummation of folly. More than half the so-called diseases of the season, and the deaths of children, which occur in August and September, arise from fashionable dissipation. No place is so good for children, if you wish them to live, as a quiet home. Country air is good for them, if they have a permanent abode. But to take them to places of fashionable resort, and stuff them with tempting viands, gravies, puddings, and pastries, is to cheat them out of two of the best things in the world, — *a good conscience,* and a *good stomach.* Even the crowded city, bad as it is, is better for them than such fashionable journeys.

Physicians ought, perhaps, not to inveigh too strongly against such travel, as, like the use of quack medicine, it brings them annually many patients. Thus, it may be profitable to the doctor, though it is destructive of health and enjoyment to the visitor.

It has always been a perplexing question with us, how the pastor, "the good shepherd, who cares for the sheep," can leave them one sixth part of the year to the mercy of the wolves. In our large cities a man must sometimes travel half a day, before he can find a church open for worship in the afternoon, in "Dog-days." It may be all right, but it looks a little like fasting too long "between hay and grass."

But we are met by the objection, would you have the pastor, already worn down, stay and die on the field? We say, yes, better die with his harness on, than at such a fashionable resort as we have described. But we have already "shown a more excellent way," in resorting to that first and most honorable occupation of man, "tilling the ground."

I would never send a person abroad when consumption had made any considerable progress. He will enjoy the short remnant of life yet before him much better at home. This disease seems to be limited to certain latitudes. It is most prevalent from the equator, where the mean temperature is eighty degrees, to the higher portion of the temperate zone, where the mean temperature is forty degrees, with sudden and violent changes. No opinion is more erroneous than that it is peculiar to cold climates.

If a person of slender habit, *before* the lungs are diseased, travel to a *warm* climate, where the air is mild, and of a uniform temperature, it will be likely to ward off the disease. If our ever-variable climate be changed for the beautiful and mild atmosphere of Italy or the south of France, or the southern portions of our own country, such as Florida or Alabama, *before* the lungs have become essentially diseased, the change may be salutary. But if the change is made *after* the disease has commenced, the effect will be to hurry it on to a fatal termination; and, to send the invalid from home, when he most needs a home, is but to give him his final home. It is but to leave the circle of his friends, to die among strangers.

It is the varying temperature of our climate which lays the foundation for so many lung diseases, and the case is similar in England. If a change is made to a more equable climate, either warmer or colder, *before the consumptive disease begins to be developed*, the effect will be good. But, it is more favorable to go to a *colder* than to a *warmer* clime, whether the object be protection against consumption, or recovery from it.

Fifteen years ago, I wrote the following sentence and published it: — "A cold climate acts as a protection against consumption, and many facts have induced me to believe that it is better to go *north*, than *south*, for consumptive patients." Such is still my opinion. Nor, am I now alone in it, though, so far as I know, I was so then; and some physicians, holding prominent positions, then scouted the idea. At this, I was not surprised, as the whole treatment of the Faculty, for this disease, during the last fifty years, until very recently, was the worst that could possibly have been devised. Starting, as they did, upon the erroneous opinion, that consumption arose from inflammation of the lungs, the treatment was as follows: — The patient was confined to his room, (the temperature of which was kept high,) and sweltered in flannel. No fresh air was admitted. If a door were left ajar, or a window raised, the nurse, or the mother, the sister or the doctor, hastily closed it. All these precautions tended to debilitate the patient, and paralyze the efforts of nature to overcome the threatened disease; and, in addition to depriving him of air, and sweltering him with artificial warmth, the direct medical treatment of the physician, was, if possible, still more pernicious. It consisted of bleeding, blistering, puking, purging, setonizing, and dosing with preparations of calomel, antimony, squills, ipecac, opium, and all that dismal array of debilitating applications, the very mention of which now sickens every well-read physician, and causes all who are old practitioners, almost to deny that they were ever addicted to such practice. Belonging, as the writer did, to a consumptive family, whose father and mother, and only brother, fell by this disease, and who himself in early life, came as near dying of it as any man ever did, who escaped, he has some knowledge of what he writes. My only brother was bled, for disease of the lungs, three or four times, for three successive years, and died on the fourth year, after he was attacked, of consumption, and before he was thirty years old. The writer submitted to all the routine of the above-named treatment, except the lancet. He would never be bled. A young sister was, for three years, subject to raising blood, and other symptoms of consumption. A physician was called, who proposed bleeding. He was a member of the regular Faculty, and a genuine follower of Dr. Rush, a very estimable man, but one, who within a few years, has been justly characterized by an eminent English physician, "as peculiarly bloodthirsty." She was not bled. She recovered, and is still living, and has lived thirty years since her early sickness, and is the mother of half-a-dozen healthy, and some of them grown-up children.

It is admitted that there has been a great change in medical treatment within the last thirty years,— so much so, indeed, that the young generation now coming upon the stage of action, will scarcely believe that their fathers were ever accustomed to such hard practice; yet, the writer can show from documentary evidence now in his office, that, the annual fee, for bleeding alone, thirty years ago, in the office of an eminent English Surgeon, (performed of course by his pupils,) amounted to a small fortune. Fortunate, indeed, is it for humanity, that the "times have changed, and we have changed with them."

But to return to the question, Is it better to go North than South, for consumptives? I have said, the North should be preferred. Now for the proof, — consumption is a rare disease in Siberia, Nova Zembla, Greenland, even in Canada, and in all northern latitudes, where the winters are long and the weather is steadily cold and serene.

Dr. A. S. Weatherspoon, in a paper read to the New York Medical Society, says, " the climate of Fort Kent, Maine, like that of the colder regions of Northern Europe, does not seem favorable for the production of pulmonary consumption. During my sojourn at the Fort, I have neither seen nor heard of a case of this disease among the French or American settlers. Assistant Surgeon Isaacs, who, during the two years he was resident at the Fort, had a much better opportunity than myself of becoming acquainted with the diseases of the country, informs me not only that he never saw a case of consumption in the country, but that some of the inmates of the garrison, who were afflicted with suspicious symptoms, recovered from them entirely. The present revenue officer at this post, a man of decidedly scrofulous temperament, had suffered a slight attack of hæmoptysis, (spitting blood,) and other symptoms of incipient pulmonary disease, when he was ordered to this post. Though liable to catch cold when exposed, his cough no longer troubles him. He has gained flesh and strength, and considers himself free from the disease.—I have no doubt, from his symptoms, when ordered to Fort Kent, he was suffering under tubercular deposition of the lungs."

A gentleman in the city of New York, of good common sense, and more than ordinary judgment, upon a recent visit to that city, remarked to the writer, substantially, as follows: "Our physicians miss it very much in advising consumptive patients to go South. They die sooner than they would at home. My oldest son was engaged to a worthy young lady, whom her physician said was in consumption. I advised him in winter to go North with her. Contrary to the wishes of her friends and the advice of her physicians, but in accordance with my direction, he took her in the winter to the northern part of Canada. They have now been there three months, during which time, the disease has not only been held at bay, but she has actually gained strength and the cough has abated."

From these and many other considerations which might be offered, I am persuaded that a great error has been committed in sending consumptives to the South. But it does not follow, because the old practice of excluding consumptive patients from the air, and dosing and drugging them, as above stated, hastened their death, that all medical advice, nor all medicine even, should be abandoned. On the contrary, medical advice is often of the greatest importance to the invalid. Not, indeed, always to tell him what he must "*take*," but what he must, and what he must not *do*.

Any mesmeric old woman, or any charlatan can tell how to "make up bitters," "salves," and "cure-alls," but this is not the grand object of medical science. If it were, it would be much better if physicians were banished from America, as Nero drove them from Rome. But it would not be so. Physicians *are* useful. They can, and do, often relieve many of the sorest "ills that flesh is heir to." They can, and do, often put a patient upon a course of living which results in the restoration of impaired health, and the lengthening out of life.

Nor, is the use of all *medicine* to be discarded, because some persons, either with or without the advice of physicians, have turned their stomachs into apothecary-shops, and shortened their lives by " dosing and drugging." It was never a dictate of common-sense, that, because a man shuns *Charybdis*, he *must* fall into *Scylla*.

Some persons, as for instance, the Hydropathist,

(and many other *pathists* might be added,) can never get more than one idea into their heads at the same time. Hence, if *water* is good for some things, it is for all, with them. *They* abominate *all* medicine.

There are now, and ever have been, men, and women too, with whom it was of no manner of use to reason. You might as well talk with the wind as with them, and you will come as near silencing an echo by loudness of voice, as convincing such by argument. Unfortunately, the profession or science of medicine is not, and from the very nature of the case, never can be, one of the *exact* sciences. The consequence is, that all kinds of quackery, charlatanism, humbug, and delusion, will crowd into, and hang about it. But the greatest of all barriers to the progress of medical science, and medicine, is, the manner in which doctors devour each other. No class of men will be respected and esteemed by the community, who do not respect and esteem each other; and, possibly, this remark applies even to the sacred profession of the clergy. If they "bite and devour each other," it, indeed, behooves them to "take heed that they be not devoured one of another." Even school teachers and other literary persons do not always express the kindest of feelings towards those of the same occupation. It is essential to our happiness to speak honorably and kindly of our own profession.

CHAPTER IV.

Mental Excitement — Its Effect on the Body — Blanches the Hair — The Miser — Vain Ambition — Fastidious Hearers — Meddlesome Parishioners — A City Call — Hope and Disappointment — Failure of Success — Trouble in the Parish — Dismission — Variety of Preaching — Anxiety for his Family — Poverty — The Apostle Paul — A True and a False Ambition.

MENTAL *excitement* and *anxiety* are prolific sources of ill health and of unhappiness. Under these terms, we mean to include ambition, and every kind of mental excitement arising from professional duties, and the wants and cares incident upon providing for the comfort and education of a family. Upon investigation, we shall find these to be the cause of ill health much more frequently than is generally imagined. It cannot be otherwise, if we duly consider the effect which the mind produces upon the body—as when fear, or grief, or anger, blanches the countenance with paleness, or reddens it as though the blood would burst from every pore; as when, in a single night, preceding an execution, it changes the color of the hair from a beautiful black, to gray, — a change produced in Mary, Queen of Scots; and, also, in the adventurer, seeking gold at our modern Eldorado on the Pacific, when he acquired

MENTAL EXCITEMENT. 63

much by hard and long toil in the mines, staked and lost the whole, in an evening's game, — and retired, not to sleep, but to *wake*, — retired a *young* man, and arose, the next morning, *a gray-haired old man*. We have some striking facts in our possession, demonstrating these sudden changes in the color of the hair, in that land of fortune-hunting and shadow-chasing. Is it then any wonder that the mind diseases the body? How true, then, must it be that happiness — the true enjoyment of life — is chiefly dependent upon the nice adjustment of the reciprocal agency of body and mind! We are confident that this real source of human happiness has been too much overlooked, especially by all studious or thinking persons.

The case of the clergyman is selected as a *specimen* for all literary and studious persons, whether they be men or women.

If such changes may be suddenly induced by strong emotions, is it at all surprising, if weeks, and months, and years, of those anxieties and cares, which cluster thickly around the path of clerical life, in these modern times, should sensibly affect the health of such incumbents? It would be surprisingly strange, if they did not operate in a very injurious manner. The case might be illustrated equally well from him who is intent upon becoming rich. There are thousands of such miserable men, from whom all the enjoyment of life has fled; whose bodies are "worn to skin and bone;" and who enjoy scarcely any real happiness. *Miser* is his name, and *miserable*, indeed, is his condition. Some of the most unhappy and wretched men and women I have ever seen, were those who lived solely to hoard up wealth. If the true enjoyment of life ever flees from the abodes of men, it is so with such families.

"Ambition! powerful source of good or ill."

We look for this, in the statesman, the hero, the emperor; in a Cæsar, an Alexander, a Napoleon. But, surely, this unholy fire will not burn in the church of Christ! Will not its sacred waters extinguish the unhallowed flame? Would to Heaven, it were so! But all church history and Christian experience demonstrate the contrary.

"Man *must* soar —
Not kings alone.
Each villager has his ambition too;
No *Sultan* prouder than his fettered slave:
Slaves build their little *Babylons* of straw,
Echo the proud *Assyrian* in their hearts,
And cry, 'Behold the wonders of my might!'"

The dispute among the immediate disciples of the Saviour, "who should be the greatest," indicates that they were not free from unhallowed ambition. A little later in the history of the church, we hear, that, "Diotrephes loved to have the pre-eminence." Some have even dared to imagine that the sin by which "Lucifer fell," introduced into the church popes, and many other hierarchs, who have not so much "served God's heritage," as they have been *served of it:* and, it is possible that, just in proportion as ambition has existed in the church, has been the tendency from simple gospel-*purity* towards the Papacy, through all the ascending grades. Be this as it may, (respecting which, we have no disposition to affirm positively,) none can doubt that ambition has too often been a "ruling passion" in the human breast, and not altogether extinct in the clergyman. We may, therefore, suppose it sometimes produces its bad effects upon his corporal system.

We will suppose a clergyman, settled in a small country parish. He "knows the state of his flock," for it is "a little one." He has pleasant friends, and those who love him: some almost idolize him. "If it were possible, they would pluck out their own eyes and give them to him."

But still, life is not all sunshine; and, he is exposed to many little annoyances. Neither men nor women "look" solely "to their *own* things; but, also, on the things of others." One thinks his wife's bonnet a little too gay, for the pastor's lady; or, her shawl too dashy; or, her dress too rich; or, the daughters are too extravagant; or, the sons are not brought up to labor. A "little matter," by a slight assistance from the imagination, "kindles a great fire."

The people do and say things very innocently about their minister, as they feel that they have a right to him and his family. They are all dependent upon the parish for their bread, and why should *it* not exercise a guardian care over their expenditures? Would they not be culpable, if they manifested no concern about that in which they are so much interested? If not, this is the reasoning of Uncle *Goodcare*, and Aunt *Watchful*, and her *Nieces*.

Little meddlings of this kind, the pastor, and especially his wife (she not having been settled over the parish) do not always bear with becoming meekness. "The field," says he, "is the world." There are other portions of this great vineyard. Why should I always remain "pent up" here? The salary is small. The garden is but "a little one." Men judge of the talents of a man by the number of the houses in the town where he lives. Great men are called to cities and populous towns. These are the "sunny places of Zion." Multitudes attend upon their ministry. The masses fly to hear them, "as clouds, and as doves to their windows." They become the centre of great power, and, often, ascend from the nadir to the zenith of the profession; receive large presents; are attired in rich vestments, and, on the Sabbath, in silken surplices, and preach from marble pulpits.

"Brother —————— has been called thither. He was

my class-mate, a man of medium stature. I could measure intellect with him; scan the Classics; comprehend Newton; analyze Butler; find flaws in Paley; read Hebrew and Chaldee; round periods, and speak in public, as well as he. In the language of the good old man of *Uz*, I can say truly, '*I* am not inferior to you.'"

Thus, prompted by ambition, and harassed by the annoyances common to this evil world, he *reasons*, instead of being satisfied with "food and raiment," and "learning in whatever state he is, to be content." He now casts about to get a call from some large town or city. Such a door opens; indeed, such doors *often* open; and, when they shut, it is only for a season. Such congregations are not diffident, and soon pass their sage judgment upon all the wares in the market.

"They can tell, in half a minute,
What's out of fashion and what's in it."

Their disposition to judge of the qualifications of a clergyman, is generally in an inverse ratio to their ability.

They are of a peculiar cast, and need a peculiar man. This man and that man may answer for other places, but will not do for them. Send him out to the West, or off to the Indians. He will do good there. But *we* want a different man; one who can build us up, stand up like others around us, and, who is a little superior to them, and, finally, one, *"who can pay our debt."* We love the gospel, and would never say, under any circumstances, "our soul loatheth this light bread," *but,* it makes a wide difference *to us* in what kind of *a dish it is served up.*

Our ambitious clergyman now gets a cousin, or a friend, to offer his name, as a candidate, to the deacon, or elder, whose office, being of the *standing* order, always entitles him to a loud voice in the introduction of a candidate, and the selection of a new pastor. "The lot, being cast into the lap" of the deacons, session, or committee, the name of our applicant comes up at the portals of fame. Discussion ensues. One doubts; another fears; till, at length, things grow climacterical. The *recommendation* finally decides the point. See what it says: he is just *the* man. He was made *for the place,* and *the place* was exactly designed for him; learned, wise, energetic, of prepossessing appearance, graceful, charming. All that fancy could desire, or imagination conceive, meet in him. He is "sent" for. He now feels almost sure that fortune is going to smile upon him. It is a long road that never turns. "Doubtless, he is the man." Aspirations of occupying a wider sphere, or of larger usefulness, and more extended influence, had long hung about him.

"Sequar vestigia rerum."

Why must he be doomed to toil through the academy, the college, and the seminary, and then,

> "—— To fix him down
> For life, in some unsettled town?
> There cull his texts, and till his farm,
> And do no good, and little harm."

He selects the best of all those which our fathers (when as yet iron horses, and steaming ships, and speaking wires were not) were wont to call *saddle-bag* sermons.

It was written in his most palmy hours, when the body was not oppressed, the girl in the kitchen, the good wife in the sitting-room, and the baby asleep. The intellect was not jaded, and "thoughts came," without call, "like spectres," of their own accord, "from the vasty deep." With such a "scrip," carefully revised, and re-touched, and legibly written, he flies, as "on the wings of the wind," to the metropolis; delivers his message to an audience, most of whom had come together, (not to *worship God*,) — to hear a new candidate.

Perhaps he is disappointed, and has the mortification to find that, in the estimation of the audience, *he is not the man.* "Happy, thrice and four times happy" for him, if it be so: for, though a defeat, in such an attempt to soar, may cause chagrin, and "take aback" the inflated sails of his earthly ambition, yet it is much better for him than it would have been to have succeeded — better than to have entered the new port "*pleno velo.*"

This failure troubles his mind. It may thus make him sick. Still, it may prove a sickness tending to health, for success might have been fatal to him. If he is a *Christian* minister, he will learn from it to "cease from man;" learn that meek, unobtrusive, noiseless piety, is of more value than "the praise of men." The great Head of the church may have designed this to deliver him from the "sifting of Satan." But it would not be strange, if, in passing through the ordeal, he should find himself "weak and sickly." How much better would this man have enjoyed life, had he been "content" to pass his days in that part of the "vineyard," where Providence had cast his lot! One is almost tempted, when he sees how much happiness is destroyed, to apply to such the language of Solomon, "Every fool will be meddling."

We will select another example, where the former was, when he first preached to the Metropolitan congregation. He succeeds — makes a clean sweep and carries all before him. The audience exclaim, "This is our man — we must have *him* at all events. Such sentences! Such elegantly rounded periods, so eloquently expressed! How *engaged!* Did you see the perspiration roll down his cheek? Oh! if all ministers were like him, "the kingdom of heaven would soon come."

He comes — is settled — takes up his abode in the city, and soon finds, if he has not mistaken his calling, he *has* mistaken the people.

For a few Sabbaths, perhaps months, when it is known that he will preach in the *morning*, the house is filled. His sermons are admired. The "birds of passage" flock thither from all quarters, there to listen and admire, till a more propitious spring dawns upon some other congregation in the gift of a more bright and shining luminary. In a word, as long as he is *new*, he has crowded houses.

"Where Paul himself oft preached,
Would scarcely fill a pew."

In every large city, there are enough of this *migratory* class to fill a house whenever there is a new and popular preacher. Who has not been amused a thousand times to witness this running after some itinerating man; or, perchance, unsexed woman?

Soon the "beaten oiled" sermons are used up; cares and duties have multiplied so thickly that there is no time, and but little disposition, *to beat* more. All seems well; and he "settles upon his lees," more and more, as time progresses. It is "like people, like priest." He disturbs their slumbers but little, and they leave it to *him* to manage the *religious* matters.

Thus affairs remain for a while. But time changes all things, and men's feelings vary. All is as "a valley of dry bones, very dead, and very dry." So soon as some begin to look around them, this discovery is made. They begin to talk about a *change* of minister: first, only in whispers, to a chosen few. Then, louder, augmenting, like the Roman poet's description of *fame*. Some wish to compromise, and advise to settle a colleague. But a torrent has started, that cannot be stayed. Like "*Report*" of old,

> "First, small with fear, she swells to wondrous size,
> And stalks on earth, and towers above the skies:
> Swift is her walk, more swift her winged haste,
> A monstrous phantom, horrible and vast.
> Beneath her plumes, the various fury bears
> A thousand piercing eyes and listening ears,
> And with a thousand mouths and babbling tongues appears."

He falters more and more, as they clamor louder. He becomes anxious; can neither eat, nor sleep. The current undermines him; and he finds those who professed to be friends, joined hand in hand with his enemies. His heart palpitates, and his nervous system becomes shattered. The crisis comes. He cuts the knot. The tie of pastor and people is severed, and, with disappointed ambition and a sad heart, a broken constitution and an empty purse, he goes out, like the itinerating "Levite" of old, "to seek a place where he may sojourn."

Sometimes, also, health fails, and happiness flees away, from another cause. The pastor has long triumphed. His word has been law, till he has become really the Pontifex Maximus, the ruler of the church, and the dictator of his peers. At length, the cord, by too much stretching, breaks. The parish refuse their allegiance, and his peers " break his yoke from off their neck." The loss of power and influence reacts upon him till it breaks the "earthen vessel," and disease lays him aside. Meekness and humility might have saved him in health and happiness.

On the other hand, disease is sometimes induced by great popularity. His activity wears him out — he dies upon the chase with his armor on. As he is popular, he must preach almost incessantly. Everything, in his hands, goes upon the "high pressure" system. He lives constantly in a state of highly excited feeling. He must have the "wind" to shake the mountains and rive the rocks; the "earthquake" to move the world's foundations, and the "fire" to consume the forests. That spirit, once powerful, when heard in "the still, small voice," will not chime in with his noisy machinery. He has yet to learn that "bodily exercise profiteth little." He has forsaken the good "old paths" of the fathers, when "beaten oil" was brought in to light the sanctuary *twice* on the Sabbath, and no more; and has introduced overmuch preaching and exhorting.

He cannot but be anxious about his family, who must eat and drink to live. He must "provide" for them bread and clothing, or come under the scriptural censure of being "worse than an infidel"—a severe censure, but one which many poor clergymen find it hard to escape. He must educate his children. He must be liberal. To do all this, and more, he has no income but his salary. He can be no lawyer, stock-jobber, broker, or mechanic. From every field of gain, the pastor is excluded, and properly excluded, by his clerical duties. If his salary does not supply the wants of his family, then, he must either "dig," or "beg." He may do something at "digging," if he have the "garden," or "farm," formerly spoken of; "to beg," he is ashamed, and his people ought to be ashamed to permit it. He belongs to that "tribe" which "has never had any inheritance among their brethren," and have always been poor; or, so generally so, that if there is a rich man among them, he is an exception to the class, and, having become the "steward" of earthly "goods," he finds the admonition often repeated, in calls upon his means, which the apostle gave to Timothy, "be ready to distribute; willing to communicate."

Of all the trying scenes that meet the eye of the

phlanthropist, few are more heart-rending, than to see a clergyman in feeble health, with a needy family, and a sick wife, cast upon the world just as he has passed the meridian of life. He needs a double portion of "Abraham's faith."

In every parish, both in city and country, a vast amount of labor devolves upon the pastor. He must marry the living, and bury the dead—preach, "in season and out of season"—visit—in a word, be everywhere, and do anything that is honest.

All these anxieties and labors soon break him down.

His only security consists in learning the lesson which the great Apostle of the Gentiles said he had learned, to wit, "in whatsoever state I am, therein to be content." This is the true way to enjoy life. Could Paul have *enjoyed* life? If not, how could he have been "content." Look at him. See him persecuted at Jerusalem, expelled from Antioch, stoned at Lystra, beaten with rods at Thyatira, exposed to wild beasts at Ephesus, arraigned before Felix, Festus and Agrippa, shipwrecked at Malta, and imprisoned at Rome.— Now, we find him "in a basket;" now, "in perils among false brethren;" now, he makes Felix tremble on the judgment seat; now, he almost persuades the half infidel Agrippa; now, he turns away the deluded worshipper from the great goddess, Diana; and, now, he produces fruit in Cæsar's household, even Nero's.

Though generally an *itinerant*, yet, when duty called, he would stay in one place for the very same reason for which ministers of our day often flee. Thus, "he would remain at Ephesus," *first*, because a great door was opened to him, and *secondly*, because "*there were many adversaries.*" Did such a man enjoy life? Hear him. "I have learned to be content;" again, "I rejoice, and will rejoice."

In all the cases of clerical ill-health which have come under my treatment for the last twelve years, (and they have not been few,) nine-tenths of them have originated in over-tasking the mind, — in anxiety and solicitude — in parish troubles — in struggling with poverty, while striving honestly to support a dependent family, and in being driven from place to place. Happily, the good man has faith in God and a hope beyond the grave, or he would be "of all men most miserable."

Let no one think from the preceding remarks that we are opposed to a holy ambition. We advocate an inextinguishable zeal in the Master's service. There is a holy, a pure, and an unholy and impure ambition. Paul had the former, when he "labored more abundantly than any other apostle." Whitefield had the same, when he crossed the Atlantic to preach the Gospel in this country. Many good men have had it. Henry Martyn, that eminent missionary, had more than an earthly ambition. His eye was fixed upon a higher reward. A heavenly impulse had taken possession of his soul. *His* ambition was to lay honors at the feet of Jesus; to consecrate his life to the enlightenment of pagan nations.

Alexander and Napoleon are examples of the latter, or unholy ambition. They sacrificed thousands of lives, and countless treasure, to obtain imperial earthly honors; while Paul and Martyn laid down their lives for the glory of Christ and the salvation of the heathen world. No doubt there are now many clergymen who have this holy ambition, and we commend it; and if there is no other, the "bow has been drawn at a venture," and "the arrow" will hit nobody. Now, the same principle here illustrated in the case of the clergyman, may be applied to any other class of men, and is equally unfavorable to the enjoyment of life. Men, generally, are the artificers of their own fortunes. *Restlessness* is the worm at the root of enjoyment in the family, the parish, the world. "A contented mind is a continual feast." But, how can one be contented when the mind is constantly warring against the body, and the body against the mind?

CHAPTER V.

The word Nervous—Nervous Diseases Numerous—The People imitate the Minister—Mesmerism—Spiritualism—A Suspicious Temper—Faith a Good Medicine—Eating Too Much—Evils produced by a Nervous Clergyman upon his Family—Remedy for Nervous Diseases—Illustration in an Accommodating Clergyman—*How* the Nerves Act—Action of the Mind on the Body—Cause of Traits of Character—Some Never Change—Others Always—Dr. Abernethy's Prescription—Value of Health—Causes which Destroy Peace—Small Salaries—Pay by Orders—Life made up of Little Things—Much that is Pleasant in the Life of a Good Clergyman.

THE word *nervous* is very singularly employed in our language. It is used in many opposite senses. It generally means, a weak, feeble state of body, and a restless, easily agitated state of mind. But, it is not always used with this meaning; for, we say, that was a very strong "nervous speech;" or he was *full of nerve,* meaning very energetic. Then, again, if a person is timid and distrusts his own powers, we say, he is "highly nervous." I shall use it in the sense first named.

Imaginary diseases are a numerous class, and of these the clergyman has his full share. We do not mean to imply that they are confined to clergymen. By no means. The progeny is *Protean,* and found among all classes of men and women. They are distressing anywhere; more disastrous when in the church; but more still to be deplored, when infesting the ministry. Such was the case with the *minds* of many of the clergy of New England in the days of the "Salem witchcraft." That great delusion was hurried forward by the diseased mind and distempered imagination of the most eminent ministers of the gospel. The people always imitate the clergy. Thus, when "the sons of Aaron" became corrupt, "the people soon abhorred the sacrifice." Thus all the abominations of every hierarchy have crept in through worldliness, sensuality, and spiritual pride.

A little incident occurred recently, which serves to verify the declaration, that the people imitate the minister. A physician of some note, and of more than ordinary learning, pronounced a word incorrectly. Some one present remarked that the word was differently pronounced. "I always," said the physician, "take my pronunciation of words from my minister. I pronounced it as he does." A minister who has preached twenty years in the same parish, leaves his "image and superscription" upon that people. You may see it in the very shrug of the shoulder, and the manner of their speaking. They imitate him as naturally as did his generals "the wry neck of Alexander the Great."

We will *first* advert to some of the imaginary diseases of the *mind*. In the so-called "Miller excitement," a part of the uneducated ministers, of some denominations, were verily befooled by the imagination. Never sprite, or witch, or demon, played more fantastic gambols with its infatuated and deluded victims. They were, indeed, led through both "dry" and wet "places, seeking rest and finding none." These were wonderful examples of the influence of diseased minds over feeble bodies. One can form but a slight idea of this wretchedness and misery, unless he has had ocular demonstration of its astounding phenomena. The whole enjoyment of life seemed to have fled from these miserable souls. A proper knowledge of the action of the mind upon the body, and a hygienic application of that knowledge, would have saved many of these poor deluded victims. Oh! when will men understand that they have minds united to bodies, and their reciprocal agency? Never till they do this will they enjoy life.

The evil might have been borne tolerably well, had it been confined to the uneducated. But it was not. We knew a clergyman, a good scholar, once a tutor in a New England College, then settled in one of the "sunny places of Zion," completely bewitched by these vagaries of the imagination. We met him in the street, and he urged us to get him an opportunity to preach in a certain meeting-house. We demurred, and endeavored to reason him out of his delusion. It was, indeed, like "beating the air!" and whenever he was about to meet us afterwards, he always shunned us, and "passed by on the other side." He evidently considered us "reprobate."

There are many cases of imaginary disease where they do not come up to such a pitch as to wholly dethrone reason — and, in these cases, where reason is not dethroned, a noisy, infatuated, suspicious demon sits down upon the throne *with* reason, and they *together* exhibit strange phantoms. Thus, we remember, many years since, hearing a clergyman pray so loudly that the over-strained vocal chords lost their tension and refused to act. But just before he thus choked up, and was compelled to stop, a good old "mother in Israel," who stood near him (for it was at a conference meeting), gently patted him upon the shoulder, with the following timely remark, "Don't, dear, *scream so*. The Almighty ai'nt deaf."

Paracelsus Theophrastus Bombastus, the discoverer of mercury, and the first who used it for medicinal purposes, (it was then called *quack salver*, instead of quicksilver, as now, from which fact the name of *quack* in medicine has been derived), believed, that "there is in man an imagination, which really effects and brings to pass things that did not before exist."

The mesmeric feats, the electro-biological jugglery, and the spiritual rappings of our own times, would not have surprised Paracelsus any more than they do persons of common sense now. Such sublimated moonshine and terrestrial nonsense would have been as well adapted to *his* mind, as it is to his wondering brethren among us. " 'T is but to *fancy* it," as Boniface said of his ale, and the work is done.

Take "Mesmerism." No fallacy or deception was ever more thoroughly exposed and refuted than were the pretensions of Mesmer and his coadjutors, by the "Commission" appointed by the King of France to investigate this matter; of which Commission, *Dr. Franklin*, then the American Minister at Paris, was one. So thorough was the exposure, and so complete the discomfiture, that the *wonder* lost all its charm, and Mesmerism sunk into degradation, only to be revived in our times.

But within a short time after that, the delusion of "Perkins' Tractors," arose in Connecticut, and passed through America, over to England, and on to the Continent, and wrought wonders sufficient to amass a fortune for their distinguished discoverer. Yet any man of common sense knows that two ten-penny nails possess as much virtue as those "metallic Tractors." But, there is no end to the vagaries of quackery. Thousands of men, and women too, otherwise sensible, are the veriest fools in these matters that the world ever saw.

The same imagination often works in the minds of clergymen, leading them to *suspect* the want of friendship and kind feelings in more or less of their parishioners. And hence, in the language of Blair, "by suspecting and hating, they incur suspicion and hatred. By suspecting others to be their enemies, they will, of course, make them such." We have no doubt many a minister has lost the confidence and good-will of some of his best people, and even incurred their hatred, by thus brooding over *imaginary* evils. A suspicious temper is always a source of misery to its possessor. But, no man who uses proper hygienic measures, and who realizes the reciprocal agency of body and mind, is likely to have such a temper.

The same distempered imagination has often led clergymen to pronounce *converted*, and urge into the church, many who were only awakened, or excited, or at most "stony ground, or way-side hearers." This has been no small reproach to vital piety — no small scandal to real "godliness," as they have soon manifested that their "conversion," in the language of Whitefield, "was but some of the minister's bungling work." It was never the work of God.

We can name but one more of these *imaginary delusions* (not for want of numbers, for their "name is legion," but for want of room), and that is modern *Spiritualism*. This is a twin-sister of the whole tribe.

All consists in a diseased mind; but not so far diseased but that, like some in the days of the Apostles, who "used curious arts," they cause strange mutations, and play well as *magicians*. When these, like their predecessors, become Christians, like them they will "burn" their spiritual "books before all men."

What renders all these delusions and vagaries the more to be deplored is, none of them are *new*. In this respect, "the thing that is, is that which has been." Not one of all the wild schemes or of all the skeptical notions of our day, which destroys so much of the enjoyment of life, but has been broached and exploded times without number. Still, they are all *new* to a new generation.

Plato, an Athenian philosopher, the pupil of Socrates, more than 350 years before the Christian era, had his *clairvoyant*, his *slave*, whom, when he wished to amuse his friends, he threw into the mesmeric state, and sent over Athens to look into his neighbors' parlors, and kitchens, and report what they were doing. Though the present age has its full share of *mummery*, yet, if we imagine that we excel those of bygone times in anything of this kind, we are greatly deceived. As with the "lost arts," so is it with the lost and forgotten mental "inventions" and delusions which "men have sought out;" they have been more numerous than at present.

The real cause of all these imaginary notions, or delusions, we will give in due time.

We have a simple prescription for these diseased minds. It is to take a few grains of faith in God, a scruple of the Saviour's meekness and forbearance, and a full draught of benevolence to all mankind.

We now turn to the imaginary diseases of the *body*. Here, also, we find many among all classes, but we will still illustrate by cases of clergymen.

A clergyman who loves good eating, and (as was fashionable till recently) good liquor, too (we mean no reflection, but simply as all drank); who is unwilling to go much abroad; in a word, who presents a fine specimen of loving indolence, is the most liable of all men to have imaginary sickness. We knew an instance of this in a young clergyman, just licensed. He was boarding at home. His good mother would get him up, breakfast him, and send him off four miles to preach.

When once set in motion, like a good clock, he would run well — ride fast — preach excellently, and come home, at night, in fine spirits. As he advanced in age, his sister used to sing to him, on a journey, to keep his spirits up, lest he should die before his journey's end: as David played off the evil spirit from Saul, so did she from him. Happy is the man who, when thus afflicted, has a sister, or wife, to charm away the evil spirit.

We have, in vivid recollection, another clergyman

who was most sorely afflicted with imaginary disease. He was a source of great anxiety and trouble to his wife, who was a healthy woman. Upon her came the weight of responsibility in taking the charge of a large family. She was accustomed to say "the imaginary sickness of her husband caused her more trouble than all the children." We once, in after life, when he had been cured of *imaginary* evils by *real* ones, heard him relate the following: "In my younger days, I was sorely afflicted with a *nervous* disease. The blood would settle under my finger-nails, and my hands become cold up to the elbows. Every one would suppose me dying. Once my wife had been up with me several times, and thus broken of her rest, night after night, until, at length, she refused to get up again. 'The old man,' which had not been wholly 'put off,' then beginning to work, I removed to the side of the bed, as far off as possible, there expecting to die; and, thought I, she will, by and by, find me dead; and then, I reckon, she will be sorry she did not get up for me. *But I didn't die that time.*"

At the age of forty years, this man lost his wife. He was left with a numerous family; and married again, in a few months, a most estimable young lady, a mere child, being but twenty years of age. This wife was delicate, extremely feeble, more nervous, if possible, than even her husband had been, and he was obliged to *put off* his imaginary diseases. He had no opportunity to cherish them. He verified the lines of the poet, for he had that disease which,

> ———— "Real pain,
> And that alone could cure."

It is a remedy somewhat similar that we would propose for clergymen, and all others who are afflicted with imaginary sickness. It is to go to work. "Up and be doing." If you wish to know whether the blood circulates, give it a trial; visit your distant parishioners on foot; lay hold of the axe, the saw, the hoe; open the air-passages to the northern blasts; you will soon see if the blood circulates, and the lungs play, and the heart beats.

Are you afraid of poverty?—go and visit the poorest, the most destitute family of your congregation; or, if you have not a congregation, visit the poorest and most miserable men and women you can find. See their wretched condition;—no bread to eat, no clothes to wear, scarcely any bed to sleep in. If you cannot find such in the country, come to the city. You may then return contented with your lot. Yea, be ready to say, "What shall I render unto the Lord for all his benefits toward me?"

We venture to suggest to clergymen one moral remedy. Is not too much of their time occupied in a controversial manner and a sectarian spirit? And may not this tend to the diminution of health? Would not cherishing the principle of the "new commandment" have a favorable influence upon health, as well as upon the moral feelings? To "contend earnestly for the faith" is an imperative duty, and a reasonable attachment to the forms and ceremonies of our own church is right. But, it is an important question to decide, as to how much of a clergyman's time is to be spent in making fine sermons, and in spinning theological criticisms. The present times seem to demand something like the course pursued by Christ, to "*go about doing good.*" He who would benefit men, must go where they are, and he who would silence opposition, and "compel" men to come into the gospel feast, must do it by cherishing and by exhibiting to them a spirit of love. "Molasses catches more flies than vinegar." The spirit of love has a happy influence upon its possessor's health and his social power. Let the clergy generally engage in carrying the gospel in its consolation and succor to the poor, the afflicted, and the imprisoned, and it would invigorate the body and nerve the mind. It would enhance their usefulness generally, and elevate *some* from feeble dwarfs to strong and full-grown men.

As illustrating the above, let me give the following. We have all seen the effect related as having been produced by one of the New England clergymen, who beat the men of the West in *chopping wood;* the result of which was, when he told them, "I can beat you just as much in *preaching*," that *they all came to hear him preach.* The people love a genial man, who can be one among them, in all innocent amusements, and in the common affairs of life. I have never forgotten the following anecdote, told me by an old country physician in my boyish days: "I was riding on horseback one Sunday to visit a patient at a distance. There came up a violent shower of rain. I came in sight of a church— thought I would stop — rode fast to get out of the storm; but, lo! when I got into the house, I found Mr. —— in the pulpit, and *it stormed harder there than it did out of doors.*" This minister was famous for *scolding* his people into obedience.

The effect of *asperity* in a clergyman is well illustrated in the following story, the scene of which was laid in the State of "steady habits," and the events of which transpired there, several years since. Two clergymen were settled in their youth, in contiguous parishes. The congregation of the one had become very much broken and scattered, while that of the other remained large and strong. At a ministerial gathering (both of these pastors being D. D.'s), Dr. A. said to Dr. B., "Brother, how has it happened that, while I have labored as diligently as you have, and preached better sermons, and more of them, my parish has been scattered to the winds, and yours remains strong and unbroken?"

Dr. B. facetiously replied, "Oh, I'll tell you, brother. When you go fishing, you first get a great rough pole for a handle, to which you attach a large cod-line, and a great hook, and twice as much bait as the fish can swallow. With these accoutrements, you dash up to the brook, and throw in your hook, with, *There, bite, you dogs.* Thus, *you* scare away all the fish. When *I* go fishing, I get a little switching pole, a small line, and just such a hook and bait as the fish can swallow. Then I creep up to the brook, and gently slip them in, and *I twitch 'em out, twitch 'em out, till my basket is full.*" Men do not always "speak the truth," even, " in love."

This is a sufficient illustration of what we mean by using, as above, the old adage of "molasses and vinegar." Therefore, whatever be your occupation, you may apply this remark to your own case or business. I might have given specimens equally illustrative of the subject from other classes. But I have preferred to let you select and apply these items where, and as you please, so that you enjoy life.

We have named some of the effects of the mind upon the body, through the agency of the nerves. Why does a mental emotion make "the mouth water," when food is anticipated? Why does it make the tears flow from the lachrymal gland, when objects of grief are presented?

How these, and a thousand other effects are produced, we know not. This is a question which has been, and still remains unanswered, though it has been agitated from the earliest ages among philosophers, metaphysicians, and physiologists. *Haller* investigated all the theories that had been put forth, upon the action of the nerves; or the influence of them through the mind, or of the mind through them, and concluded that the nerves operated through the medium of a very subtle fluid permeating their cavities, and called *spirit*.

What *Haller* called *spirit*, *Von Helmont* denominated *Aracheus*. *Stahl* called the same *anima*, and *Hunter*, *materia vita*. All these meant, that which we call the *vital principle;* and, it must be confessed, we have but a very imperfect knowledge of it, even now, in the latter half of the nineteenth century. *Hunter* considered this invisible spirit to be added to inert matter, as magnetism is to iron, and that it bears some analogy to electricity and magnetism. *Hartley* thought all the action of mind upon matter was produced by an elastic ether; or by the "vibrations" of infinitesimal particles of the brain and nerves. *Newton* conjectured the same. *Le Gallois*, a very learned Frenchman, believed there was a secretion of the nerves themselves, by which their power is transmitted, and through the medium of which the brain and spinal marrow perform their action upon the animal body.

In the midst of all these opinions, after a somewhat careful study of the nerves, and *nervous* diseases, and of various temperaments, as well as the reciprocal agency of the mind and body, it seems most probable to us, that nervous energy, by a wise arrangement of the Creator (yet secret to science), depends upon the principle of galvanism, or modified electricity.

The nerves are the telegraphic wires of the body by which the brain sends out its messages to the various corporeal organs, and receives back reports from the external world. If the telegraphic wire be broken, the machine will not work. So if the brain, or the nerves running from it, be disorganized or broken, the animal machine will not work — the organs of the body will not act. "The wheel is broken at the cistern, and the pitcher at the fountain," and the man is laid aside.

Considering the curious construction and operation of the nerves, and of the mind upon the body, and the body upon the mind, we need not be surprised at the number of nervous diseases and the singular phenomena which take place among men.

We may see, from the remarks already made, the cause of some peculiarities of character. We do not mean that character is ever formed by such physical properties, that every man is not responsible for his own. But we do mean that there is a wide difference in men, *by nature,* as to their temperament, or mental and bodily qualities. Thus, one is quick to decide, to make up his opinion; and when he has done it, he is "fixed as in a frost." Move him! you might as well think to move Ararat. Shoot arrows, either of truth or error, at him; they make no impression. They rebound as from the hide of the rhinoceros. There are no seams in his sheathing, no joints in his armor. He has taken his side, and he took it never to retreat. He is prepared " to stand,"—stand against every shaft. He has anchored, and never means to let his anchor drag. No matter how long, or how short the time he was in fixing down, he is moored for ever. He has clenched his hand, and like the grasp of the spider upon the poor fly, who happens to be his victim, even death does not unclinch it. In common phraseology, "he has '*got kinked,*' and all creation can't unkink him." He glories in never changing. No windows exist in his mind to let in the light. No reasoning is argument with him. He *knows* he is right; and all we would say to such an one, is to repeat the remark of an old Scotch divine, " It behooveth a Scotchman to be *right,* for if he be *wrong,* he be for ever and eternally wrong." Stability is a good characteristic, but obstinacy is the source of much unhappiness, and ought to be shunned by all. It too often very much resembles what the colored man said his *conscience* was— "Something that say, *I won't.*"

Another seems to be, constitutionally, all vacillation. Yesterday he was here; to-morrow he will be there; and the place, or the opinion, in which you left him last, is no pledge of where, or how, you will find him next. In the morning, he was pursuing this opinion, and he *thought* he was right; at evening, he has imbibed another, and he now *knows* he is right. The opinion of the last man he conversed with is his opinion, until he converses with another.

"He is to nothing fixed,
But love of change."

He wishes to remove from one parish to another, at least as often as once in two years. A permanent residence is no *home* for him. He was destined for "a bird of passage;" and causes, real or imaginary, for such removal are never wanting. The death of a *good* deacon, or the asperity of a bad one, and the alienation of a few who were once friendly, are with him sufficient cause for change. Indeed, change seems bound in his nature, and one might as well think to fix the weathercock to one point, as to bind him to one opinion or place. This love of change influences his whole conduct; and this seems to be so inherent in his nature, that it is inaccessible to reason or argument.

INDECISION OF CHARACTER.

Now, these traits of character are with some men constitutional. We knew a clergyman who had, at different times, belonged to three or four denominations of Christians. He said, "his brethren called these changes, but *he* called them changes only from glory to glory."

Of the former, we may say they usually remain inflexible, till some terrible storm comes and tears them up by the roots, and they die suddenly. They may be compared to a beautiful apple, which looks fair and red without, but which is rotten at the core. When the disease appears upon the surface, the whole is gone. They sink at once; "the whole heart being faint, and the whole head sick."

The latter may be said to die by piece-meal, or by inches; or, as *Dean Swift* said, when he looked up and saw the dead branches of a tree—"I shall be like that tree—*I shall die at the top first.*" They are whirled in perpetual eddies, till by little and little, of disease of both mind and body, they finally fall off. These are specimens of the mutual action of body and mind.

For the former, we would prescribe alternate doses of the modifying oil of gospel tenderness, and of fellow-feeling with all men, "specially of the household of faith," and of that "charity" which "thinketh no evil, and is kind." For the latter, ten grains each, morning and evening, of the ingredients composing the Christian armor, as enumerated in Paul's Epistle to the Ephesians.

We think these will prove as efficacious as Dr. *Abernethy's* celebrated prescription to the hosts of *dyspeptic* patients who were accustomed to throng his office. It was this, one and the same to each, " Go home, sir, read my book at page —, eat your food slowly, and live like a Christian." Our prescription need not be confined to clergymen. It will suit the case of many others, and it should be understood that there are many in every calling who do not enjoy life so well as they might, if they would follow our prescription.

There are one or two thoughts connected with this subject which claim further attention.

The health of a clergyman is often injured by the losses, perplexities, and trials into which he is thrown by the indiscreet, unwise, niggardly, and sometimes cruel conduct of his parishioners. If he is of that nervous, sensitive diathesis (to use a physician's phrase), which we have been considering, almost any of the following circumstances would prove injurious to his health.

We knew a clergyman, long since entered into his rest, who, under a wild-fire religious excitement (so called) in which certain young girls, under the guidance of some itinerant holder-forth exorcist, "or vagabond Jew," took it upon them to admonish him that he was a "formalist and hireling; a blind leader of the blind."

Some of them were very young, not more than a dozen years old. The good pastor had labored faithfully "in season and out of season," and seen but little fruit of his labors. Being of a sensitive and nervous temperament, their reproaches were to him as "vinegar to nitre," disturbing his peace, rendering him miserable and sick. The best remedy for their foolish and impertinent vociferations would have been a faithful application of that little instrument which Solomon recommends as very successful in driving "foolishness from the heart of a child."

We have known a clergyman disqualified from study, and really made sick, by the niggardly and deceitful dealing of one of his deacons. It was by simply deceiving in a load of wood. It was not the value of the wood, but the thought, on his part, of being overreached in a case where he could not complain; or, if he did, where the last error would be worse to him than the first; and, on the part of the deacon, that he should have a professor and an officer in his church who was devoid of common honesty, and willing to commit sacrilege. Had this pious man been less pious, and possessed of a different temperament, he would have shaken off this "viper and felt no harm." In this respect, it seems, sometimes, desirable to be *thick-skinned*, and to partake largely of the properties of a

"Boanerges;" but forbearance and charity are more comely for a Christian pastor.

We knew another clergyman, who had the misfortune, or the good fortune, to be, like Christ's early disciples, from the humble walks of life; his father having been a basket-maker. When, (as was customary in those days,) a load of basket-stuff was brought along for sale, in the absence of the good man, some of his parishioners would purchase it, and order it to be left at the front door of his residence; there, on his return, he would find it, and weep over the depravity of his people for the deed. A little more firmness of nerve, or of that independence which prompted the reply of some of the apostles, when the serjeants said, "the council had sent to let them go; they have beaten us openly uncondemned; and now, do they thrust us out privily? Nay, verily; but let them come themselves, and fetch us out." Or, of that feeling which Paul conveyed to the chief captain, when he inquired, "Is it lawful for you to scourge a man that is a Roman, and uncondemned?" Or, that which led him on another occasion to say, "I appeal unto Cæsar," would have answered a better purpose. Many a man would have thanked them for the basket-stuff for kindling-wood.

We also remember a case somewhat similar, where a portion of the people did not manifest a disposition to "pluck out their own eyes and give them to" their pastor, because they loved him so much. A member of the parish, who had been absent on a voyage, but not long enough to forget the right, on his return, was soon visited by a neighbor, who wished to enlist him against the minister. "Why," said he, "the minister is the worst man living — he will not even attend a funeral of one of his opposers." The cool reply of the sea-captain was, "Well, he *is* very different from me. If you had used me as you have him, I should *rejoice* to attend all your funerals."

Another cause of ill health to clergymen is found in the scantiness of their salaries, and the non-payment of even the small pittances usually promised. People often settle pastors, calculating that they shall grow, so that they shall advance upon the salary. But it too generally turns out, on their part, as was stated by a certain lady respecting the *growth* of clergymen. She said, "they had settled several young ministers, calculating that they would *grow*, but they grew backwards, and she hoped, when they settled another, he would be a *full-grown* one."

In many parishes, the salary is absolutely too small for the minister to live upon, even if he received it promptly. But, in addition to not receiving it when due, some have a way of paying it *by orders*. We remember a clergyman, who, upon being told when he bought a load of wood of one of his parishioners, that he might pay him with an *order* upon the treasurer of the society, remarked that he preferred to pay money for his purchases. The parishioner said, he "thought it was less trouble to give *orders,* and the people generally preferred it." Upon finding the minister firm in his decision of paying money, he said, "their former pastor was more accommodating; they paid most of his salary in orders." Of that, this clergyman had already been apprised by the pastor himself.

In other parishes, the money comes in driblets — a dollar or two at a time, as the treasurer happens to receive it. Thus no calculation can be made upon regular payments, and consequently the money is not worth as much as it otherwise would be. We once heard of a treasurer of a society who was quite offended because a minister would not take his salary in driblets.

It may be said these are all small matters, scarcely worth naming. We know they are, and we know, also, that it is of small affairs that life is composed. We know also, that it is much easier to bear, occasionally, a large disappointment, than an everlasting repetition of smaller trials. "A continual dropping wears the stones," and all enjoyment of life.

A minister's cup of trials, too, is generally full, and it is the last drop that sinks the ship. Like an everlasting round in the treadmill, to grind and grind and know no end, is the great trial of too many. "Save me from my friends," is not unfrequently a phrase full of meaning. Now all these, and a thousand more, contribute to destroy the health and wear out the life of clergymen.

There are other important considerations connected with this subject. The gospel must be preached. The world will go to perdition without it, and "how can they hear without a preacher?" Some must be ambassadors of "the Prince of Peace." They must not desert the field, but fight on till death; or, till they can say, as did the great apostle, "I have fought a good fight."

These considerations give vast weight to our subject. No one is justified in withdrawing from the gospel field who has health sufficient for the work.

Meekness, patience, forbearance and long-suffering, become all who hold the sacred office. Clergymen must be "examples to the flock." They must also have a "good report of those that are without," though this is what neither the apostles nor their Master had.

Religion being the most important of all concerns, and the prevalence of religion in the world having, by divine appointment, been made dependent upon the preaching of the gospel, it becomes a question of vast weight to decide, when, where, and how a minister should preach—where the point is at which forbearance should cease—when he should take injuries from "false brethren" and from the world calmly, and when he should "rebuke sharply." In all these, it certainly becomes clergymen to "ask wisdom of Him who giveth liberally, and to come boldly to the Throne for grace to help in every time of need."

We need to guard ourselves against thinking too much of life. It is the gift of God continued, taken, when he pleases; and, while "little things are great to little man," in the most trying of them, it is important to remember that life has been given us for usefulness, and that in it no evil can befall us which is not under the guidance of our heavenly Father.

Another consideration worthy of attention, is, that all things work for good to the Christian. The fiery furnace of a pastor's life may be necessary for his purification, or for that of any other man.

Then, also, it is important to remember how much there is which is pleasant and refreshing in the life of a good minister. He is an object of endearing affection to many. They love him as they love their own souls. They esteem him highly for his works' sake. They remember him in their blessings, and often administer to his necessities. They pray for him as one whom they love and delight to honor, and to see honored. These good people are to be found scattered all over the land — ready to do good to the minister — or to lay down their lives for his sake. Much of his enjoyment arises from their kindness.

While, therefore, we speak freely of his trials and of many things which impair his health and wear out his life, we would never forget that he has "not yet resisted unto blood," and that should he even fall upon the field of battle, it will be only to be embalmed in the memory of the good, and to rise to a crown of glory of unfading lustre. Let every clergyman then feel that trials and loss of health are the well-intended chastisements of a benevolent Father, and that it is "through much tribulation that we must enter into the kingdom of heaven," but let him never be instrumental in bringing them upon himself by his own imprudence or neglect. The true enjoyment of life consists in the exercise of the benevolent affections, the proper care of the body, and a well-ordered management of the mind. This happiness can be had by all, and the writer has chosen the case of the minister of the gospel, as an illustration for all others, because *he*, more than any other one, in imitation of the great Exemplar, is bound to have in exercise all these *talents*, namely, body, mind, heart, and not to bury one of them; but so to improve them that at the coming of "the Master," He may "receive his own with usury."

CHAPTER VI.

Locality Important to Usefulness — Frequent Removals—Cause originated with the Clergy—The People soon learned it—Sleepy Hearers—Advertising Ministers—No Excuse—Ministerial Tones—Sermons too Nice — President Wayland — Archbishop Usher.

WHILE man has no permanent home on earth, it is not desirable only, but necessary to his highest usefulness and greatest enjoyment, that he should have an abiding place while he remains in this world. Few men who have often changed their residence, or their business, have ever had great enjoyment of life, or been greatly useful to the world. This is the general *principle*, while there have been exceptions to this, as to all other rules; and following out our plan of selecting the clergyman as an example for all classes, we will proceed to show the illustration of this *principle*, in the case of the clerical profession, or by the frequent change of their location.

It has been hinted, in a previous chapter, that frequent *removals* of clergymen often prove injurious to their health. A word more on this point may not be amiss.

If a man is worth anything, the longer he remains in one place, the more useful he will be. If he is worthless, the oftener he resembles the "rolling stone, gathering no moss,"—doing no good,—either to himself, or others, the better for all concerned. But no clergyman of common feelings, and especially of sensitive nerves, can have all his plans of usefulness thwarted, and all his social relations (save those of his family, and sometimes these even) broken up, without a severe shock to his nervous system, often so severe as to impair health.

For the last few years, these frequent and sudden removals may have been chargeable, chiefly to a restlessness among the people; to "itching ears," and to "covetousness, which is idolatry." The people are in fault. But though, as often happens, they may be *now* more blameworthy than the clergy, yet they were not "first in this transgression." Now the question here arises, who were the *original* transgressors? Did this evil first spring up from among the clergy themselves? Whoever looks back upon the relation of pastor and people, for the last thirty or forty years, and calls to remembrance the permanency of the pastoral relation then, will see, not only that a great change in this relationship has come over us, but, also, that it *originated* in the ministry. So seldom was the removal of a pastor in former days, and his re-settlement, that an eminent lawyer was accustomed then to say, "he would as soon marry a woman who had been divorced from her husband, as vote to settle a minister who had been dismissed from his first charge." The present unsettled state of parochial affairs, seems to have originated on this wise. Some leading ministers thought they needed a great man in a particular place. Hence, they went to any parish where, in their estimation, the field was smaller, or of less importance, and said to the "feebler folk" (no matter how well contented they were in their pastor, or how ardently attached to him), "you must give up your minister." He must "go to yonder high place of Zion," and to *him*, also, they said, "go, and he went." The "little flock" remonstrated, but always had to yield. The weight of influence from the "great," sometimes conjoined (as was natural) with a desire in the candidate for a larger field, preponderated, and the lesser "flock" was left like "sheep without a shepherd." They sometimes hinted that metropolitan power was waxing too strong, mourned the loss of their good pastor, which the influence of the bishops and the richer parish had removed from them, and submitted "according to the grace given unto them," though they did not enjoy it.

But "the end was not yet." The people soon found (to use a trite phrase) that "this was a game that two could play at as well as one"—to wit: if their minister could be taken away by others, or take himself away against their wishes, *they* could send him away, if they

FREQUENT REMOVALS. 107

pleased, against *his*, even when combined with *those* of his peers.

The breaking up of the pastoral relation, having been thus commenced by the clergy, and the people having become like the priests (in this matter at least), the work went on until removals became so general that *permanency* in the pastoral office became the *exception*, *change* the rule. Indeed, change in the ministry became so rife, that in many cases the parish settled their minister *on wheels*, with a *proviso* in the contract that he might or *should* go, on "six months' notice" of either party," *nolens volens* the other.

Nor was it found that our ecclesiastical polity presented any barrier to such removals. "*Councils* were only advisory, called to sanction what the parties had done." Thus they really became a dead letter, or acted a mere *farce*, and their *results* read as follows — "This council, after prayer and mature reflection, sincerely regret that things are so in this church and society, that the dissolution of the pastoral relation between the Rev. A. B. and the church in ——, has become necessary, and we are of the opinion that it ought to be, and it *is*, hereby dissolved. We hereby recommend the Rev. A. B. to the fellowship of the churches, wherever he may be called 'to sojourn,' as a pious, devoted, and accredited minister of the Gospel; and this bereaved people to the Great Head of the church, praying that he will soon send them a faithful shepherd to 'watch over and break to them the bread of life.'"

In many parishes this scene has been acted over almost every year, certainly every five years, for the last twenty. Any wicked man "of wealth and standing," in most of our country parishes, by the influence which money and family friends give him, can accomplish the removal of the faithful pastor simply by withholding his pecuniary aid, and raising a hue and cry against him, either with or without cause.

Such a deplorable state of things must not only destroy ministerial influence, but also affect ministerial health and happiness.

These remarks of course apply to that system of church polity which has *Councils;* in a word, to *Congregationalists* or *Independents*, including *Baptists;* and it is doubtful whether any other system of government among the American churches has presented much improvement upon this as it respects frequent removals in the pastoral office; so that, though the above was written for the latitude of New England, yet, like the "Old Farmer's Almanac," with very slight variation, it will answer for any other latitude.

Indeed, if *preaching the gospel* is the great work of the ministry, it becomes an important question, how often, and when, should a pastor be removed from his appropriate duty, **to take "the oversight"** of a college, seminary, or school? Judging from appearances, it would seem, that every board of trustees of these institutions, from the highest to the lowest, conjointly with the bishops, or professors already there, feel that they have a perfect right to pounce upon any pastor, especially any one who is popular, beloved, and doing good service in the "vineyard," or among "the flock over which the Holy Ghost has made him overseer," and transfer him to their service.

We should like to know "by what authority they do these things, and who gave them this authority?"

It is seriously doubted whether any such course is authorized, either by Christ or his apostles, or can find any precedent, or support from the New Testament. It is questionable whether the system of *advertising*, so prevalent at present in cities, that such an one will preach on a certain subject, at a certain time and place, is wise or right. Does it not look a little too much like the *catch-penny* advertisements of itinerant lecturers? More especially is this practice questionable in a *pastor*, for two reasons: *first,* because the parish, having settled him, *expect* he will preach without publishing it in a newspaper; and, *second,* it may seriously interfere with the arrangements of some more humble, but less ostentatious brother, who may preach at the same hour, but not choose to herald it by a flourish of trumpets.

We have only one other point to glance at, in this chapter, in which the clergyman's temper, patience, and long-suffering, are often tested, and, consequently, his health affected, and his enjoyment of life destroyed.

No greater insult can be offered to the minister by a hearer, than to go to sleep while the gospel is being preached to him; and scarcely any conduct can desecrate the sanctuary more than to make it a *dormitory*. No healthy person can be excused for sleeping in church. If an apostle rebuked those who abused "the Supper," by language like this, "What! have ye not *houses* to eat and to drink in? or despise ye the church of God, and shame them that have not?" may it not be said to those who come to church to sleep, What! have ye not *beds to sleep* in at home, that ye come here to slumber? Who ever knew a man *sleep* at a *political* meeting?

It must affect any minister to see his hearers asleep. It is recorded of Dr. Young, the author of the "Night Thoughts," that "having failed, on one occasion, to get the attention of his hearers, and seeing some of them asleep, he stopped preaching, sat back in the pulpit and burst into a flood of tears." Such an effect, from such a cause, should be expected in a faithful, devoted, but nervous man.

It has been said of one of the most eminent clergymen of the nineteenth century, that nothing so seriously disturbed his temper, or affected his health, as the sleepiness or irreverence of his hearers. This man possessed one of the warmest hearts, and quickest intellects, and most sensitive nerves that ever fell to the lot of man. He could almost make the breezes of heaven fan his hearers, and the songs of the redeemed break in melody upon their ears; or so vividly describe the lost as to make them see the gaping pit, witness the lurid fires, and hear the wailings of the lost. Yet he could not endure a *sleepy* hearer.

But this part of our subject must not be left, without seeing whether ministers themselves are not sometimes accessory to the drowsiness of their hearers. Still, if this shall be made to appear, it is not a sufficient excuse to justify such an insult, both to the preacher and to his Master, as sleeping in church. But it is feared that clergymen do become, in a degree, aids to sleepy hearers in the two following ways. First, by getting into the habit of speaking in a kind of *sing-song*, affected, and pious *tone*. A medical writer, in a recent article in "The Medical World," assigns this as the cause of so many persons going to sleep in church; and argues the justness of his supposition by stating it as a fact, that when such a *sing-song* pastor *exchanges* with some brother, the peculiar *phase* or tone of speaking being changed, these sleepy hearers keep awake.

It is quite probable that the above is as really the cause of sleeping with many, as the following, which we have heard assigned. "A clergyman who had a deacon that always slept when he preached at home, and kept awake when a stranger preached, asked him how this happened?" The deacon replied, "Why, when you are at home, you understand all our matters, and I know every thing will go on right. But when we have a stranger, he needs watching."

The other cause which may make sleepy hearers is, ministers make *too fine sermons*,—they are *so* nice that common people do not understand them, consequently they lose the ideas, the *thread* of the discourse, and go to sleep. But, as words have influence just in proportion to the *height* of the place from which they come, I will let the *Rev. President Wayland* and others tell the rest of this story.

"The vice of preaching at present, in most of our pulpits, is that we do not aim correctly. We strive to please the few, and not the many; and the result is that the conscience of both parties is unmoved. The pulpit is dying of the proprieties. We dare not introduce an anecdote into a sermon. We shrink from an illustration unless we can count it classical. We are averse even to the delineation of character, lest we should detract from the dignity of the pulpit. When a man is afraid of losing his dignity by attending to his own business, we generally think he has very little to lose. We fear that the pulpit is liable to create a similar impression. Look at the highest example of preachers. How simple is the teaching of Christ, how perfectly adapted to the audience by which he was surrounded! How it abounds in illustrations, parables, and even every-day proverbs, so that the common people heard him gladly! Paul tells us himself how he preached in Corinth, and Ephesus, and he is surely a good model for a cultivated man. Look at Bunyan, one of the most eloquent and effective preachers of his time,— how plain, how simple, how earnest, and yet how full of incident and illustration were his discourses. Observe President Davies,—how plain, forcible, earnest, and direct were his discourses. We sacrifice vivacity and interest to a vague pedantic notion of what is *proper* for the pulpit, as though a preacher of the Gospel were lecturing to a class on the proprieties of rhetoric. Is it not time that a change came over us, and that a preacher aimed more at interesting and converting men, and less at the reputation of refinement of style, and exquisiteness of propriety? A minister once said that a sermon without a fault would spoil a revival. Are not such sermons the reason why revivals are so rare among us?"

Paul says, "I used great plainness of speech." Archbishop Usher says, "It requires all our learning to make truth simple."

It is believed that the crowning excellency of the preaching of the late Dr. Nettleton, and the prime cause of his great success, was the simplicity of language which he used. A child could comprehend every word.

CHAPTER VII.

Enjoyment of Life dependent on Speech—The Voice—Where formed—Power of Habit in Speaking—Its Sounds—Much Culture required to make an Orator—Power and Beauty of the Human Voice—Aphonia—Clergyman's Sore Throat—Treatment—Written Sermons—Supposed Ignorance of the Clergy on the Common Affairs of Life—The Literary Lady.

So much of the enjoyment of life is dependent upon the power of speech, which God has vouchsafed to the human species over all other animals, that the hygienic and proper management of the vocal organs is of momentous importance. Pursuing our usual plan, the use and management of this wonderful apparatus will be explained and illustrated, and its blessings pointed out by the case of public speakers; and, especially, in the clerical profession.

In a former chapter, reference was had to "the Clergyman's Sore Throat." But some more extended notice of the voice, its formation, use, and disease of its organs, seems necessary. The voice is formed in the larynx. This organ properly belongs to the respiratory apparatus. Its structure is very complicated. Did we not know this from an actual examination of the organ, we should infer it, from the wisdom and design manifested throughout the whole animal organism, when we consider that two of the most important functions of life, viz., breathing and speaking, are accomplished through the instrumentality of the larynx.

It is a cartilaginous tube, or box, located at the top of the windpipe. The anatomy and physiology of this organ are exceedingly curious and interesting. At the base of the tongue we find the *thyroid* bone — a bone shaped like the letter *u*. From this bone, a ligament passes to the *thyroid,* or shield-shaped cartilage. This cartilage does not pass round the *back* part of the larynx. The windpipe is surrounded by a strong cartilaginous ring, called the *cricoid* cartilage, and this is embraced by another, called the *thyroid*. Two cords, formed by the folds of the mucous membrane of the larynx, pass, the one above and the other below, the little hollow, called the *glottis ;* forming a *buttonhole-*like opening between them, called the *chink* of the glottis. The voice is formed by the lower cords, which are made of the most elastic material found in the human body. The experiment has often been made upon animals to ascertain precisely where the sound is made, and has been found to arise from the *lower* cords; and hence these have been called the *vocal cords.*

It is wholly by the power of habit that we are able to contract or lengthen these cords, so as to give a high or a low sound, by moving in certain ways the muscles attached to them. When we consider what a difficult and intricate matter this is, it is truly wonderful that a child ever learns to talk. The sound being thus formed in the lower vocal cords, all the parts above serve only to increase or lower, or in a word, to modify, the voice.

There are seven distinguishing characters of voice in men and women. In men they are termed bass, baritone, tenor, robusto or full-tenor, and tenor-leggiadro or counter-tenor. Those of women are termed contralta, mezzo-soprano and soprano. The compass will be found to vary according to the length of the vocal cords and windpipe, the longest possessing the power of producing the greatest number of notes. Thus, one voice may comprise a range of twelve notes, and another of sixteen, yet both may be of the same character. The change which occurs in the voice in the decline of life is the result of the ossification of the cartilages of the larynx, and the hardening of its ligaments, which produce a hard and cracked sound.

In the change of the voice from the boy to the man, those parts *above* the vocal cords become much enlarged, and hence operate as a *sounding* board. Constant efforts give power over the voice, this wonderful instrument. This is the reason that it requires long practice to make an orator. Of the truth of this remark, Cicero and Demosthenes are examples. It must be supposed, therefore, that "Apollos" practised much, before he became what Luke calls him, "an eloquent man." With the beauty, power, and excellence of the human voice, nothing can bear comparison. It is the sweetest music that the ear can hear. It is the glory of man; it is, also, his bane. Without it, the gospel cannot be preached. It is characterized in Scripture under the term, the *tongue*. "It is a fire, a world of iniquity among our members. Therewith bless we God, even the Father, and therewith curse we men, which are made after the similitude of God." It is more untamable than beasts, birds, or serpents.

From the delicacy and intricacy of the vocal organs, we should naturally infer the vast importance of their function. Signs may express thoughts, wishes, emotions. A savage, beholding the golden apple, might make a gesture indicating that he wanted it; a dog has been known to make a sign that he wished for human aid to relieve his master in distress. But how insignificant are these pantomimic representations to human speech! No device for expressing thought or volition, but dwindles into insignificance before the human voice. A single vocal utterance awakens thoughts in hundreds of bosoms. "Words, fitly *spoken*, are like apples of gold in pictures of silver."

Like all other parts of the animal economy, this vocal apparatus is liable to disease; and in no class of men does this occur more frequently than among clergymen. So often, indeed, has it prevailed within a few years, that it has been technically called "*the* clergyman's disease."

Aphonia, or loss of voice, may arise from several causes. It may be caused by a cold; by thickening of the mucous membrane of the larynx; or by injury to the vocal cords — by their becoming permanently enlarged, relaxed, or inflamed; or by the nerves becoming diseased or paralyzed, which run to the muscles which move these cords. Or, we may have *aphonia* from extreme debility, as is sometimes the case in the last stage of consumption; or, from ossification of the cartilage of the larynx. *Hoarseness* is often caused by an enlargement of the vocal cords; the cords becoming like the strings of a bass viol which has laid out all night in the dew, or become soaked with water. Not unfrequently, a roughness of the voice is caused by a chronic inflammation of the membrane which lines the larynx and trachea. This inflammation is sometimes coming on for years. Every sermon preached tends to augment it. When it is taking place, the throat feels raw, or, as elsewhere described, as though it were *scraped*. I have known a patient in such case make an almost constant effort to *swallow* for an hour, especially after preaching.

This kind of sore throat commences usually in **the**

fauces or *pharynx*, above the root of the tongue, and extends downwards to the larynx; and, eventually, unless checked by proper remedies, to the lungs. On examining the *velum*, or soft palate, as seen in the mouth, it is found to be of a deep red, interspersed with light or ash-colored spots. The membrane is inflamed, and these spots are caused by a concretion of albumen upon the palate and surrounding parts. As the disease progresses, these spots coalesce, and finally coat the whole secreting membrane. Small sloughs take place, and beneath, the membrane is of a deep red color, deprived of its epithelium, or inner lining. It is only in severe cases, that this inflammation extends into the larynx, and down the windpipe, running into what was formerly called *tracheal* consumption. The disease is usually slow in its progress; but, sometimes, there is an acute inflammation of the epiglottis, or valve covering the larynx, and the lining of the larynx itself, and of the air-tube, and an adhesive substance poured out in such abundance as to prevent the entrance of air into the lungs,—thus causing death, as by suffocation or loss of breath. It was from such a form of this acute disease, that General Washington, the Father of his Country, died; though, undoubtedly, the medical treatment he received hastened on the disease to a fatal termination.

In the commencement of this disease, there is simply

an enlargement, irritation, or slight inflammation of the *follicles*, or glands of the pharynx and larynx. These glands are very numerous in the membrane which lines the upper parts of these passages. The increase and extension of the disease are in the glands of the tube running to the lungs, becoming diseased in a similar manner. The access of this disease is so insidious, that it may have continued months, or years even, without manifesting any other symptoms than a desire to *hawk* up, or to *swallow* something which seems to lie at the top of the larynx, with a slight roughness, or occasional huskiness of the voice, and an unnatural relaxation, or enlargement of all the parts of the throat. It must not be inferred from these remarks, that this disease is limited to any one profession or occupation; nor to any particular age or climate. It pervades, to a certain extent, almost all classes, and I have known it to exist even in females.

The causes conspiring to induce this disease are various; but, in a word, may be said to be anything which depresses the vital powers; such as too close application to study, anxiety, over-exertion, exposure to cold, fear of not succeeding, disappointed ambition, a torpid condition of the liver, &c. The immediate exciting cause is often too much and too loud speaking. Frequently this disease is induced by singing. In most instances, it is accompanied by an extremely nervous state of the whole system. Every nerve in the body seems to be on the stretch. In many cases, it is accompanied by indigestion; and, in some, it is excited by acid eructations from the stomach, which excoriate and roughen the throat at the top of the œsophagus, or meat-pipe. Rarely have I ever seen a case where the tone of the whole system was not *below* the usual standard of health. It more frequently arises from a deranged stomach than is generally supposed. Indeed, many diseases which seem to be *local*, as often an affection of the eyes, is caused by abnormal action of the stomach.

In the *treatment*, the first requisite is rest, absolute rest from public speaking, and, as far as can be, from using the vocal organs at all: together with this, there should be relaxation from care. In a word, both mind and body should be quiet. But as *prevention* is better than *cure*, let all strive to ward off this disease. To do this, the hygienic management of these organs becomes very important; and, no small share of the enjoyment of life is taken away when the vocal organs are diseased.

Some remedies must be addressed directly to the diseased organs. Within a few years past, means have been devised for entering the box of the larynx, and of applying to its surface, and to the whole of the trachea, reaching even into the bronchial tubes, and some say into the lungs, certain chemical salts, held in solution in water, which check this irritation and inflammation, and induce the mucous membrane to take on a healing action. The principal, and the first one chiefly employed, was the nitrate of silver, in the strength of from ten to eighty grains to the ounce of water. Other remedial agents have sometimes been used, and I have occasionally employed the nitrate of silver, in the form of an impalpable powder, by inhalation. In either of these ways, this agent often produces a salutary effect upon this disease. But, as an abuse of the *nitrate* has sometimes given the skin a permanent dark tinge, the oxide of silver has by many been substituted for the nitrate.

But the local application alone rarely effects a permanent cure, as the disease is generally accompanied with indigestion, or a torpid condition of the liver. Hence, if none but local applications are made, the disease will be but half treated, and the apparent cure will not prove real and permanent.

If public speakers wish to avoid the disease in question, it will be important for them to attend, among others, to the following particulars: They must not study too hard, nor at improper times. They must be moderate in the amount and loudness of their voice. Often much more effort is made in speaking than is necessary to be audible. Many of the best and most effective speakers have put forth but little physical power, and spoken uniformly in a moderate tone. Such clergymen practise as though they believed the declaration of holy writ, "*bodily* exercise profiteth little." The ignorant alone consider that the *louder* the preaching is, the better it is; while the wise and considerate know that *empty* things make the most sound. It is much easier for the vocal organs to speak without than with notes. I would have every minister preach, ordinarily, without writing his sermons. I would have him study his sermon as long as it would take him to write it, and then make his brief, and go into the pulpit and preach from it. It will fatigue him much less, and he will have the accompanying influence of the eye, which is much more valuable than is generally imagined, and his audience will be better pleased and better edified. This is the way many eminent preachers have done, and the way every one can do, who can preach in any way acceptably. In the opinion of the writer, a chief reason why the lawyer can do twice as much speaking as the clergyman, without injury to his vocal organs, is, the former speaks *without*, and the latter *with*, a written discourse. It is important, also, that clergymen relieve themselves from all undue anxiety, and it would not be injurious, but beneficial, if they should occasionally be found, like the great "Apostle of the Gentiles," laboring at "tent-making," or some other manual labor. It is a relic of the "dark ages," that clergymen should never know anything, nor do anything but study and make sermons. So thought not Paul; so practised not our great Exemplar. Neither the celibacy of the clergy, nor their monkish austerity, nor their ignorance of every-day affairs, and the common duties of life, ever contributed to their happiness or usefulness.

It has almost passed into a proverb that clergymen know nothing about business matters. Witness the following: A clergyman once inquired at a "Savings Institution" what per cent. they paid for money. Upon learning that the per cent. was small, he so remarked. "O," said the bank-man, "we don't take large sums, and a large part of it comes from *old maids* and *clergymen*, of the class who don't know how to manage for themselves." The same remarks apply far too generally to all studious men and literary women. Secluded from the world, they know but little of its plans and doings. Devoted to science, to books, or to one of the learned professions, when they descend into the world of business, it is almost as though they came from another planet. Who has not heard of the *literary* lady, of whom, when the girl was absent and she was herself compelled to get a dinner, her husband said,

"She undertook to get it by the book,
And she booked it, and booked it,
And, at last, never cooked it."

How much of the enjoyment of life depends upon knowing something besides *books!*

11 *

CHAPTER VIII.

Misery or Happiness from the Feet — The Feet — Their Proper Use and Management — The Anatomy of the Foot — The Turks and their Feet — Boots and Shoes — Cotton and Woollen Stockings — Sympathy between the Feet and other Organs.

WE have known the health much impaired, and the enjoyment of life greatly diminished by the want of proper hygienic care of the feet. These very necessary and useful organs can never be slighted without making it known that they belong to the body and require their proper share of attention. The function they fulfil, and the skill of the great Architect evinced in their formation, both proclaim that much of the happiness of life is connected with their healthy and usable condition: enjoyment or misery often proceed from the foot.

The *anatomy* of the human skin is very curious. The *scarf*, or outer skin, is hard and dry. The true skin beneath is composed of minute fibres, first gathered into bundles, then into each other, so as to form a web. This web is very compact, yet porous. The pores grow larger as they descend deeper, until, in the lowest part, they have a diameter of about one-twelfth of an inch. The pores are nearly round, and separated by strands of fibres of double their own diameter. Hence, the lower surface of the skin resembles a coarse net. The strands or fibres are connected with the fat under the skin.

It is a curious question to know how we can support the whole body upon so sensitive a layer as the skin of the foot.

The wonderful mechanism of the foot alone can explain the phenomenon. The wisdom of the Maker may be seen in it.

A membrane is so constructed, as to present different *qualities* at different *depths*, upon the same surface, giving an *even* support to the sensitive layer which is placed upon it. Then a coarse net-work that will expand every way, and again return to its original form, composes another membrane. The open meshes are filled with a cushion of fat. Thus, the construction is more complete for elasticity and yielding to pressure, concussion, or contusion, than any *spring* cushion which art can construct. Such is a small part only of the curious anatomy of the foot, with which it is not now necessary to proceed further.

We might learn a profitable lesson from the Turks respecting the management of the feet. It may be deemed unnecessary to dilate upon the severity of the manner in which we treat our feet, because every one knows where the shoe pinches. We crowd them into black moulds, deprive them of the benefit of air, and too frequently of water, and never allow them to raise themselves from a low grade of existence; and, as these very useful organs of locomotion have never been raised above this state of degradation and suffering, we imagine such degradation to be necessary, and such suffering unavoidable. But if we would take a lesson from the East, from whence report says "light has always come," our erroneous ideas on this subject might be corrected. There, certainly, the privileges of the feet are far superior. There, they share an equality of rights with their brother hands, and are allowed to take upon themselves an equal share of duty. Their presence offends no sense. Their aspect excites no aversion. They are respectfully placed on the great man's sofa, in the full enjoyment of air, light, and water. There *they* use boots and shoes, instead of *being used* by them. Our boot and shoe despotism does not reign there

Wo shrink away from, and despise the slave who can kiss the toe of his Holiness the Pope, or of any Eastern monarch. This, we think, is quite too much for young America. It would, indeed, be so, if *the* foot of the Western were the foot of the Eastern world. Here lies our error,—*the* foot there is not the abject, offensive, cabined, cribbed, confined, unclean thing which we often carry about with us, and hide in a boot. The foot there rejoices, as of old, in a buskin, like that which covered the head in the days of Roman grandeur, denoting the quality of the man. An Eastern traveller has well said, "When the festal henna imparts its dye to the rosy fingers, it disdains not to bestow it on the toes; and the artful coquette, conscious of the power of a pretty foot, calls attention thereto by dyeing the nail of the third toe, when she tinges that of the third finger."

But we need not go to ancient or modern Turkish, or other heathen record, or modern travellers, to learn the value of a proper attention to the feet. We have it from the pure fount of Inspiration. Abraham washed the feet of his visitors at the door of his tent, and our great Exemplar washed his disciples' feet.

Many have ruined their health by not giving proper care to their feet. Not one boot or shoemaker in a hundred knows how to construct a boot or shoe properly. They are almost never shaped like the foot, and often quite too small. Hence, pressure is made upon various parts, and corns, bunions, and inverted nails, are frequent companions of those who wear them. No one deserves pity or compassion for *corns* but the poor child or idiot. A frequent result of obstructing the growth of the nail of the great toe is, the surgeon has to come and cut off the toe. The late Dr. John C.

Warren was accustomed to say to his medical students, "I have cut off more than forty for such a cause."

A boot or shoe made of leather only, no matter how thick the sole, will never protect the feet from wet, because the skins of all animals are porous, and the process of *tanning* never obliterates the pores. Hence, all leather is permeable to the slightest exposure to wet or dampness. Every shoe should have inserted between the soles a slip of bladder or gum elastic, or a piece of one of these should be worn inside.

The best kind of stocking for a covering next the skin, in most cases, is made of *cotton*. The feet of most persons perspire so much, that with a thick woollen stocking they very soon become damp and uncomfortable. Often there are catarrhal and bronchial difficulties which arise from, and are kept up by, this constant dampness of the feet.

A clergyman once applied for medical advice for a bronchial difficulty which had troubled him for some years. To the questions, "Do you wear woollen stockings? Are your feet damp and cold? Do they perspire freely?" he answered in the affirmative. He was relieved of the difficulty, and the chief medical advice was to exchange his woollen for cotton stockings, wash and rub his feet daily, and get them well warmed before going to bed at night.

In my own case, I have found my feet much more

comfortable, even in the winter, with cotton than with woollen stockings. I learned the value of using cotton instead of woollen stockings, for damp and moist feet, from a gentleman in New York, who had worn the cotton for twenty years; and I would not be induced to go back to the use of the woollen upon any consideration.

A missionary, now entered into his rest, but who lived to a good old age, once told me he was in early life troubled with an irritation of the throat and constant bronchial expectoration for several years. During all this time he wore woollen stockings, and his feet were constantly damp. Soon after exchanging them for cotton, he lost his bronchial trouble.

It is true the feet should be warmly clad; but, in all such cases as have been above described, they will be much warmer with cotton than with woollen stockings.

Nothing tends more readily to produce irritation and inflammation of the throat than damp feet. But the worst kind of damp feet, that which is constantly present, arises from wearing woollen stockings, when the feet naturally perspire. It would be much preferable to wear no covering to the feet, as the Indians of this country often do, than to bandage them with a mass of wool. Some years since, a portion of the Penobscot tribe visited Squantum, in the town of Quincy, Massachusetts, in the month of October. The weather was unusually cold for the season. To one who had little or no clothing on his lower extremities, the question was asked, "if he were not cold." Putting his finger significantly to his nose, he said, "*Why ain't your nose cold?*" and then added, "*I am all face.*" Reader, you will never enjoy life till you take a proper care of your feet. It may appear a trifling affair to you, but if you, upon experiment, do not find these remarks true, send me your experience, and I will correct my statement in the next edition.

CHAPTER IX.

Insanity the Child of Civilization and Education — Clergymen and all Students should be Acquainted with Diseased Minds—Their Special Charge over the Sick—Mather and Burroughs—Insanity Hereditary — Many are Insane on one Thing — The True Cause of Millerism and Spiritualism — Men have supposed themselves Beasts, Dogs, Cats, Wolves — Cruden — Cunning of the Insane in Concealing their Malady — Improved Treatment of the Insane — Their love of Freedom — One Case — How to prevent Insanity and escape Mental Decay—Combine Study with Amusement—The Poet and the Philosopher — Religious Excitement sometimes causes Insanity — Cause of Fatuity in Old Age — Why called Lunacy — Insanity usually comes on Gradually — Incipient Symptoms of Insanity — Drs. Parker and Gilman.

It is among civilized nations only, that we find insanity. This is very wonderful. What is there in education, or in any part of civilization, that causes this alienation of mind, which exists from the slightest derangement up to madness? Does it not arise chiefly from the way in which we pamper and enervate our bodies by our manner of living, and from overtasking our minds with study, and in anxiety for worldly honors and distinction? If so (and there is but little doubt that it is), what a drawback upon the enjoyment of life arises from our so-called refinement, civilization and education! When we see the direful consequences of this evil, may we not almost sigh for the freedom of body and mind of the wild man? Dr. Rush said, "Insanity is never found among the American Indians." I asked a young lady, who had spent some years among the Indians in our north-west settlements, if she ever saw an insane Indian? She said, "Yes, one; but he had lived among the white men."

Insanity is a mental disease with which clergymen have much to do. Indeed, quite as large a proportion of their profession, comparing it with the whole number of other classes, in the opinion of the writer, become insane. In an institution for the insane, where he was a "Director," some little time since, out of one hundred and sixty patients, three had been of the clerical profession.

Not long since, he was called to visit, professionally, at a friend's house in Boston, a clergyman, an old acquaintance. He had just escaped from a "Lunatic Asylum." He was very feeble, but perfectly self-collected. "What," said he, "doctor, do you think would be the effect of a man's jumping from a window, three stories high, and falling upon his feet on the frozen ground?" The reply was, "It would give him a pretty good shaking." "I tried that experiment last night," said he. He had made his escape, with his face blackened, and with carpet-bag in hand, and taken the cars, by which he arrived in Boston. It was afterwards ascertained that he did not jump the whole distance from a three-story window to the ground, but that, by making a ladder of his bed-clothing, he lowered himself at least half the distance.

Several clergymen have been known to become insane. But, if such were not the case, there are reasons, arising from their professional duties, which demand of them some knowledge of such cases. Indeed, it is in these mental diseases, these "hurt minds," these shattered nerves and distracted spirits, that the duties of the clergyman and the physician pre-eminently meet. It was part of the commission of those whom the Saviour first sent out to preach, "As ye go, heal the sick;" and, it is a well-known fact that for many centuries the office of the minister of the gospel and the physician was filled by the same person; and some have even doubted whether anything has been gained, either to the church or the world, by removing these ancient "landmarks;" or, by divorcing what the "Great Head of the Church" first "joined together," in the great commission of preaching the gospel. But, be this as it may, one point is certain. He was the great "Physician," and "went about doing good, healing all manner of diseases among the people." In his "labors of love," under the grand diploma which he received from heaven, no class of persons partook more largely of his benefactions than did the *insane*. The maniac, who had fled from the abode of man, and who had his "dwelling among the tombs; whom no man could bind, no, not with chains — who had often been bound with fetters and chains, and the chains had been plucked asunder by him, and the fetters broken in pieces,— neither could any man tame him; and always, night and day, he was in the mountains, and among the tombs, crying and cutting himself with stones"— this raving maniac was healed by this great "Physician," and was "found sitting at the feet" of his Deliverer, "clothed, and in his right mind." The same was the case with the *epileptic* child, who "often fell into the fire, and into the water, and who wallowed foaming," before Christ when brought to him by his distressed father. As had the first commissioned ministers of the cross much to do with distempered imaginations, diseased brains, and insane minds, so have all their successors in office, from that day to the present; and, far better would it have been for the world, and more creditable to the church, if modern clergymen had understood more of the true character of mental diseases. Had *Cotton Mather* understood the nature of diseased minds, when his brother clergyman, *Burroughs*, was "hung, at Salem, for witchcraft," he would have allowed the people to have heard the address of the dying martyr, instead of declaring it to be "the words of the devil, speaking through" his reverend brother. Happily for the world, and for "Christ's sake," too, most modern clergymen are better enlightened on the subject of mental diseases than were their predecessors.

Excessive study tends to mental derangement, engorging the brain and capillary vessels of the head with an undue proportion of blood. The mental excitement and anxiety of clergymen, to which allusion has formerly been made, tend to produce the same effect. Derangements of the digestive organs, and even constipation of the bowels, have produced insanity.

Dr. Edward Jarvis, who has given much attention to insanity, has enumerated eighty causes of this disease, and, probably, there are still others not named by him. It is not necessary here to repeat the catalogue. Suffice it to say, in a person *predisposed to insanity*, an apparently small cause may excite the disease. It should be distinctly understood that insanity *is hereditary*. We mean by the use of this term *here*, precisely what we said, when speaking of *consumption* as a hereditary disease, viz., a *predisposition* to this disease,— such a condition of the bodily organs and mental powers, as may readily result in insanity. That such is the natural condition of certain families, no well-informed physician can, and no clergyman ought to doubt.

Esquerol, a distinguished physician, says, "One half the cases of insanity, among the wealthy, arise from a *hereditary* family taint, kept up by intermarriages among the same kindred, to keep the property in the family." He also says, "he has found seven sisters and brothers in one family who were insane." *Halsam* mentions ten families, in every one of which several cases of mental derangement occurred. The writer has had personal knowledge of a family, where the father and two children committed suicide, in mental derangement, and one or more of the remaining children have been insane. Indeed, this fact of hereditary tendency to insanity should never be overlooked in intermarriages; nor, should it be, in reference to anything which would naturally tend to produce this disease.

The *predisposition* to insanity is generally found in families of dark hair and dark complexion.

The *liability* to insanity is the greatest between the ages of twenty and forty years, and a larger number become insane between twenty-five and thirty, than in any other five years of life.

We have called insanity *a* disease. This term needs to be explained. It is not intended to convey the idea that it is one and the same disease. By no means. It is not generally composed of the same elements; nor, do any two cases present the same form; nor, the same case, the identical expression, at different times. It presents all phases and all degrees, from the slightest alienation, up to the entire dethronement, or loss of reason. Though insanity may have generally the same form and elements, yet the *combinations* of these elements are numberless.

This is a point which is too often overlooked. The *monomaniac*, we call insane on one subject. Such persons are sometimes found; but, generally, the wall of partition between sanity and insanity is broken down in more than one place. Reason is lost on more than one subject. Still, monomaniacs are numerous.

Many, never supposed to be insane, however, are so, upon some points. We have seen a man insane upon the subject of *religion*, and upon nothing else. He would talk for hours on any other subject, and appear perfectly sane. But the moment religion was named, his reason left him.

Dr. Eberle says, " I knew a man who for more than twenty years supposed himself to be the President of the United States."

Professor Fetch, of Jena, continued to lecture in the University, long after he believed himself to be the Emperor of Rome, and Judge Edmonds sat upon the bench some time after he was deranged with his "spiritual" hallucinations.

We promised, in a former chapter, to assign, in its proper place, the cause or reason for certain abnormal conditions of mind, as we find them manifested in society. This is the proper place for those reasons; and, as a specimen of what represents a whole tribe, whose name is "legion," we will select modern "*Spiritualism.*"

Several clergymen have written and published upon this subject—thus, the *Rev. Mr. Beecher,* and the *Rev. William R. Gordon, D. D.*, ascribe it to "the influence of the *devil*," and the *Rev. President Mahan* to "*Odylic Force,*" and the *Rev. Mr. Corning* to, he knows not what. Now these opinions of this vagary of diseased minds, forcibly remind one of good "Cotton Mather riding around, at the execution of Burroughs, and exhorting the people not to listen to him, because it was the *devil speaking through Burroughs.*"

It is a little singular that, at such a day as this, we should have returned so nearly to the vain imaginings of those dark days of New England's shame. But many an insane man (I mean *insane* upon one subject) has been the executioner of a *sane* one, as was "Mather" in the case of "Burroughs."

These "spiritual rappers" are insane upon this subject, and this is their pitiable case. When they get a little further advanced, and become insane upon some other points, they are taken up and sent to a "lunatic asylum." This has been the case with many. But they were no more REALLY insane *then*, than they were before; it was only an increase, or extension of the same disease, which existed equally before in *kind,* but not in *degree.*

Some insane persons imagine themselves transformed into inferior animals. Such was the case of Nebuchadnezzar, " eating grass," and the daughter of the " King of Argives," described in Virgil. The same was the case with a nobleman in the court of Louis XIV., who imagined himself a *dog*, and would pop his head out of the window and bark at the passengers. Similar was the case of those of whom Lorenzo Dow gave a description, some years since, at the camp-meetings of the West. They had the "*shaking*" disease — he says, " many who went to mock, kicked and shook with others, all the while cursing the power which produced these effects." Rollin and Hequet have recorded a malady by which the inmates of an extensive convent, near Paris, were simultaneously attacked every day, at the same hour; when they believed themselves transformed into *cats*, and a universal mewing was kept up throughout the convent for several hours. But, probably, the most strange and direful form which this kind of insanity, or hallucination, ever took, was, when the impression spread over a large portion of Europe that the people were *wolves*, and the miserable sufferers went prowling about the forests, uttering the most terrific howlings, carrying off lambs from the flocks, and gnawing dead bodies in their graves.

Hundreds of other cases might be cited, in which all would say these poor creatures were insane upon these particular subjects. But they were not a whit more so in reality (though they might have been in degree) than are the "spiritual rappers," "mesmerizers," and "Simon Maguses," of our day; or, than many who walk our streets and attend, more or less, to their business. Hundreds are insane on some one point, though it may be unknown either to themselves or their friends.

I here quote some of the many cases which often appear in the journals of the day: — "*Rev. Joshua Upson*, of Dayton, Ohio, became infected with the 'spiritual' disease some time ago, and, under the impression that he was directed so to do by 'spirits,' abstained from eating, and actually died of starvation."

All will admit insanity in such a case. But was he any more insane, in *reality*, than all who believe in the "spiritual" mania? It is admitted he might have been so in an augmented *degree*, but not a whit more in reality.

The Superintendent of the Lunatic Asylum at Utica, N. Y., says, "Insanity is fearfully on the increase in this State." Recently, within five days, seventeen new patients were admitted into this institution; the greatest number ever before admitted in so brief a space of time. There is no doubt but that this increase is owing, in a great measure, to the excitement caused by the "spiritual," and other kindred humbugs of the day.

It may be asked, why do this and other hallucinations

reach some of the well-educated and higher classes in the community? The answer is, because among all classes there are those unfortunate persons in whom the *nervous* temperament predominates, and tyrannically rules over all the mental faculties, — rendering them highly susceptible to "spiritual-medium" influences. Such persons are more highly charged with magnetism than common sense, and hence readily become *monomaniacs.*

The editor of "The Medical World," in a recent number, well says, "Two harmless monomaniacs have been permitted to intrude themselves into all circles and places in this region (Boston, Massachusetts), for the past few years, who announced themselves Presidential candidates. One of them has finally been provided for in a hospital."

But he has been thus diseased for years; and so are many others who still go at large.

Alexander Cruden, a Scotchman, well known to the clergy, as the author of the largest and best "Concordance of the Bible" ever printed, during the pursuance of his theological studies, fell so desperately in love with a worthless daughter of a clergyman of Aberdeen, that his friends were obliged to send him into confinement. Whether this malady was really excited by love or not, it followed him, occasionally, during his life; and yet he was one of the best and most inoffensive of men, and went through with a literary operation which alone would be sufficient to crack the brain of any student of our day. Speaking of his relinquishing his studies for the ministry, his biographer has the following sage remark: " Possibly, some symptoms of that aberration of mind, which more strongly discovered itself at a subsequent period of his life, rendered the abandonment of *a profession so replete with mental anxiety and labor,* when its duties are properly performed, highly prudential, if not essentially necessary."

Nor is it any proof that a person is not insane on some point, because he has great power and tact in concealing it. The insane are often brighter and more sprightly, on many points, than they ever were before. I have often heard a man preach who was subject to periodical excitement, frequently amounting to insanity. When he was not *too far* excited, or only sufficiently so to rouse up his *nervous* energy, he was most powerful—such pathetic eloquence would burst from his lips, accompanied by such apparent emotion, that every eye would be wet, and every heart touched, and the admiring hearer would depart saying, "*That* is the connecting link between angels and men, and *that* eloquence was from the *angelic* part of him."

The insane have great acuteness in disguising their malady. In a case of madness, tried before "Lord Mansfield," the patient evaded questions in court for a whole day, and seemed perfectly sane to all present. But *Dr. Batty*, who knew the particular point upon which he was deranged, was called into court and asked him, "What had become of the princess with whom he had been in the habit of corresponding in cherry-juice, dropping his billets into the stream below, where the princess had received them in a boat?" In a moment, he was thrown off his guard, and confessed that, "Having been confined in a castle, where he was deprived of pen and ink, he had written his epistles in cherry-juice, and thrown them into the stream, where the princess had received them in a boat." Yet this same man evaded all the questions of one of England's most acute judges for a whole day.

"Lord Erskine" could not catch a man on any question, who maintained that he was *the Christ*, till *Dr. Simms* demonstrated his hallucination.

"I understand," said an insane woman to the medical "visitor" to the Institution, "that you are the medical attendant here, and that one of your duties is to see that no person is here improperly confined. Now, sir, as I assert that such is my condition, gauge my intellect."

When insanity is brought on from hard study, the patient rarely ever recovers.

The *treatment* of insane persons has been much improved within the last thirty years. Within the recollection of the writer, the course pursued with this class of persons was chaining, whipping, half-drowning; and the *medical* treatment was but little better. It consisted in *depleting*, by bleeding, physicking, &c.,— a course always tending from bad to worse, in all *nervous* affections. It is now well understood, that the *milder* the treatment, both hygienic and medical, the better for the patient. Much praise is due to the directors, superintendents, and all who have the management of asylums for the insane, for their kind efforts, and great success in alleviating the condition of lunatics.

Still, every one confined in an asylum desires to be liberated. I have yet to find an exception; and, notwithstanding all the modern improvements in dealing with the insane, I would say of *it* as *Cowper* of the *Sofa* and the *Gout*—

> "The sofa suits the gouty limb;
> But gouty limb, though on a sofa,
> May I never feel."

So, if it be the will of Heaven, may *I* ever be spared the horrors of a lunatic asylum, with all its alleviations! This desire to escape from confinement is exceedingly intense, and often prompts the most desperate efforts:

"Among the inmates of the Northern Ohio Lunatic Asylum is a once highly respectable citizen in good circumstances. For some time past he has manifested a strong disposition to escape, and the utmost care and vigilance have been exercised to frustrate his designs, but not always with success. Before being placed in his sleeping-room at night, he has been always stripped and carefully examined to prevent the secreting of any instrument, and all his clothes but his shirt, pantaloons and stockings taken away. In spite of these precautions, he has succeeded three times within a few days in escaping from his room.

About two weeks since he took a set of false teeth out of his mouth, and by constant work contrived with a saw thus fabricated to make a hole through the floor of his chamber sufficiently large to admit of his dropping through into another part of the house, and then escaping. He was traced and caught.

"A few days since he secreted a pin, and with that exceedingly unlikely instrument, managed to pick the lock of his door and escaped into the hall, where he was fortunately arrested. He then stated that a pin was of more value than ten thousand dollars when he wished to escape from a room.

"Last Saturday night he was carefully examined, as usual, before being placed in his room, but succeeded in secreting a small brass ring, split at one part, in his hair. On being locked up for the night, he set to work, and with the ring he cut through the window-sash and shutter, so as to enable him to remove them from the window. He then took the coverlid of the bed and tore it into strips, with which he made a rope reaching nearly to the ground, a distance of some twenty-five or thirty feet. Some of the cotton batting with which the coverlid was wadded, he placed in his stockings to protect his feet, as he had no shoes. Then dressing himself in shirt, trowsers and stockings, he slid down the rope and escaped."

In connexion with insanity and the decay of the mental powers, a question of some moment arises; that is, *how* can insanity be avoided, and those powers preserved?

The answer is, by never overtasking them; and by keeping them from rusting by a proper degree of activity; and by placing the body in such condition that it shall not injure the mind.

First, then, let the mind never be overtasked. The brain, the seat of the intellect, much resembles the muscles — exercise invigorates, strengthens, refreshes. Intense labor fatigues, exhausts. Intense thought, or emotion of any kind tends to produce insanity. On this point, an intelligent writer has just given the following note of warning. "In one of our lunatic asylums, there are several gentlemen who were one year ago in full health and active business, and, in each of these cases, mental alienation is traceable directly to overworking the brain. They are men of wealth and social eminence, and, until their sad affliction, were distinguished for usefulness in the church and the community. But to these we must add, perhaps, thousands of cases in which premature old age, and mental imbecility, have arisen from similar causes."

The case of *Sir Walter Scott* is a wonderful verification of the same sentiment. With a giant intellect, and a more than Mercury's swiftness in imagination, embarrassed in the decline of life, the brain, tasked to labor beyond its willing supply, sunk; and the towering Polyphemus of all writers of fiction, died a bodily wreck — a mental idiot.

The same has been the fate of many clergymen. Their mental labor and excessive emotion have early broken down their intellects. Pope, who was a rare genius, by excessive study, fell into a state of exhaustion, a sort of torpid, indistinct existence; and it was only by totally relinquishing study, and by riding on horseback, that he regained comparative health. Sir Humphry Davy, by over-excitement of the brain, in his chemical researches, brought on a severe illness, in which both body and mind participated. *Byron* has the following touching lines upon the course of Henry Kirk White:

> "Oh! what a noble heart was here undone,
> When Science' self destroyed her favorite son!
> Yes, she too much indulged thy fond pursuit,
> She sowed the seeds, but Death has reaped the fruit.
> 'T was thine own genius gave the final blow,
> And helped to plant the wound that laid thee low."

But, in the second place, the mind must not be withdrawn entirely from its wonted stimulus. It must not be allowed *to rust*. Intellectual exercise and mental relaxation must go hand in hand, or rather alternate, and it has been by a wise *mingling* of these two, that mathematicians and philosophers have usually lived to old age. With Sir Isaac Newton, study and recreation were prophylactic, and prevented him from breaking down or from becoming insane. Thus he lived to his eighty-fifth year. Upon this principle, old Plato called "mathematical demonstrations, the purgatives of the soul." Lord Bacon said, "If a man's wits be wandering, let him study mathematics."

The *poet* is much more liable to become insane than the philosopher. His imagination is ever *flying*, while his reasoning powers seldom act. Twenty poets become mentally diseased to one philosopher.

Religion, falsely so called, has often produced insanity. The mind, perhaps, weak by nature, overwhelmed with sorrow, depressed by the loss of friends, or disappointed by living dead ones, retires within itself—reflection and meditation enhance its already overstretched powers, and insanity follows. Reason abandons the helm, and *suicide* is often the result. But at the same time, the migratory holder-forth, with vociferous speech, and apparently superabounding zeal, while he frightened hundreds into insanity, would never shake, either by thought, or anxiety, a single nerve in his own system.

Fatuity in old age arises from want of that employment which has occupied the earlier years of life. This is sometimes found in aged retired clergymen. Accustomed during the early part of life, and in the maturity of manhood, to all the labor, care, and anxiety of a parish, when the people no longer wish to hear them preach, and force them into retirement, the mind is very liable to decay. We can call to mind more than one case of this kind, in which fatuity has been the result.

There is much weight in the following reply of an aged clergyman, when his people informed him that they did not wish him to preach any more, — " Why, surely, after I have been a minister for forty-five years, I can *preach* as well as I can do *any thing.*" The best way to preserve the mental powers is to keep them actively employed.

That eccentric and wonderful man, Dean Swift, died an idiot; and Dr. Samuel Johnson ascribed his fatuity to two causes: — first, to an early resolution that he would never wear spectacles, which precluded him from reading in the decline of life; and, secondly, to his avarice, which led him to exclude visitors, or to deny himself company. In this manner he deprived himself of all food for the mind. Hence, it languished and collapsed into idiocy. He died in the hospital, which he had himself founded for just such persons as he became. Clergymen, who reside in the city, are not so likely to become fatuitous, or fall into mental decay, as those in the country. First, because they do not usually live so long; and, second, because they have more to occupy their attention. The mind of any man, who has nothing to do, preys upon itself, till it presents the singular anomaly of having devoured itself.

Dr. Franklin presented a case just the reverse of that of Swift. His was a remarkable instance of the influence of reading, writing, and conversation, in preserving to the age of eighty-four years a sound and active state of all the mental faculties.

Most old men, of every profession and occupation, when they give up active life, soon fall into mental decay, unless they read and converse much with the younger members of the community.

The insane were anciently called *lunatics*, because it was believed that this disease was caused by the *lunar* changes. The writings of the older physicians abound with superstitious ideas upon this and kindred subjects. In ancient times, the changes of the moon were all the *almanac* they possessed, and it was not uncommon for whole tribes to worship "the Queen of heaven."

While I have but little faith in the prevailing opinions that the moon rules the growth of vines and plants, and influences the *shrinking* of meat, and the *coming* of soap, and many other such like notions, still, as this "silvery orb" rules the tides, and thus exercises an influence upon our planet, it is natural to suppose she *has* an influence upon our atmosphere, and in this way operates upon our bodies. Our health and spirits are greatly dependent upon atmospheric changes, and upon the electrical phenomena of the air. An eminent physician, who long had the charge of an asylum for insane persons, says, "he has arrived at the conviction that an excited and unsettled state of mind prevailed more at the moon's changes than at other times."

Shakspeare seems to have understood this matter, and, what thing connected with human nature did he not understand? He says:—

"Sure, 'tis an error of the moon that comes
Nearer unto the earth than she is wont,
And makes men mad."

Epileptics are more affected by the phases of the moon, than persons laboring under other forms of madness; but of these, the writer has already spoken in a work now before the public. Having, probably, treated more epileptics than most physicians, he has carefully watched for this *lunar* influence, and is compelled to admit that this unfortunate class of patients are afflicted as here stated.

The third, and last preservative, that of the proper

management of the body as to study, food, medicine, sleep, narcotics, exercise and relaxation, will be elsewhere pointed out in this work.

Insanity, usually, comes on gradually. It is, therefore, the more difficult to *diagnosticate*. This, also, is an additional reason why clergymen should have a knowledge of this disease — of the agency of the mind upon the body, and of the body upon the mind.

It is a question which the physician is called upon to decide, Is this person insane? And, I scarcely need add, it is often one of the most difficult duties which he has to perform. So, also, the clergyman, if he understands the true condition of his melancholy parishioner, will be able to say, when he needs *physic*, and when he needs gospel instruction and consolation.

Here, again, we find the older divines, in their knowledge of medicine conjointly with that of theology, possessed an advantage over those of more modern times. Doddridge, in his "Rise and Progress," speaks of a case of religious melancholy and despondency, where the person might have soon been set right by medicine, when all arguments and religious instruction were of no avail.

As the approach of insanity is often gradual and insidious, where the least hereditary tendency is suspected, any change in the habits and natural disposition should be carefully watched. Does the eye shrink from the popular gaze, and catch furtive glances at the visitor; is the look sly, or fixed, and downward; or the expression vacant, or quick and restless, you may reasonably fear mental alienation. Thus, a practised eye will often detect insanity where the nearest friends have never even suspected its existence.

Alienation towards friends is often an early symptom of insanity. The nearer and dearer the relationship is, the more intense is often the hatred.

The testimony of the two physicians of New York, given in the case of Huntington, the forger, lately convicted there, shows of how little value and how totally absurd are the views of physicians on this subject. We direct the reader's particular attention to the following details in relation to it.

Dr. Willard Parker was examined at great length as to the insanity of Huntington. The conclusions he arrived at were as follows:

"He seemed to me to have a mind which operated very differently from the mass of minds; my conclusion was, that he was insane; self-preservation is one of the laws of our nature, and he seemed to have no sort of tendency or care with regard to it whatever; the all-absorbing subject was the mere matter of making paper and carrying on operations in Wall street; I should not regard this affliction as monomania — still, the making of 'paper' seemed to be the all-absorbing subject with him, and if he were out, he would make this paper again.

Q. What do you mean by monomania when you speak of it?

A. I should define it, that a man's mind operates naturally, rightly (so to speak) on all subjects, excepting one subject, or one or two subjects; in reference to that subject, the moment it is touched, it awakens a new train of thought, action and manifestation, which actions are entirely at war with what is called the action of a sound mind; the opinion which I formed about his mind was entirely dependent on his statements and my own examination of his condition; the forms of insanity are infinite; the medical profession do not undertake to give a separate name to each peculiar development of insanity — that is admitted to be quite impossible by the most eminent medical men; in treating of some peculiar forms of monomania, those terms are made use of as expressive of this monomaniacal condition, but though some forms are thus defined by name, I suppose there are a great number that have no name."

Dr. Charles R. Gilman testified as follows: "All that I mean to say is, that I believe him to be insane; I pronounce him insane; a man manifests his insanity in a particular way; I suppose Huntington has that mixture of mental and moral insanity which is very often found; I believe he has a diseased brain; I don't believe he would be responsible if he rose up at this moment and drove a knife into you, which God forbid; if he should commit any offence whatever, I believe he should not be responsible; he would know what he was doing if he did what I said; that, however, would not affect the question of his insanity. The fact of his committing murder and knowing that he would be hanged for it, would not affect the question of his insanity; neither would his commission of forgery or stealing. He might know that all this was wrong; delusion or hallucination has nothing to do with it; I believe that he has moral and mental insanity, with a little of intellectual insanity; intellectual insanity in that he was reckless in the use of money, in the way he committed the forgeries and his making no attempt to escape; in reference to this matter of forgery I have my doubts as to whether he is insane; the question is, if he were placed in circumstances where he would commit violence, would he not have done so? I think he has general insanity; it is doubtful whether it is right to call it monomania; I differ with Dr. Parker in regard to this man's insanity being monomania or a general mania; I use the words 'unsound,' and 'madness,' and 'unsoundness' as being 'identical;' I asked him if he had a boy, and blurted out, 'What a horrible inheritance he had grown up to;' he was perfectly cold, and said 'it would all blow over;'

though he knew it was forgery, he did not appreciate it; I think the light manner in which he spoke of his wife and child showed his insanity; I think this taken with other things is a proof of his insanity; I know of one case in which the insane tendency was to commit forgery; there was a case of insanity; I would not pronounce Monroe Edwards insane; I read the case of Fontleroy, who was hung for forgery in England; I suppose that Huntington committed forgery, although he knew it was wrong, but his power of resistance was diminished by the mental effects dependent on his physical organization; it is my opinion that Huntington had an irresistible tendency to commit crime; my opinion is, that if a man is insane it would be unsafe to calculate on what he might or might not do; the definition made by twelve judges in England of insanity is all wrong in my opinion; I regard it as nonsense."

What enjoyment of life can there be when the mind is deranged? and how much our happiness depends upon the nice adjustment of this reciprocal agency!

CHAPTER X.

Our System of Education — The Body should receive Attention First — No Necessity for Early Mental Pressure — Meaning of Education — The kind of Schools for Little Children — Physical Training to keep pace with Mental — Moral and Religious Instruction — A Parent's Opinion — No Study out of School — Rewards for Intellectual Superiority Condemned — For Moral Conduct Approved.

THE writer has been more or less connected all his days with the education of the young, as he is at present; and the remarks in this chapter, as connected with this subject, are the result of much experience in the management of children. Reference has already been made to both physical and mental disease, as arising from excessive study, connected with the neglect of proper care of the body; and it has, also, been already said, that *epilepsy* and *insanity* are the result of such a course, both among children and adults. But, it seems to the writer that enough has not yet been said upon the popular system of education which produces such direful results to the health, happiness, and lives of children. The present chapter will, therefore, be devoted to the American education of the youth of our land; or, more particularly, to the stimulation early applied to the mind, while the body is neglected.

This course has well been denominated by Lucius M. Sargent, of Massachusetts, the gifted author of the famous "Temperance Tales," as "a system of child murder." I would have the first ten years of the child's life devoted chiefly to cultivating and strengthening the organs of the body. This is but the prompting of nature. It is the principle upon which all builders act. They lay the foundation first. "The house we live in" is the body.

This premature development of the mind, and neglect of the body, have long been prominent evils in our educational system. Some years ago, "infant schools" were in vogue. Little children were taught reading, arithmetic, grammar, Latin and Greek: and we were soon to have learned men and women, almost from the cradle. Men looked on, and wondered "whereunto this thing would grow," and what kind of men and women these precocious children would make. But they were soon relieved of this anxiety; for it was found that *such* children rarely lived to become men or women; or if they did, they dwindled down into mere commonplace persons, mere intellectual pigmies, verifying the old adage, "soon ripe, soon rotten." If the body did not die, it was so enfeebled as to be useless, or worse, and the mind deranged or idiotic.

It is often very pleasing to the fond parents to see how bright, intelligent, and witty their child is; and, not unfrequently, they find great satisfaction in showing to others the brilliancy and mental sprightliness of their precocious darlings. Such parents know not what they are doing. All the praise lavished by such parental folly, and fond aunts, doting grand-parents, and injudicious friends, tends to the serious injury and almost certain destruction of these children.

Their keen flashes and sparkling witticisms are but the indications of an over-stretched mind and a neglected body. Every parent who *thus* rears his child, instead of preparing him to be the comfort and solace of his declining years, is fitting him to bring down his "grey hairs with sorrow to the grave."

I knew a child, naturally frail, bright and intelligent, the idol of his fond parents and doting friends, whose mind was altogether too active for the body. At the age of seven years, he could read Latin, Greek, and the Hebrew alphabet. At the age of eight years, nervous spasms commenced, and constantly increased, till, at ten, he died of epilepsy. This is but the history of multitudes.

They are indulged, neglected in physical, and stimulated in mental education, till the nervous system breaks down, and an early grave, or a diseased body, and an idiotic mind, become the final result. Many are thus destroyed every year by our system of education, which all begins at the wrong end. Then pursue this course, and train the body first, and there will be but little danger of too much study.

This neglect of the physical and stimulating of the mental man, is the more to be deplored, from the fact, that this early *precocity* is wholly unnecessary; because, many of the best educated and useful men the world has ever seen, were very *dull* pupils in their childhood. Andrew Fuller, Sir Walter Scott, and Daniel Webster, were all very dull scholars in their childhood; and yet, who has ever done more in theological discussion than the former? or who, in the whole world of fiction, than the second? or who, at the bar and in the Senate, than the latter—well called the "Defender of the Constitution?" Many such men there have been. They have lived and written, and labored, and blessed the world, after the *hot-house plants* of precocious intellects have long been dead and forgotten! What a lesson to all parents and teachers, who wish to raise up a generation of intellectual *giants* and corporeal *dwarfs!*

Let all the friends of education, parents, teachers, physicians, clergymen, boards of education, guard this whirlpool in which so many bright geniuses have been engulphed. Better be, in early childhood, yes, during the first ten years of life, intellectual *blockheads*, than hastened to a premature death.

"What manner of child shall this be?" was a question once asked, and the same question may be put respecting every child. I need scarcely say, any child will be very much what his education is. Who can tell what the infant, now lying in its cradle, will one day become? What dormant powers are there to be unfolded? What will be the future development of that living germ? The work of education is to develop this germ,—to show this intellect how to expand. It is not to pour into it knowledge, as the quack pours his gilded pills and panaceas into the stomach of his foolish patient, but rather to *lead out* the mind, as the scientific physician, by judicious advice, puts his patient upon a course of living, which, if properly followed, will result in health.

Starting, then, with the great principle that education (as its derivation from *educo* implies) means to *lead out*, let us take the child from infancy, and follow it up till its school education is completed; I say *school* education, for its *general* education will never be finished till the intellect ceases, or is removed from earth. In this respect, the following expression of the immortal RUSH, of Philadelphia, was not peculiar to him, but belongs equally to all mankind: "I expect to be always learning as long as I live."

But some one says, this idea of education cannot be correct, for the mind of the infant is a blank, or rather, there *is* no mind there. Not so. If there *is none* there, never will there be any there. It was a graphic and favorite expression of my old preceptor, REV. ASA MESSER, President of Brown University: "There must be some *substratum*, some foundation, upon which to build; you cannot build a house upon nothing."

There is a mind in every infant, and it is not long before the mother sees it. Soon, both parents see it, and, if they do not exercise judicious government over it, *feel* it, too.

Till the child is two, or two and a half years old, I would have it chiefly under the watch and care of its mother. One grand error here, in the management of young children is, they are left mostly to the care of servants, and often to those who are, of all persons, the last that should have charge of them.

When the child is between two and three years old, I would have it sent to *a* school; not, however, to *such* a school as were those for young children, so popular for a short time, and so pernicious among us, called *infant* schools.

The school that I would propose for these young children should be very different from those; not designed to serve a mere educational purpose, nor to receive regular instruction in any department. I would have no books of any kind. Half the time should be devoted to amusements, plays, or innocent games, constructing block houses, &c.; the other half should be employed in simple work, such as would interest children, and not only keep their little hands busy, but teach them how to use their fingers. This employment might be imitating outlines or drawings of animals, birds, houses, &c., by pricking them on paper; making them like basket-work with various colored strips of pasteboard or paper; marking the forms of letters, &c. In a word, I would have these schools do no more than amuse these little minds, and employ these little fingers, at that tender age when study would be not only useless, but irksome. Still, much instruction would be communicated by these schools; and, what is better, it would be given in such a way that it would be always pleasant to receive it. It is of much advantage to obviate the irksomeness usually attached to that word, *study*, at any age. More especially is it so with young children. How to enjoy life is the great thing to teach the young child.

A lady fond of children, possessing adaptation to instruct by amusing (a rare talent), would do great good in such a school. In summer I would have her, with her charge, almost "dwell," as "DEBORAH" did, "under a palm tree," or some other tree, in "a garden." I would have this school made so amusing and delightful, that the little child should account it a great deprivation to be kept away from it for a single day. Thus much, for what I would have the *primary* school to be;

and, it would be better to have it extend, under various modifications, to the age of five years, if not longer.

Let us now enter upon our *second* school. This should take the place usually occupied by what is generally denominated the *Primary School;* commencing with the child at the age of five years, one year older than the law usually recognizes him as entitled to attend any of our Public Schools. This school should be very different from such schools at the present day. But previous to giving particulars, I will make a few remarks as to the *importance* to be attached to these schools, usually called *Primary*.

No schools can be more important than these. Here has been one great error in our Common School system. It has too often been supposed that any one can teach a Primary School. Often has the expression been used by parents, and, sometimes, by educators themselves, respecting a young lady, only half educated herself, "She will answer to teach a Primary School." With such language, the true friends of education should have no fellowship. With it, those entrusted with the selection of teachers should make no parley. This principle strikes at the root of all correct education. For such schools, the best teachers should be selected, inasmuch as error here is fundamental.

"Just as the twig is bent,
The tree's inclined."

If it is important that any child should be *correctly* taught, most emphatically is it so, that the *young* child should be thus taught. I would be more particular in the examination of a teacher for a *primary*, than for an *advanced* school. Often have I done this in Boston when examining teachers for such schools; especially in those branches which they were to teach. Fifty-four candidates for a vacancy in one of these schools, were once examined, and a large majority of them failed in giving the various sounds of the letters of the alphabet, and in other parts of Orthography; and many of them had been teachers for several years, and some were graduates from the Normal Schools. Some of them, affected to tears, said: " We learned these things when we were children, but have since given no attention to them." The reason was, they were small matters, upon which they never expected to be examined.

I would have schools of this kind take the children at the age of five years, and keep them till they are ten. During the five years spent in them, they should be taught the alphabet, spelling, the sounds of various letters, reading, geography, mental arithmetic, historical stories, drawing various letters, animals, and other things, on the slate, or with pencil and paper. These, and perhaps some few other simple matters, are sufficient to fill up the five years allotted to such schools.

The children of this age should not be confined to

their seats, nor to the room (unless it be a very large one, and then the open air would be preferable), for two or three hours at a time, and compelled during that time to *study*, as is generally now the case. On the contrary, they should, as often as every half hour, be allowed to leave their seats, or the room; or, as is the case with some of the Swedish schools for older pupils, be taught to exercise and amuse themselves *in their seats*. It would be well to alternate, every half hour, between these two modes, in, and away from their seats and the schoolroom. It is both folly and cruelty to confine children, of such an age, to their seats for nearly six hours a day, requiring them to study during this period. In the first place, the confinement is unnatural to them, and calculated to render them not only restless, but debilitated. In the second place, it renders their lessons irksome, which should by all means be avoided. The great secret of a successful teacher is to render the task of the pupils pleasant. What a child does voluntarily and pleasantly is done with zest, and with all the heart, and such pupils are always ready to do their duty with alacrity. What teacher that has tried this plan has not seen the eye sparkle and the sweet smile of childhood light up the countenance, as a new thought and new light flash into the mind, and *it* expands, like the rosebud under the bright radiance of a summer's sun! Such are the *oases* (if they occur at all) in the teaching of some; especially was this the case under the old iron rule of the *schoolmaster*, in the days of our fathers; while under the benignant guidance and mild demeanor of others, they are like the bright beams of the "King of Day" on a May morning, when no cloud obscures the horizon.

These schools should be governed mostly by *love;* by which is meant, what is generally termed *moral* suasion. To accomplish this end, the loveliness of virtue, the peace of conscience, which always attends well doing, and the approbation of associate pupils, teachers, parents, and, above all, of our Heavenly Father, should often be portrayed to the pupils. *This* kind of *stimulus* ought always to be used; other kinds, never. Then, also, these children should be shown the deformity of disobedience, vice, and all that shows itself in the forms of falsehood, ill temper, unkindness, and the like.

In the next place, I would have religion, *the religion of the Bible,* taught in these schools. If we were heathen, the heathen mythology might properly be taught in them, as religion. But, as we are a *Christian* people, the *Christian religion* should be *the* most prominent feature of the education of our children. In respect to religious instruction, the legislation for our Public Schools is a *burlesque* upon our Christianity.

Thus much for schools for children till they are ten years old; for what I call *model schools* for such children. Next comes the *tertiary*, or third schools, made up of girls (for I prefer to write of schools for females, for no other reason than that such is my own school), from ten to fourteen years of age. These four years include the period when a great proportion of pupils are carried through their school-education. It is not, however, for such that I design these remarks, as in *model schools* for a thorough course of education, a higher class still remains.

In this class of schools, the same studies, with the exception of those of the alphabet and powers of the letters (which, it is presumed, have been already acquired), are to be pursued, with the addition of a few others, among which should be the rudiments of the English language, written arithmetic, history, a more extended course of geography, natural philosophy, modern languages, and also Latin.

The *moral* lessons during this period of school education, should have great prominence. The *heart* should be cultivated largely. Now is the time to fix deeply in the affections, as well as in the understanding, the great duty of love to God, to our neighbors, and ourselves; reverence for instructors, parents, and superiors, and especially for the aged; the latter of which is at present very much wanted among the youth of our land. "Those shall stand up before the aged, and honor the old man."

During this period, also, innocent amusements and physical training are by no means to be omitted. Here let me say that *girls* need looking after much more than boys, in this respect. They are naturally more given to sedentary habits; more inclined to be quiet and inactive, and less disposed to exercise in the open air. Boys will be out of doors, and when out, will run, and jump, and sport, and custom has sanctioned many games among them which it has prohibited to girls. The consequence of this is, that unless much care is exercised over them in such matters by the teacher, they will grow a feeble, pale, degenerated race, so far as their bodies are concerned. This neglect of the *physical* education of girls was the starting-ground of the school established by the writer. Of the *fourth* class of schools for girls, it need not vary in the *studies* pursued much, if any, from those in our girls' high schools and seminaries, as these are generally now well chosen. But, the *physical* and moral training should receive very much more attention than it does at present.

Lessons should never be given pupils who are regular attendants upon school, to be studied out of school hours. The children ought to have these hours for healthy amusements. Nor should they be required to study during vacations. Some teachers tell the children to take their books home and study during the vacation. This is wrong.

A parent in Boston wrote as follows—

"I have two sons attending the public schools, both of whom are in delicate health, owing in a great degree to overtasking the brain, and not having sufficient time for play. If I remonstrate with them about studying so much out of school, the answer is, 'I *must* get my lessons, and I have not time enough given me *in* school, to accomplish all that is required.' They study until late in the evening, when nature requires sleep, and request the housemaid to awake them early in the morning, that they may study as much as possible. Two-thirds of the hours of the Sabbath day and evening are given to their secular tasks, and when the Sunday-school teacher gave tickets for their admission to the Bunyan tableaux, much persuasion was necessary to induce them to go (although on Wednesday afternoon, when there was no school), on account of having such long lessons to learn. I know not exactly whom to blame, as the teachers are requested by the school committee (many of whom are ignorant of the proper way of educating children) to urge them on, and are desirous of making a brilliant exhibition, no matter at what sacrifice. I am afraid I shall get too much excited if I write more, and will close, only adding, that I wish all who have charge of children may have discretion given them to duly regulate their requirements of them."

All attempts to gain intellectual knowledge by filching from children the time that nature requires for the fullest development of their bodily health, is "penny wise and pound foolish," and tend to diminish, not the enjoyment of children only, but to detract largely from their happiness in after-life. A proper view of the reciprocal agency of body and mind will destroy all such attempts.

Another thing greatly destructive of the health and enjoyment of children, the consequences of which often follow them through life, is the system of *rank* and *rewards* practised in many schools, in bestowing favors merely for intellectual superiority. The whole system of *medal distribution*, in some schools, is made upon this plan. Now, this is all wrong—all injurious to the true enjoyment of life, tending to the ruin of both mind and body, and for the following reasons:

1st. The stimulus of securing a prize, by excelling others, operates the most powerfully upon *precocious* children — a class which always require holding back rather than urging forward. It is among this class of pupils (when their health does not become too far destroyed, or they do not die before the prizes are awarded) that the medals are distributed. It is among this class of children that chorea, nervous headaches, epilepsy, and numerous diseases of mind and body, are generally found, which arise from over-action of the brain, and induce general debility and prostration. For this cause many of these children are weak and sickly, and many sleep "the sleep of death." It is believed that every physician of this city, who has any considerable amount of practice, has had a number of these cases, where the disease was induced solely by overtasking the intellect.

2d. We object to such distribution of medals, or rewards, as here named, because it recognizes and acts upon a principle which flows neither from God nor nature; to wit, that the capacity, or mind and body of all children, is equal. This principle, as it is carried into operation in many public shools, *tasks all alike*, then holds out the tempting bait, and says, the one who can intellectually outstrip his companion is "the best fellow," and shall have the prize. This resembles the giant's bedstead, fitting only the few, and stretching or cutting off the many. Every man who has been at all conversant with children, and especially with teaching, knows very well that some can learn, in the same time, twice as much as others. Who, unless void of discretion, would think of assigning the same task to these very different capacities? And yet this is precisely the course pursued in some schools. No allowance is made for the native quickness or genius of one pupil over another. Each must bear his own burden. But this is not all, though this, of itself, is sufficiently disheartening to any one who is hard to learn. What is still a more objectionable feature is, no allowance can be made, upon such a system, for physical *indisposition*, or for those of slender constitution. There are many of this class, possessed of the finest intellects, the brightest talents, and the most sensitive feelings; but they are corporeally unable to apply themselves. "The spirit is willing, but the flesh is weak." It is not only unwise, but unjust and cruel, to place such where they must necessarily compete with those whose constitutions are tenfold stronger than their own. It is reproaching the God of nature, who alone has "made them to differ." It is placing the feebler in a position where they must inevitably fail of success, and that, where their native sensitiveness (always too great) will be augmented an hundred fold, by their failure. To place the stimulus of medals before such children is wrong; the effect is "evil and only evil, and that continually."

3d. This distribution of medals is an injury to the *successful* candidate. It destroys all his enjoyment. It stimulates his pride — excites those very feelings and passions which every wise and prudent parent or teacher, who desires to cultivate the *heart*, finds it the most difficult to suppress. As long as human nature *is human*, it will avail but little for His Honor, the Mayor, or the committee man, as he puts the blue ribbon around the child's neck, to say, as has often been said, (and which seems to spring from a consciousness of wrong doing,) " This is a distribution of merit; and now you must not be proud of it, nor think more of yourself than you ought to think, or less of the unsuccessful pupils than you do of yourself." The intellect of the child, which has been stimulated in a wrong way for months, perhaps years, quickly reasons as follows : " For what have my parents, and teachers, and friends been stimulating me so long, by constantly urging upon me the importance of gaining a medal? For what have I labored all this time, depriving myself of amusements, of exercise, and of all the innocent sports which are the delight of children, and which promote health? Surely it cannot be, after all, to think that I am no more deserving than others who have not received such reward! This exhortation condemns me, and reproaches my teachers, parents, and the committee."

The result is, the child is made prouder, vainer, more intolerant of caution and rebuke, and instead of cherishing sentiments of kindness towards his classmates, the unsuccessful candidates, he despises them; and, to believe otherwise, in the present state of human nature, is like cherishing the vain chimera of the non-resistant in self-defence. It has a more pernicious effect upon the *heart*, than all the good the intellect ever gained from such stimulus.

4th. It is productive of evil to the *unsuccessful candidates.* They have hearts, consciences, which must feel — what is often but too true — that these rewards have been bestowed out of *favoritism.* Many of them have labored as zealously, and, by the confessions of the teachers and the awarding committee, are almost as much entitled to a medal, as those on whom it has been bestowed. This idea was well illustrated a few years since, in the case of one of the girls, who declined the prize because she felt conscious it did not belong to her. One of the daily papers characterized this deed as worthy of the angelic nature. What a pity that such natures should be so strongly tempted *to fall!* and alas, that the temptation should come from the teachers and the committee — their moral guardians! Would that all the children to whom medals are distributed, upon the present principle, were *such* angels! It would put an end to this direful practice, and teach the parents, instructors, and School Boards, a lesson which would elevate them all an hundred fold above their present standard of the Christian morals, and the higher and better feelings of the heart.

It is devoutly to be hoped that Boards of School Committees will never be the occasion of unduly spurring and expanding the intellect, at the expense of the bodily health, and that reciprocity of kindness and good feeling among the children, which is the perfection of beauty and wisdom, and productive of the greatest earthly happiness.

5th. Such a system of awarding medals injures the good influence of the teacher upon the pupils, and greatly perplexes him in the discharge of his duty. It places him often in very trying circumstances, and where he is obliged to ask for more medals, to satisfy his own conscience, and to reconcile the feelings of the pupils and the parents. This perplexity is often so great that he is constrained to wish that the medals were wholly dispensed with.

6th. It also injures the parents; and if any one doubts it, let him go a day or two after the examination of the schools, and distribution of the medals, and visit them. If he does not find *ten* dissatisfied, murmuring and complaining, to one satisfied and pleased, we are much mistaken. It is, therefore, a great detriment to human enjoyment.

7th. Another reason why the management of many schools is injurious to the health of the pupils is, it allows them little or no opportunity for relaxation and exercise, at the recess. It was once thought that the recess was a time for sport, exercise, and amusement. This was as it should be. After an hour and a half of study, children need relaxation,—to start up and throw themselves about. It is their nature to do so. Now, if instead of walking down stairs, face to back, with hands folded, and standing in a similar position in the yard, like criminals in the " House of Correction," as they are compelled to do in some schools, they could unbend themselves, and have ten minutes for exercise, it would be a very great improvement upon the present plan. If there be no room for such exercise in the yards attached to the school-houses, it would be very advantageous to them to take a walk in the streets. Every school-house should have a yard connected with it sufficiently large for the physical recreation and exercise of the pupils.

But, rewards for moral deportment, for benevolence, kindness, good behaviour, and such things as *all can excel in*, are not open to these serious objections. Such rewards are just and right. In the subjects presented in this chapter, there is very much room for an improved system of hygiene for both mind and body, by which the enjoyment of all concerned would be greatly enhanced. Not only *too much*, but *too many* studies are required of children. The consequence is, they get a little knowledge of every, and not much of any thing. I always regard a school as suspicious, when I see the pupils lugging their arms full of books home every night, and back every morning.

The following is from the pen of Hon. George S. Hilliard, of Boston, and fully sustains our views:

" We were present at the School Festival in Faneuil

Hall on Tuesday last. We will whisper a confession into the ear of the public that we have doubts and misgivings — growing with our growth and strengthening with our strength — as to the whole system of medals, Franklin and City; and as to the wisdom of selecting a few boys and girls out of a school for these conspicuous decorations, and leaving the rest unnoticed.

"We doubt whether the intellectual advantages, especially in the case of girls, are not counterbalanced by injurious moral influences; and even in an intellectual point of view, we question whether the effect be not to stimulate the quick and bright, who need it not, and to depress the slow and timid, who need encouragement. But for a Boston editor or a Boston man to hint any doubts upon the subject of the Franklin medals, is like speaking disrespectfully of the equator, or suggesting an inquiry whether the sun and moon are not beginning to break up a little, and to show a failure in their faculties; and we therefore say what we have said timidly and deprecatingly."

CHAPTER XI.

Value of Opium as a Medicine — Injury by its Habitual Use — Its Effects — Difficulty of breaking off its Use — Ministers, Lawyers, and Ladies use it — Use of it in England — De Quincey, the Opium Eater.

THE excessive use of *opium* seems to demand a more extended notice than the other *narcotics*. Opium is one of the oldest of our medicines, and the fact that it is a valuable *medicine* should operate against its daily use. It is the most important narcotic of the *materia medica*. "If I were allowed but two weapons with which to combat disease," said Sydenham, "opium would be my first choice." But we may ask, What has a man in health to do with medicine? especially with the most potent of all medicines?

It is a powerful poison, and operates, as such, upon the whole animal kingdom, causing paralysis, convulsions, stupor, fatuity, and death. Says Dr. Allen, in his inestimable essay on the use of this drug: "The greater the development of the nervous system, the more marked and diversified are its effects. On the Indian and negro, who have a predominance of the sanguine lymphatic or muscular temperament, its effects partake more of an animal nature; but where there is a greater development and activity of the brain, together with the nervous system, it operates more directly and effectively on the mind. At the same time, its deleterious effects on the body are by no means diminished.

"The effect of opium on the human system depends very much upon the quantity and frequent use, as well as the age, temperament, habits, idiosyncrasy, &c., of the individual. Its first and most common effect, is to excite the intellect, stimulate the imagination, and exalt the feelings into a state of great buoyancy and activity, producing unusual vivacity and brilliancy in conversation; and, at the same time, the most profound state of self-complacency. All ideas of labor, care and anxiety, vanish at once from the mind. Then follows a succession of gorgeous dreams, or a continued state of ecstasy, almost indescribable. Mr. Tiffany, in his late works on the 'Canton Chinese,' attempts to sketch this happy state of the opium-smoker. 'The victim inhales his allotted quantity, and his senses swim around him; he feels its subtle nature; he floats from earth, as if on pinions. He would leave his humble station, his honest toil, his comfortable home. He would be great. He runs with ease the paths of distinction; he distances rivals. Wealth and power wait upon him; the mighty take him by the hand. His dress is costly, his fare sumptuous, his home a palace, and he revels in the pleasures he has read of and believed to be a fiction. Music sounds through his lofty halls, sages assemble to do him honor, women of the brightest beauty throng around him; he is no longer poor, lowly, and despised, but a demi-god. The feast is spread, the sparkling cup filled to the brim with hot wine, and he rises to welcome one whom he has left far behind in the path of glory; to tender to him triumphant courtesy; and, as he advances a step, he reels and staggers wildly, and competitors, guests, minstrels, magnificence, all fade from his vision, and the grey cold reality of dawn breaks upon his heated brain, and he knows that all was nought, and that he is the same nameless creature that he has ever been. A cold shudder agitates his frame; weak and worthless, he seeks the air, but finds no relief. He cannot turn his thoughts to his calling; he is unfit for exertion, his days pass in sloth, and in bitter remorse. And when night comes in gloom, he seeks again the sorceress into whose power he has sunk, and whose finger mocks while it beckons him on.'"

Wasn't it worthy of the *Christian* name of *England*, to force upon a Pagan nation, at the mouth of the cannon, and the point of the bayonet, a drug, the curse of which is but faintly shadowed forth in this description? Oh, shame! where is thy blush, not for Christianity only, but for *humanity?*

No drug, no means of intoxication, captivates, bewitches, and chains down its poor victim to misery and woe like this. It is the "Goliah of Gath" among intoxicating agents. Its complete power over its votary is not wholly to be ascribed to the natural love of stimulus (though even this is sufficiently powerful), but that he has heard or experienced the ecstatic heaven which it creates.

There is no escape from the *fascination* of opium, when once its use has been commenced. The pleasurable sensations experienced, at first, soon pass away, and give place to the most horrid dreams and appalling pictures of death. Spectres of fearful visage haunt the mind. The light which once seemed to emanate from heaven, is converted into the gloom of hell. The countenance becomes pallid; the eye assumes a wild brightness; memory fails; mental exertion and moral courage sink, general atrophy comes on, and the poor victim has ceased to live before he really dies. This fearful state of things is not reached by all who use opium. But there is a strong tendency to it in any case where it is used. Its customary use is like a whirlpool from which there is no escape to any who come within the eddy.

The inebriation from alcohol can scarcely be compared with that arising from opium. Its worst feature is, that none return from its use, who have once embraced it. This cannot be said respecting alcohol. From the latter there are many reformed inebriates. From opium there are none, where the drug has been within their reach. The Chinese, when he has become addicted to its use, will steal, sell his property, his children, and finally, even murder for it. But a few days ago a man called on a physician and wished to be sent to the Boston Almshouse as a vagabond, that he might be delivered from the use of this drug. He said it had ruined him, and he had no power to escape from its influence. He was sent at his own request, as a vagabond, to Deer Island, and is now being successfully treated by Dr. Moriarty of that hospital.

It is surprising what an amount of this drug may be taken, when one has become accustomed to its use. Physicians sometimes give one, two, and three ounces in twenty-four hours, in cases of great pain. Its use is much more frequent in the community than many suppose. Even among the higher classes, it prevails to an alarming extent. At a meeting of physicians held in Boston, it was stated by one of the oldest and most experienced, that "he knew a lady, who took seventeen teaspoonfuls of laudanum every morning, to set her up for the day; and, it must be made of the best opium, as she would know in a minute, if it were in the least adulterated."

It is believed that many sedentary and studious men,

and many clergymen are in the habitual use of this drug, and that under its stimulus many literary works, and many sermons are written, and lawyers' pleas made. We scarcely need add that no habit can be more ruinous to the health of the body and the faculties of the mind, or more destructive of happiness.

Since the discovery and introduction of the use of chloroform and ether, these agents have been much employed to produce intoxication. Many persons keep themselves half inebriated by them. The effect is very similar to that of other narcotics, and lays a foundation for many nervous diseases. It cannot be too strongly condemned. We advise all who value health and happiness wholly to forego the use of these injurions agents.

When the above was read, some time since, it was stated by several ministers present, that they had known many cases where opium had been habitually used by clergymen, and names were given of some, eminent in that profession, who had seriously impaired their intellect and judgment by its use. We forbear to give these names, as some of these gentlemen are now no longer among the living. We will add, only, that it was the unanimous opinion of all present, that this was a subject which ought to be brought to the notice of the profession, and to that of students of all classes.

The writer has given the alarm, and candor obliges

him to say that, he thinks this drug is used quite as much among *lawyers* as ministers, and much more among fashionable ladies in high life than in either of the learned professions.

Mr. De Quincey (it is remarkable, that though this man impaired his health very much in early life by the excessive use of opium, yet he lived to the advanced age of seventy-four years, and his mind was bright to the end of life), the author of "Confessions of an English Opium-Eater," says, "Who are they?" (opium-eaters.) "Reader, I am bound to say, a very numerous class indeed. Of this I became convinced some years ago, by computing, at that time, the number of those in one small class of English society (the class of men distinguished for talent and notoriety), who were known to me directly, or indirectly, as opium-eaters; such, for instance, as the eloquent and benevolent William Wilberforce; the late Dean of Carlisle, Dr. Isaac Milner; the first Lord Erskine; Mr. ——, the philosopher; a late Under-Secretary of State, Mr. Addington, brother to the first Lord Sidmouth (who described to me the sensation which first drove him to the use of opium in the very same words as the Dean of Carlisle, viz.: 'that he felt as though rats were gnawing at the coats of his stomach'); Samuel Taylor Coleridge, and many others hardly less celebrated."

John Randolph, of Roanoke, Virginia, that most

eccentric and remarkable man, according to the testimony of Dr. Joseph Parrish, of Philadelphia, in which city he died, May 24, 1833, was in the habitual use of opium. Dr. Parrish was his attending physician, at the time of his decease. Randolph had started for Europe, but was taken sick before reaching the packet, and died in the City Hotel at the time above stated. His eccentricities accompanied him to the last. "I told him," says Dr. P., "he had been so long an invalid, he must have acquired an accurate knowledge of the general course of practice adapted to his case. He replied, 'Certainly; at forty, a fool or a physician, you know.' I remarked," continued the Doctor, "There were many idiosyncrasies in some constitutions, and wished to ascertain what was peculiar about him. He said, 'I have been an idiosyncrasy all my life.' He informed me that all preparations of camphor invariably injured him, and, as to ether, 'it would blow me up.' Not so of opium and its preparations, for I soon discovered, he was in the free use of this drug in some form or other. He told me, he 'could take opium like a Turk;' and I certainly received from him the impression that he was in the habitual use of opium."

Was not Randolph's a case in verification of our declaration, it causes wit to unfurl her proudest banner? And may we not conclude that many of those retorts which petrified his hearers, or shook the Halls of Congress with laughter, originated in the stimulus of this potent drug?

Dr. Jacob Bigelow was long in the habit of relating to the medical classes in Harvard University, the following anecdote, illustrating what we have said of the use of opium: "An Englishman in this city used to be invited to all parties and public dinners, on account of his *wonderful conversational powers*, the result of taking opium. On one occasion, he took a little too much, and went to sleep so that he could not be awaked. This revealed the secret of his powers of speech."

The reader may be astonished to find such men as have been named classed among opium-eaters. But his astonishment would be much augmented, if the writer were to give the names, now in his possession, of the recent dead, and present living, among the talented and respected in the learned professions in America, not excepting even the clergy. Suffice it to say, the daughter, America, is by no means outdone in the use of this narcotic by her mother, England.

CHAPTER XII.

The Skin—Scarf—True—Pigment—Capillaries—Perspiratory Tubes —Of the Skin—Sympathy between, and other Organs—Hygienic Uses of Water—The Cold, Plunge, Shower, Sponge, Bath—Caution in using the Cold Bath—Quotation from Dr. J. C. Warren—The Warm Bath—Mr. Wilson—Dr. Combe—Whitefield's Remarks —Water the best drink—The Feet and Water.

SOME of the older physiologists considered the skin the most important organ of the body, as has been already said—both for the prevention and cure of disease. Nor were they much mistaken, if one organ can be more important than another.

What is the skin? It is a soft and pliant membrane which invests the whole body, both its internal and external surface, following closely every winding, every prominence and hollow of the body.

The skin is composed of two layers; some make *three*, the scarf-skin, pigment, and *cutis vera*, or true skin; others do not consider the *pigment* as a separate layer. We have a very delicate sense of touch in the pulps, or ends of the fingers. This is owing to the scarf-skin being very thin here, and to the parts being fully permeated with nerves.

What *is* the scarf-skin? It is a transparent fluid,

exuded or poured out from the blood-vessels, and spread thinly over the true skin. As it hardens, the solid particles are gathered together into minute roundish granules, which seem to have a vital affinity for each other, and thus collecting together, and imbibing the fluid, as it is poured out, they at length form little *cells*. One layer is thus completed; the same operation going on forms another. The moisture evaporates from the outside portion, and leaves little hard dry scales, with which the whole body is covered. These are composed chiefly of albumen, of which you will see a fine representation in the white of an egg. Simple water will not readily dissolve this substance, but soap and water will, because the alkali of the soap dissolves the adhesive or hardened albumen.

Suppose we never washed or purified the skin? We should not only become filthy, but benumbed, losing all delicacy of touch.

The scarf-skin has one peculiarity which is very striking, It never wears out. Our clothes wear out; but this skin, the more we wear it, the thicker it grows. This is one of the wonderful productions of nature, and shows how superior her operations are to those of art.

The scarf-skin cannot be prevented. It is a natural healthful secretion. It should be removed by friction and ablution, but all promises to *prevent* it, as in what is called *dandruff* on the head — all the lotions and mixtures used for this purpose, are mere charlatanism. Spots are sometimes visible on the scarf-skin. These are best removed by some acid, as lemon-juice.

The *pigment,* or paint, the seat of color, is in the lower part, or under the scarf-skin. - This accounts for the black, red, or white man; and the color of the skin is in proportion as this paint is light or dark. The fairest skin becomes brown, if exposed to a tropical sun.

> "The toiling youth who seeks an olive crown,
> Is sun-burnt with his daily toil, and brown."

If we would have a fine clear skin, we must be careful to preserve health, and avoid exposure without, and irritants within.

As the scarf-skin is a mere belt, or scabbard for the true skin, so it prevents the true skin from being bruised or injured.

The first object of the skin which I shall name, is the sense of *feeling.* This is in the nerves. But it is greatly augmented by the thinness and softness of the skin. Hence the allegorical expression, when persons are very sensitive, they are called *thin-skinned.*

The tanned skins of animals are used for leather. The strength of the leather depends upon the true skin; but its smoothness and delicacy depend upon the papillary layer. No other material known can bear comparison with skin in the manufacture of leather; and yet, how much more wonderful is the living, breathing skin as it invests the animal!

The second layer, called the *cutis vera*, or true skin, is composed of minute fibres, which are gathered' together in bundles, and interwoven with each other, into a compact, but porous web or net. It is full of pores, which grow larger as they descend deeper, till their diameter is about one-twelfth of an inch. These pores are round, or nearly so, and are separated by strands of fibres, of double their own diameter — so that the lower surface of the skin resembles a coarse web, or net, the meshes or apertures of which are filled with little bags of adipose matter, called fat.

The external skin differs in thickness in different parts of the body. Upon the back, and outside of the limbs it is thick, evidently to protect these parts, which are much exposed, from injury; while upon the front of the chest, and inside of the limbs, it is thinner, because these parts are less exposed to contusions. The sensitive layer of the skin is thin, soft, and uneven. It is filled with blood-vessels which give it a reddish hue, and nerves, which bestow the power of feeling.

The little conical prominences upon the skin are called papillæ. They are too small to be seen with the naked eye. Each of these little prominences, or each papilla, has an opening, through which a hair-like vessel passes, and a small nerve. This little blood-vessel is called a *capillary*. These capillaries are called *intermediate* vessels, because all the blood in the body passes through them, from the arteries to the veins.

In the palm of the hand and the pulps of the fingers, the sensitive layer of the skin is raised into small ridges. These ridges are very variable — some being in concentric circles, some oval, others winding, or more or less parallel; some of them separate very abruptly, and diverge widely.

The skin is so permeated, or filled with blood and nerves, that the point of a pin cannot be inserted without giving pain and drawing blood.

The capillaries are porous, and permit the passage *outwards* of oxygen and the nutritive elements of the blood; and *inwards* of the carbonic acid gas. The grand object of the blood, therefore, in its outward course, is to convey oxygen, and the elements of nutrition, to supply the wants of the body,—and in its *backward* course, to carry the elements of *decay*, or that which is unfit for further nutrition, to be thrown out through the lungs. Various degrees of color (except that which flows from the *pigment*) are proportioned to the quantity, velocity, and composition of the blood flowing through the capillaries. Thus, in *blushing*, a mental emotion causes a sudden turgescence or fulness of blood in these vessels. Fear, a different emotion, drives the blood from the capillaries, and sometimes causes *death,* by congestion of the brain or heart.

A person is said to be "purple with cold," when the nervous energy is overcome, and the circulation in the capillaries retarded. The little blood remaining in them gives a blue tinge to the complexion.

The *pores of the skin* are the openings of small tubes, which traverse the whole thickness of the skin, and are imbedded in the fat under it. These tubes are connected with the perspiratory glands, the oil glands, and veins. Each perspiratory tube forms a beautiful spiral coil. The pore or mouth of the tube opens obliquely, and answers the purpose of a valve.

Mr. Wilson, in his admirable work on the skin, enumerates 3528 of these pores in a single square inch on the palm of the hand; and each tube, of which the pore is an opening, being a quarter of an inch long, it follows that, in a square inch of skin on the palm of the hand, there exists a length of tube equal to 882 inches, or 73 feet. Taking 2800 as a fair average for each square inch of surface, in a man of ordinary stature, the number of pores will be 1,750,000 inches, or nearly 28 miles. It is no wonder, then, that such marvellous effects are produced by the perspiration.

These general remarks upon the structure of the skin, and especially upon the *perspiratory* system, are made to show the great value of a proper and judicious hygienic use of water.

All acknowledge the importance of cleanliness, but few know the *sympathy* between the skin and the internal viscera. There is an intimate sympathy between the skin and the lungs. This is often seen in the case of those persons who are troubled with a severe cough during the cold season of the year, and who are free from it in the warm season, when the perspiration from the skin is profuse. The first effect of external impressions from the atmosphere is on the skin and lungs. We are unable fully to explain this sympathetic effect between the skin and lungs and other viscera. But, that such a sympathetic action takes place between these organs, is demonstrated in the cold bath. When the body is immersed in water of a temperature considerably below that of the body in its natural state, the vessels on the skin are rendered torpid, and the blood is thrown upon the internal organs. At the same time, a sympathetic torpor takes place in the capillary vessels of the lungs, which occasions the *panting* for breath experienced upon suddenly entering the cold bath. But reaction soon takes place, and the functions of the skin are renewed with increased energy. This is but a repetition of what takes place in sudden atmospherical changes. In our climate, proverbial for its sudden changes, the *lungs* are the organs which suffer most.

In the greater part of the derangements of the lungs

and other viscera, we shall find the functions of the skin first impaired. The insensible, and even sensible, perspiration is checked. The balance of the circulation is deranged. Hence the chills and flushes which alternately succeed each other. Here commence the slight effects of pulmonary difficulties, and these troubles are in proportion to the violence of the atmospherical influence upon these organs, through their sympathy with the skin. This point being settled, we can readily see the course of relief pointed out, and the remedial measures to be pursued. *It is to restore the proper functions of the skin.* This may often be accomplished by various kinds of bathing, but the judicious use of the bath exerts its most salutary effects in *preserving* these functions. It is often a remedy for disease, but it is more than a *remedy* for disease by *preventing* it, inasmuch as, according to the old proverb, "an ounce of prevention is worth a pound of cure," and as, he is a greater surgeon who *saves* limbs than he who *cuts them off*. Upon this principle, it is said, the Chinese pay their physicians so long as they themselves are in health, but take away their salaries as soon as they are sick. Many of the most grave diseases which "flesh is heir to," are cutaneous, and would never exist, were proper measures used to cleanse and purify the skin. The truthfulness of this maxim undoubtedly led the Jewish Lawgiver and the Arabian Prophet to prescribe so many ablutions in their canons. It is not intended by this remark to place the writings of Moses and Mahomet upon the same footings; but, simply, that in their frequent purifications of the surface of the body, both of them prescribed a course, and made compliance with it a religious duty, which was calculated to promote the health, happiness, and longevity of their followers. Bathing was much practised by the ancient Greeks and Romans. They expended vast sums of money, not from the coffers of individuals only, but also from the public chest, in erecting stupendous and beautiful baths. These, at the present time, like all the other works of art in those countries, are in ruins. Still, the ocean, lakes, and rivers supply their places.

It is not simply in reference to *cleanliness* that I would call the reader's attention to the use of the bath, but also in relation to its very important agency as a means of *preventiny* and *removing* disease. I suspect the bath is in much more frequent use in this country now, than it was a quarter of a century since. But its use here, even now, is little in comparison with what it is in the Eastern world. According to modern physicians and others who have travelled in Asia and the northern parts of Europe, baths are frequently used at the present time. One of the most eminent physicians of modern times says: "It is a mistake to suppose that it is only in a hot climate, where the perspiration is abundant, that ablution is necessary. In the wilds of Russia, the peasant steams himself in a hot vapor, and then rolls himself in snow. By early inuring himself to these transitions, he preserves health to old age, and seldom requires medicine."

No one can study and understand the proper functions of the skin and the sympathetic influence exerted by it on the internal organs, without realizing the truth of what is said above, relative to the effects of the bath in preventing and curing disease. It is, beyond doubt, the best preventive of disease known, when properly used, and it certainly exerts no inconsiderable influence in removing disease. But it should never be resorted to by the invalid without the advice of an experienced and judicious physician. I mean, when there is the slightest probability that any of the internal organs are diseased, or greatly debilitated. I have known both the cold and warm bath prove highly injurious to invalids; and it would not be too much to say, I have known them to convert slight diseases, and those that might have been remedied by proper treatment, into grave and incurable ones; especially, the *cold* bath when used improperly and indiscriminately. To point out *when* bathing may be employed with safety and utility, is very important.

The *cold bath* — when may it be safely and usefully employed? This question may be the most properly answered by the effects which its use produces.

It may be used by *sponging* a part or the whole surface of the body, and wiping and rubbing the skin, first with a soft napkin; and then, with a coarser one, or with a brush, or with the hand, which some consider the best flesh-brush. This manner of using the cold bath is generally safe, if commenced in the warm season. In the case of those who are feeble, it is the best and safest way of applying cold water to the surface of the body.

A *second* method of using the cold bath is by *immersing*, or *plunging* the whole body into the water. This produces a greater shock to the system than *sponging* the body. The blood is suddenly driven from the extremities and capillaries of the skin, and thrown upon the large vessels and trunks of the interior.

A *third* method is by *showering* or *affusion*. In this, also, the shock is greater than in *sponging*, and may exceed that of plunging, if the amount of water used is considerable, and descends from a great height.

These *three* are the usual methods in which the cold bath is administered. In all of them, the effect is similar in kind, though it may vary in degree. The shock given to the system produces a *reaction* in proportion to the strength and vigor of the constitution. The collapse of the capillary vessels is soon overcome by the power of the heart and arteries, and a general *warmth* and *glow* of the whole system succeed, which are both pleasant and salutary. A new and more vigorous impulse is given to the perspiratory vessels of the skin and glandular organs. The excretory vessels are roused to renewed action, and the whole system is invigorated, which is evinced by a sense of elasticity, flow of spirits, and pleasing sensations.

If this reaction take place soon after the bath, it is the best indication of its beneficial effects. If a gentle glow or warmth *immediately* succeeds the shock of the bath, it is a sure proof of its utility; but, if the reaction is slow in taking place, it is of doubtful benefit; and, if it does not follow the bath at all, it is proof that the use of it, instead of having a salutary effect, is hurtful and dangerous. I have known instances where the bath has been persisted in for some time, when, instead of a *glow*, it was followed by a chill, and it was ruinous to the constitution. No person should use the cold bath, when, after bathing, it leaves the system cold or chilly. If there is any organic disease of the large viscera, such as the heart, liver, or spleen, or functional derangement of the heart, it will be injurious or dangerous to use it; and, as this may be the case, while the invalid himself knows it not, he should never use the bath until he has been carefully examined by a skilful physician. The seat and cause of the disease should be thoroughly explored, and the chest and abdomen examined by percussion, compression, and auscultation, and all the physical signs of visceral disease strictly scrutinized, before he is advised to resort to sea-bathing or to the use of the cold bath in any of its forms. I cannot too strictly enjoin upon the invalid the absolute necessity of consulting his physician, before he ventures upon an experiment an which his future health or life may be so dependent.

It is a good way for the invalid to commence with the tepid bath, and gradually lower its temperature, if its effects do not prove injurious, until it be of the coldness of the atmosphere.

The cold sea-water bath, or salt dissolved in the water, is always preferable to fresh water. This seems to depend on the stimulus of the salt upon the skin.

If the cold bath is commenced in infancy, almost any child may be inured to its use, and its constitution so tempered, as to be but little affected by atmospherical vicissitudes. If commenced at adult age, before disease has begun its ravages, or the constitution is greatly undermined, any one may so far harden himself to our climate that its sudden changes will do him but little injury. I consider the cold bath, if commenced early, and properly administered, as the greatest safeguard against the various diseases with which we are acquainted. If it be true, as has been said, of the aborigines of this country, that they immerse their newly-born infants in cold water, it is, to say the least, not a very unwise or injudicious practice. No person can live in this climate without exposure to its vicissitudes, and there is no guard so effectual, as the use of cold water in some way applied to the surface of the body. As a *remedy* in certain diseases, it is invaluable; such as small-pox, scarlet-fever, measles, and other rashes. In all these we may wash the skin freely with cold water, from the commencement to the close of the disease. It is thus rendered soft, the acrid matter passes off more freely through the pores, and the fever is abated. In small-pox the cold sea-bathing has been found highly salutary. Dr. Eberle, in his Practice of Medicine, on scarlet-fever says: "The application of cold water to the surface of the body cannot be too strongly recommended in the higher grades of this affection." And he quotes the following passage from Bateman. "As far as my experience has taught me, we are possessed of no physical agent, by which the functions of the animal economy are controlled with so much certainty, safety, and promptitude, as by the application of cold water to the skin, under the augmented heat of scarlatina and some other fevers. This expedient combines in itself all the medicinal properties which are indicated in this state of disease, and which we should scarcely expect it to possess, for it is not only the most effectual *febrifuge*, but it is in fact, the only *sudorific* or *anodyne* which will not disappoint the expectation of the practitioner." "I have had the satisfaction, in numerous instances, of witnessing the immediate improvement of the symptoms and the rapid change of countenance produced in the patient by washing the skin."

The following quotation is from Dr. Warren's book on the Preservation of Health.

"The application of cold water to the human body is beneficial principally in two ways; first, as a purifier; second, as a tonic. 1st, it purifies the body by removing from its surface those excretions which are continually poured out. The skin is an outlet, by which are discharged matters necessary to be thrown out of the system, for, if retained, they would produce disease. These matters cause an incrustation over the surface of the skin, and this, to a certain extent, obstructs the little orifices, through which these exhalations take place. Physicians and surgeons are in the habit of observing deplorable instances of filthy concretions on the skin of poor patients, and this kind of neglect, unfortunately, is not wholly confined to the lower classes.

"Besides these exhalations, the surface of the skin becomes more or less charged with cuticular exfoliations, which ought to be daily removed. The linen taken from the body of a poor person is sometimes seen to shed a shower of flakes of separated cuticle. The regular removal of these substances not only gives a more free outlet to cutaneous exhalation, but the act by which they are removed, also serves to promote the healthy action of the capillary vessels of this organ.

"2d. The effect of cold water as a tonic is well known. The refreshing influence of water applied to the face, neck, hands, and arms, is a matter of general experience. The operation of cold water, applied to the whole surface of the body, is to produce an agreeable and refreshing sensation. This is followed by a glow more or less considerable, depending partly upon the difference between the temperature of the water and that of the body, and partly on the state of the body itself, to which the application is made. Immersion of the hand, or any other part of the body, in cold weather in tepid water, is followed by a sense of chilliness, while immersion of the same part, for a limited time, in iced water, is followed by a sensation of positive heat. Immersion of a part, or the whole of the body in cold water, causes an increase of vigor. This is particularly obvious in hot weather. When one, who is exhausted with heat and fatigue, plunges into cold water, or receives the affusion of it over the whole surface of the body, the languid frame is immediately invigorated and prepared for new labors. This change is probably attributable to a uniform contraction of the small vessels, and a more regular flow of blood through the relaxed organs, thus reviving their vigor.

"In the same way congestions, by which the vital

actions are impeded, are removed, and this not only in the external or cutaneous portion of the body, but also by the reflex nervous action of Dr. Marshall Hall, or sympathy as it has been formerly called, in the great central organs, the heart, lungs, stomach, and intestines. Thus a great many diseases may be removed in the incipient stage; for vascular congestions, or accumulations of blood in particular vessels, by which the circnlation is obstructed, constitute the origin of a great number of diseases. All those who have been in the habit of using cold water know, that an incipient catarrhal affection often disappears on its judicious application to the surface of the body. This disease is a congestion of the blood in the vessels of the membrane lining the nostrils, trachea, and lungs, arising in this instance from the application of cold air to the surface of the body. When cold water is applied to the skin it produces increased circulation in this part, and the blood is thus diverted from the internal organs. A similar train of occurrences takes place in the germination of many diseases. The effect of the judicious application of cold water to the surface of the body is, therefore, to relieve temporary languor, remove incipient disease, and give permanent tone to the animal system."

I now proceed to make some remarks upon the *warm bath*. Says the distinguished writer, Dr. Johnson: "As the first instance of cold bathing, *as a remedy*, was that of Melampus bathing the daughter of the king of Argos, so Medea's cauldron is supposed to have been the first record of the warm bath. From the derivation of the word, 'care destroyer,' and the fabulous stories of old age restored to youth by the effects of Medea's boiler, we may suppose that the *warm* bath was highly appreciated in ancient times." I have no doubt that a general use of the warm bath in our country would produce the most salutary effects upon the health and longevity of its inhabitants. The time will come when a change, "so devoutly to be wished," will take place, and the bath be generally used. There are, at present, many objections which are utterly unfounded, but which must, nevertheless, be removed, before this desirable era will dawn upon us with its blessings.

It is objected to the *warm* bath, that it renders persons *effeminate and debilitated*. This is proved to be an erroneous opinion, from the fact that in those Southern and Eastern countries where it is in general use, the inhabitants are healthy and live to a good old age. That the *warm* bath, like every other good thing, may be so abused, carried to such a pitch of excess, luxury, and extravagance, as to prove deleterious, there can be no doubt. That it was carried to this extent among the Romans, is readily granted. But it was when they were luxurious in everything—when vice of every kind so abounded, that *even the use of the bath, salutary as it is*, could not save them. Then (as music, the daughter of heaven, when she had been exiled from her proper place, has been made to serve the purposes of Satan), the bath was made subservient to their sensuality and effeminacy. What good thing may not be abused? When used with moderation, it neither *debilitates* nor tends to promote effeminacy. In debilitated subjects, it strengthens the system, and is much safer than the cold bath. It has already been said that the *cold* bath is improper and dangerous in many diseases. Not so, the *warm*. Its effects are the reverse of the cold. It elicits the blood to the surface, causing it to fill the whole cutaneous system, and thus relieving the internal organs. It is very salutary after exhaustion. It improves the pulse, elevates the spirits, and increases the appetite.

As a *remedy* for disease, it is far preferable to the cold bath, but not as a *preventive*. It may be employed with safety in a far more numerous class of diseases than the cold bath. It relieves, or greatly mitigates, among others, the following diseases:—scrofula, indolent swellings of the joints or lymphatic glands, gout, incipient consumption, chronic obstructions of the liver and other viscera, old syphilitic difficulties, stone, inflammation of the bowels, and the whole host of cutaneous diseases, numerous as they are. A judicious use of the warm bath in the relief of diseases cannot be too highly appreciated.

To those who are not specially diseased, it is one of the greatest luxuries of life, and as such, it has ever been esteemed in the Eastern world. Homer tells us that Ulysses refreshed himself with the warm bath when he had returned from his toils and wars. It may be administered at any time, but promotes perspiration the most, when taken in the evening. It may be taken to good advantage when the person can retire immediately after it to bed. I think this the best time to receive the warm bath. When taken during the day, it should be followed by gentle exercise for an hour or more. There are various kinds of baths now administered, such as the Russian vapor, medicated, sulphur, iodine, &c. All these, when judiciously and properly used, may be serviceable and worthy the attention of the valetudinarian or invalid.

Every person must see the great utility of purifying the skin, when the amount of perspirable matter which passes through its pores is duly understood, and the sympathy between that and the internal viscera fully appreciated. This sympathy has already been glanced at. Lavoisier, a celebrated French chemist, and many others, have estimated the exhalations from the skin, alone, to be about two-thirds of the whole amount of meats and drinks taken into the system. How powerful, then, must be the free perspiration from this covering of the body, to preserve the whole internal structure in health; and what a potent energy is it capable of exerting in relieving disease and restoring the deranged and disordered functions of the whole animal economy!

The Vapor Bath is spoken of in the following language by Dr. Erasmus Wilson, in his treatise on Healthy Skin.

"The vapor bath offers some points of difference from the preceding, in the circumstance of extending its influence to the interior, as well as to the exterior of the body. The bather is seated upon a chair, in a position agreeable to himself, and the vapor is gradually turned on around him, until the requisite temperature (from 90° to 110°) is attained. The vapor is consequently breathed, and thus brought into contact with every part of the interior of the lungs. The vapor bath has undergone much improvement within the last few years, and its powers, as an agent for the cure of disease, have been increased by the discovery of various vegetable substances, whose volatile elements are susceptible of being diffused through the vapor, and, thus introduced into the blood, are made to act upon the system.

"Bathing and exercise are very closely allied to each other—they both stimulate the actions of the skin, and both, if carried too far, are productive of fatigue.

Bathing, again, is indebted to exercise for some of its useful properties. In like manner, the rules of bathing and those of exercise are very similar. Bathing, to be efficient in preserving health, should be regular, should be commenced by degrees, and increased by a process of training, and should not be permitted to intrude upon hours devoted to some important function, such as digestion. It must not approach too near a meal, that is to say, if it be attended with the least fatigue; nor, must it follow a meal too closely, three or four hours being permitted to elapse. The time occupied in bathing in cold water by invalids should not exceed a few minutes, ranging, perhaps, from two to ten; but persons in health may carry it to the point of satiety, provided always, that they combine it with active exercise. The period for the tepid, warm, or vapor bath, is from a quarter to half an hour, unless special indications require to be fulfilled.

"Another curious and important law is associated with the influence exerted by the bath over the state of the pulse, which is, a power of absorption by the skin below the natural range, and an augmented transpiration above it. The absorbing power is modified by various circumstances, such as the quantity of fluids already contained within the tissues of the bather, the state of the body in relation to food, activity of nutrition, &c. In this sense, medicated baths have the power of acting upon the system. The process is, however, slow, and requires long immersion when the water bath is used, but more active with the vapor bath."

The following extract is from Dr. Combe:

"The vapor bath is calculated to be extensively useful, both as a preservative, and as a remedial agent. Many a cold and many a rheumatic attack, arising from checked perspiration, or long exposure to the weather, might be nipped in the bud by its timely use. In chronic affections, not only of the skin itself, but of the internal organs, with which the skin most closely sympathizes, as the stomach and intestines, the judicious application of the vapor bath is productive of great relief. Even in chronic pulmonary complaints, it is, according to the Continental physicians, not only safe, but very serviceable, particularly in those affections of the mucous membrane which resemble consumption in so many of their symptoms. Like all powerful remedies, however, the vapor bath must be administered with proper regard to the condition and circumstances of the individual; and care must be taken to have the feet sufficiently warm during its use. If, from an irregular distribution of the steam, the feet be left cold, headache and flushing are almost sure to follow. If one-tenth of the persevering attention and labor bestowed to so much purpose in rubbing and currying the skin of horses, were bestowed by the human race in keeping themselves in good condition, and a little attention were paid to diet and clothing, colds, nervous diseases and stomach complaints would cease to form so large an item in the catalogue of human miseries."

Perhaps no man was ever more happy during a long life than Benjamin Franklin, and he found no greater enjoyment than when *swimming*.

Whitefield said "there never was a lazy Christian," and we may add, there never was a *dirty* Christian. Whatever they might have been before, when they have become Christians, it can be said of them, as the great Apostle said to the Corinthian converts, "ye are *washed*." Filth is incompatible with Christianity, which, from beginning to end, is a cleansing process, both of the outer and inner man. "Know ye not that your *bodies* are the temples of the Holy Ghost, and will the Holy Spirit dwell in a polluted body?" It is not only "with a true heart, in full assurance of faith, and hearts sprinkled from an evil conscience," that we are "to draw near to God," but also "having our *bodies washed with pure water*." The Church which Christ loves, and which is presented to Himself glorious, without spot or wrinkle, or any such thing, "is *cleansed* with the washing of water by the word." A filthy, dirty Christian cannot be. A clergyman should be a pattern of neatness. He cannot have health without cleanliness. A physician of Boston ascribed the sore eyes, and frequent loss of vision, which he met with in his travels in the East, to want of cleanliness. To be unclean in body indicates an impure heart.

No indulgence in filth nor libations to Bacchus can so calm the distressed mind as cleanliness. The Poet Thomson had this in view when he said —

> "Even from the body's purity the mind
> Receives a secret sympathetic aid."

It is doubtful whether Christianized nations use water for purposes of cleanliness as much as do uncivilized and unchristianized. Lord Kames, in his "Sketches of Man," said, many years since: "In the Island of Otaheite, both sexes bathe freely, and never eat without washing before and after. The Negroes, in general, on the Slave Coast of Africa, wash themselves, morning and evening." When our missionaries first visited the South Sea Islands, amid all their degradation, they found the heathen washed twice and thrice a day. No nation ever made a more free use of water both for ablutions and cold and warm baths than the ancient Greeks, and they were long-lived. Arcadia and Etolia, indeed all Greece, were celebrated for longevity. Pythagoras, Pindar, Sophocles, Anacreon, Plato, and Zeno all lived to advanced age. Italy was also famous for its baths, and in the 76th year of the Christian era, when a census of the people was made, there were 265 persons over one hundred years of age in that part of

Italy which lies between the Po and the Apennines. An unclean plant is disgusting, an unclean bird is still more loathsome; but there is nothing more disgusting and loathsome than an unclean man, except an *unclean spirit*.

Cold water is one of the best tonics we have. It gives vigorous action to the stomach and the whole alimentary canal. It should not be taken *with* food, nor immediately *after* eating, as a certain degree of heat is necessary to the proper digestion of food. If a gill of ice-water is thrown into the stomach when recently filled with food, at its common temperature of 100° of Fahrenheit, it is cooled down to 70°, and digestion stops till the temperature rises again to 100°. Hence the impropriety of drinking cold or iced water with our meals. But water taken when the stomach is empty, or nearly so, has a highly invigorating and beneficial effect.

Water-drinkers ordinarily outlive spirit-drinkers. We have a remarkable verification of this statement from an old physician of Natchez. After having enumerated the deaths of most of the physicians of that city, who lived there thirty years ago, who were spirit-drinkers, and given the names of those who were not, and who are still living, he says: "As it was with the doctors of Natchez and vicinity, so has it been with the lawyers. The lawyers of that city and vicinity, thirty years ago, who were in the habit of using alcoholic beverages, in the place of plain water, between meals, are all dead long ago. There is not one left. Even to bring down the time to twenty years, there is not one left. While of the temperate lawyers of the same locality, from twenty to thirty years ago, all are living at the present time, June, 1853, minus a number *less* than the natural decrease of mankind, incident to the most healthy countries, as set forth in the Carlisle tables of mortality. The bench and the pulpit have scarcely lost a member, except from accident or old age. The temperate lawyers, with the exceptions just mentioned, are not only all living, but they are all rich, although they began life poor. The contrast arrived at, by consulting time and experience, is so great, that it may be said death is in alcohol and life is in water, when used as a common beverage. That plain, good, pure water is better than alcohol in any form, to enable the human system to endure fatigue and exposure, and to give both body and mind strength and vigor, the history of the above-mentioned classes plainly proves."

He gives the names of many of those temperate men, and the posts of honor which they have or do now fill. Among them are Major-General John A. Quitman, a model of a temperate man in all things except politics; Hon. Robert J. Walker, late Secretary of the Treasury; Capt. John B. Nevitt, a master spirit at political meetings, yet he never drank half a pint of ardent spirit in all his life.

Verily, by these statements we are reminded of a remark of an old clergyman, in our boyish days, respecting a man by the name of Drinkwater. He had turned exhorter among the Smithites, and one night advised the audience all to flee into *Lot's* ark. Some one asked our old congregational clergyman, after his exhortation, what he thought of him. He said, he thought he had better keep *drinking water*.

The *feet* require attention, if any one would preserve health. No person who neglects his feet, can long be in the enjoyment of comfort, cleanliness, or health. It is very uncomfortable to any one to have dirty feet; more disagreeable to smell them, and most destructive to health to possess them. Every person should wash his feet daily, and then rub them thoroughly with a fine napkin, and then a coarse one, and then, if they are moist and cold, they should be rubbed daily with warm dry sand, and washed again and thoroughly dried. The stockings should be changed every day. I have known persons afflicted with bronchial disease and a little hacking cough for years, when the whole trouble arose from damp, cold feet, which were seldom washed or cleansed; and I have seen the same persons enjoying comfortable health from simply attending in a proper manner to their feet. But we have spoken of the feet in another place.

Remember the good old proverb, "Keep the head cool, the feet warm, and throw physic to the dogs," so long as you are well, and I add, you will not be likely to be sick. This is the best way to enjoy life. "Health consists in temperance alone."

CHAPTER XIII.

The Poets on Sleep — A Source of Enjoyment — Sleep a Mystery — A Means of preserving Health — Want of Sleep a cause of Disease and of Insanity — When, where, and how long should we sleep? — Napoleon — John Wesley on Sleep — Curiosities of Sleep.

Sir Philip Sidney says:

"Come sleep, oh, sleep! the certain knot of peace,
The baiting-place of wit, the balm of woe;
The poor man's wealth, the prisoner's release,
The impartial judge between the high and low."

Sancho Panza says: " While I am asleep, I have neither fear nor hope, neither trouble nor glory; and, blessings on him who invented sleep, the mantle that covers all human thoughts; the food that appeases hunger; the drink that quenches thirst; the fire that warms cold; the cold that moderates heat; and lastly, the general coin that purchases all things; the balance and weight that makes the shepherd equal to the king, and the simple to the wise."

About one-third of the life of man is spent in sleep. He who lives to reach the age of three-score years and ten, will have spent more than twenty-three years of this period in unconscious repose. This simple fact alone is sufficient to proclaim the overwhelming importance of sound refreshing sleep to the health, happiness, and longevity of man.

But the personal experiences of each individual speak still more impressively upon this subject, because they appeal to his sensations. Deprived even for a single night of the balmy influences of

"Tired nature's sweet restorer,"

we are oppressed with languor and exhaustion. Long-continued wakefulness disorders the whole system. The appetite becomes impaired, the digestion weakened, the secretions diminished or changed, the mind dejected, the nervous system exhausted, and soon, waking dreams occur and strange phantoms appear, which at first may be transient, but which ultimately take possession of the mind, and madness or death ensues. A writer in the American Journal of Insanity thus speaks: "We wish we could impress upon all the vast importance of securing sound and abundant sleep; if so, we should feel that we had done an immense good to our fellow-beings, not merely in preventing insanity, but other diseases also."

The origin of much of the nervousness and impaired health of individuals who are not decidedly sick, is owing to a want of sufficient and quiet sleep. To procure this should be the study of every one. It is to be feared that the great praise of early rising has had *this* bad effect—to make some believe that *sleep* was of but little consequence.

We have heretofore stated that in our opinion the most frequent and immediate cause of insanity, and one of the most important to guard against, is the want of sleep. Indeed, so rarely do we see a recent case of insanity that is not preceded by want of sleep, that it is regarded as almost a sure precursor of mental derangement.

Notwithstanding strong hereditary predisposition, ill-health, loss of kindred or property, insanity rarely results, unless the exciting causes are such as to produce a loss of sleep. A mother loses her only child, the merchant his fortune — the politician, the scholar, the enthusiast, may have their minds powerfully excited and disturbed; yet, if they sleep well, they will not become insane. No advice is so good, therefore, to those who have recovered from an attack, or to those who are in delicate health, as that of securing, by all means, sound, regular, and refreshing sleep.

The old poets were well aware of the value of sleep. Not only Shakspeare and Dryden and Young have sung its praises, but Drummond thus extols it:

> Sleep, silence, child, sweet father of soft rest,
> Prince, whose approach peace to all mortals brings,
> In different host to shepherds and to kings,
> Sole comforter of minds which are oppressed;
> So, by thy charming rod all breathing things
> Lie slumbering with forgetfulness opprest.

Many allude to the fact that while it is the solace of the poor and needy, it often flies the perfumed chambers of the great. Says Cowley:

> Sleep is a god too proud to wait in palaces,
> And yet so humble, too, as not to scorn
> The meanest country cottages;
> His poppy grows among the corn;
> The halcyon sleep will never build his nest
> In any stormy breast.
> 'Tis not enough that he does find
> Clouds and darkness in the mind;
> Darkness but half his work will do,
> 'Tis not enough — he must find quiet, too.

It is true that some few persons are able to perform much mental labor, and to study late at night, and yet sleep well. Some require but little sleep. But such individuals are very rare. General Pichegru informed Sir Gilbert Blane that, during a whole year's campaign, he did not sleep more than one hour in twenty-four. Sleep seemed to be at the command of Napoleon, as he could sleep and awake apparently at will.

M. Guizot, Minister of France under Louis Philippe, was a good sleeper. A late writer observes that his facility for going to sleep after extreme excitement and mental exertion was prodigious, and it was fortunate for him that he was so constituted, otherwise his health would materially have suffered. A Minister in France ought not to be a nervous man; it is fatal to him if he is. After the most boisterous and tumultuous sittings, at the Chambers, after being *baited* by the opposition in the most savage manner — there is no milder expression for their excessive violence — he arrives home, throws himself upon a couch, and sinks immediately into a profound sleep, from which he is undisturbed till midnight, when proofs of the Moniteur are brought to him for inspection.

Let not the importance of sleep, then, be disregarded; but on the contrary, let its sweet and soothing influences be cultivated. Let it not be regarded as an evil that comes to interrupt enjoyment, but as a *great accomplishment* and a pleasure of itself. Says Keats:

> What is more gentle than a wind in summer?
> What is more soothing than the pretty hummer
> That stays one moment in an open flower,
> And buzzes cheerily from bower to bower?
> What is more tranquil than a muskrose blowing
> In a green island, far from all men's knowing?
> More healthful than the leafiness of dales?
> More secret than a nest of nightingales!
> More serene than Cordelia's countenance?
> More full of visions than a high romance?
> What but thee, sleep? Soft closer of our eyes!
> Low murmurer of tender lullabies!
> Light hoverer around our happy pillows!
> Wreather of poppy buds and weeping willows!
> Silent entangler of a beauty's tresses!
> Most happy listener! when the morning blesses
> Thee for enlivening all the cheerful eyes
> That glance so brightly at the new sunrise.

Sleep is a very wonderful phenomenon. — Why we should have been so constituted, as, that it should be necessary for us to spend one-third of our lives in an unconscious state, we are unable to say. But so it has been ordained by our Creator. The Redeemer once said, "Our friend sleepeth;" "the disciples thought he spoke of taking rest in sleep!" It is a consoling thought, that what is called the death of the righteous, is represented in scripture as "falling asleep;" and we all know what it is to rest in sleep.

When, where, and *how long* should we sleep? These are the inquiries we will endeavor to answer.

When should we sleep?

Our Creator seems to have answered this question by making day and night. When light, and noise, and bustle cease, and heat is mitigated, — when "tired nature" seems to rest; *then* the mind and the organs of the body, the muscles and senses, should sink into forgetful quiescence; and remain so, till the "powerful king of day" and harbinger of action, folds up the mantle of darkness, and throws over creation the brilliancy of his power. This would seem to be the dictate of nature. This dictate the animal creation obeys, with the exception of a few beasts of prey, which the sons and daughters of etiquette and fashion (mostly in cities) by devoting the day to repose and the night to dissipation, have deemed worthy of their imitation. The night which brings repose to sober men and sober beasts, only rouses their powers to action by gathering around them those artificial stimulants which steep them in the fumes of debauch till morn, and toss them on the ocean of dreams till noon. This is the best way to live a short life. It is like editing a daily journal; or like a pastor succumbing to all the whims; or attempting to satisfy all the demands of his parishioners; or like the atmospheric road, not only exhausting the air, but annihilating space; or, to use the graphic language of another, "burning the candle at both ends." He, then, who would live long, and possess a sound mind in a healthy body, and enjoy life, must shun such a course. He must proscribe such a fashion, though it be "the god of this world;" especially the *presiding deity* of all large cities. He must learn the lesson which Dr. Franklin told the Parisians the American Colonies had learned,— "that it is cheaper burning day-light than candle-light."

But we have almost forgotten that we are writing for students, as it is doubtless unnecessary to dwell upon this subject for *them:* and, if not necessary for them, it will be useless for others, for it is in vain to write, or speak, or philosophize on such a matter to people in general.

Hundreds of iron pens, and thousands of tongues, with brazen lungs, could never write or talk away the evil. So long as present pleasure is esteemed a certain good, and future suffering and disease uncertain, the great mass of the population will pursue the former, and risk the consequence of the latter. It is doubtful whether this evil is checked in the least, among those in health, by all that has been written and published against it. "*Morbios odimus et accersisimus,*"

As to the *time* of sleep, the old adage is as true and important, as it is quaint.

> "Early to bed and early to rise,
> Makes a man healthy, wealthy and wise."

We knew an individual who possessed, at the age of eighty-three, an unusual vigor, and presented the characteristic marks of a sound mind in a healthy body. Though he once occupied a prominent professor's chair in one of our first theological seminaries, and, both from his position, and having reared up a large family, must have been exposed to much company, yet his testimony upon this very point was, " I have always been a good sleeper. Whatever company may be at my house, when nine o'clock comes, I uniformly take my light, bid them good-night, and retire to rest."

We have no doubt of the wisdom of such a plan, and there is much reason for believing that sleep is much more refreshing in the early, than in the later part of the night.

It must, however, be evident that any rule for sleeping in the night, and laboring in the daytime, if it is to be applied the world over, cannot be adopted; for, in hot climates, the natives cannot labor after the sun has been up a few hours, and they can then sleep, and work better after sunset. But even then, the ground has become so heated during the day, that it is uncomfortable to labor in the evening. The best time for them to labor is two or three hours before sunrise. Hence, the natives of India often take their sleep in the daytime.

So, also, if this rule were made to apply all over the earth, those in the coldest climates must sleep months together. But the rule answers very well for us, to sleep in the night and labor in the day; and that is sufficient for our purpose.

The next question is, *where* should we sleep? We should never sleep on, or near the ground. The vapors arising from the surface of the earth are pernicious to health. In some countries, where they ride all night in coaches, the drivers are accustomed to admonish the passengers not to go to sleep on the route, as the consequence will be "the *chills*," or fever and ague.

It is believed that, in those countries where fever and ague prevail, no one has been known to have the disease who has uniformly slept in an elevated place; while those who are accustomed to sleep upon the ground, and in cellars and basements, are almost always subject to this disease. This rule should never be forgotten by those who reside in countries visited by intermittents.

We should never sleep in a small, ill-ventilated room. In the bed-room, we spend from seven to eight consecutive hours—we may safely say, on an average, one-third part of our lives. The demand of air for respiration, to a single person, is seven cubic feet a minute. At this rate, for eight hours, or one-third of the twenty-four, it would be three thousand three hundred and sixty feet. Suppose, now, our sleeping-room does not contain more than six hundred cubic feet. It is no unnatural supposition, for we can find hundreds of such bed-rooms around us.

A person goes into one of these rooms with the door closed. How long will this air last him? Not two hours. Even if we suppose the sleeping-room to contain one thousand cubic feet, it would last its occupant, but about two hours and a half. What is he to breathe the other five or six hours, while he usually remains in this room? Carbonic acid gas. In other words, a deadly poison. And, what is still worse, as our beds are usually located nearer the floor than the ceiling of the room, and as this gas, from its greater density than air, falls to the bottom, the poor sleeper gets the larger share of the poison.

It will be asked, if this be so; if this gas is so poisonous that a person immersed in it will die, as soon as if he puts his head under water, how it is that he will live at all? To this very natural question, we reply, there are some mitigating circumstances. None of our sleeping-rooms are perfectly air-tight.

And then, though people do not die often suddenly, yet multitudes of them are suffering with dizziness, head-ache, dyspepsia, and a host of kindred diseases induced by sleeping in such contracted and ill-ventilated rooms. To augment the evil, frequently there are several persons, with one or two cats or dogs, and plants, together with an air-tight stove, or a pan of coals, in the same room. When all these things are taken into the account, the wonder is, not that so many " are weak and sickly," but that they are not all of this class; not, that there are so many aches and pains, and apoplexies, and palsies, dyspepsias and consumptions, and sudden deaths; but rather, that there are no more. We have all heard of the *"Black Hole,"* at Calcutta. It was a room eighteen feet square. In this room one hundred and forty-six persons were confined. It had but one window, and that a small one. The weather was hot and sultry. Dr. Dunglison, in his Elements of Hygiene, says: "In less than an hour, many of the prisoners were attacked with extreme difficulty of breathing; several were delirious; and the place was filled with incoherent ravings, in which the cry for water was predominant. This was handed to them by the sentinels, but without the effect of allaying their thirst. In less than four hours, many were suffocated, or died in violent delirium. In five hours, the survivors, except those at the grate, were frantic and outrageous. At length most of them became insensible. Eleven hours after they were imprisoned, twenty-three only, of the one hundred and forty-six, came out alive, and those were in a highly putrid fever."

There are many *black holes* like this, used for sleeping-rooms among us; the difference between *them* and the one at Calcutta, is, they are not crammed quite so full of human beings. In a word, then, we may say, a sleeping apartment should be lofty, large, and airy. It is a poor economy for health, to have large and spacious parlors, and small and ill-ventilated bed-rooms. Fashion, however, is a reigning deity in this respect, and will no doubt continue to bear sway, notwithstanding the gratuitous advice of the doctor against her dominion.

Even when the sleeping room is large, it is advisable to have it communicate with an adjoining apartment. into which the air is freely admitted, as by this means, the air is prevented from becoming stagnant. If this cannot be done, a window may be left open, provided the weather is clear, and a current of air from it does not fall directly upon the bed.

On an average, from fifty to sixty degrees of temperature, is the most wholesome for a bed-room. Fire and lights, as a general rule, should never be allowed during the night in a sleeping room. Damp rooms and damp bed-clothes must always be shunned. In fine, as to *places* to sleep in, it will do much better for *hearers* to sleep in *churches* than for *ministers*, though even of the former, when they sleep there, we might ask: "What, have ye not" beds to sleep in at home, "that ye shame the house of God?"

The last particular is, *how long* should we sleep? We are aware, that we are now entering upon a disputed point, and that it behooves us to be careful what we say. The so-called "immortal Alfred," divided his time into three portions, of eight hours each, allotting one to refreshment and the health of the body, by sleep, diet, and exercise; another to business; and the last third to study and devotion. But the life of Alfred was not a long one, and hence his example cannot be adduced as a rule for those who desire longevity.

No one who wishes to accomplish great things should deny himself the advantages of sleep, or exercise. Any student will accomplish more, year by year, if he allow himself seven or eight hours to sleep, and three or four for meals and amusements, than if he labors at his books, or with his pen, ten or twelve hours a day.

I knew a young man who labored in a boot manufactory seventeen hours a day, for a year. The result was a total prostration of health, and partial paralysis of one side of the body. He repaired to one of the medical Gamaliels of Boston, and was depleted to a considerable degree. Getting no better, he went to another, who reversed the treatment, and put him upon Scotch-ale and beefsteak, upon which he gained a little. He was finally cured in three weeks, by the treatment at first recommended to him, namely, electricity and out-of-door occupation. Sir John Sinclair, speaking of himself, says: "The author has studied twelve hours a day, for three months; but that was in the prime of life, and for a particular purpose, and he would not recommend any other person to try the same experiment, for any length of time."

It has been said of Dr. Priestley, that he wrote more, and on a greater variety of subjects, than any other English author; yet, at no period of his life, did he spend more than six or eight hours a day in business that required much mental exertion. A vast amount of labor may be accomplished, at this ratio, in a life of medium duration.

John Wesley said, he could command sleep even on horseback. He lived to be eighty-eight years of age. In some very curious remarks which he has left upon sleep, he admits that no one measure will do for all; nor will the same amount of sleep suffice, even for the same man, at all times. A person debilitated by sickness requires more of "tired nature's sweet restorer," than one in vigorous health. More sleep is also necessary when the strength and spirits are exhausted by hard labor or severe mental efforts.

Those who have allotted but three or four hours for sleep, and who have maintained that this amount would suffice for all, have made a "bed shorter than for an ordinary man to stretch himself upon, and a covering narrower than he can wrap himself in." Indeed, it partakes a little of the character of the Procrustean bedstead. Bishop Taylor and Richard Baxter, the former supposing that three, and the latter that four hours' sleep were sufficient for any man, both fell into this error.

Whatever may have been the case with some few persons, of a peculiar constitution, it is evident that health and vigor can scarcely be expected to continue long without six hours' sleep in the four-and-twenty. Wesley says, during his long life, he never knew any individual who retained vigorous health for a whole year, with less quantity of sleep than this. Women, in general, require more sleep than men.

Mr. Wesley once wrote a sermon entitled "Duty and Advantage of Early Rising," founded on Eph. 1 : 16— "I cease not to give thanks for you, making mention of you in my prayers." Though, doubtless, it was a subject of thanksgiving to the founder of Methodism that its ministers rose early, yet it must be confessed, this was a remarkable text upon which to found a sermon on early rising. But what is to our point here, is, the following plan which he gives for ascertaining the quantity of sleep required by each person. "I had been accustomed to wake every night at about twelve or one, and to lie awake some time. I concluded that this arose from lying in bed longer than nature required. To be satisfied on this head, I procured an alarm watch, which awakened me at seven, nearly an hour earlier than my previous hour of rising. Yet I lay awake as usual, at night. The next morning I rose at six. But notwithstanding this, I also lay awake the second night. The third morning I rose at five, but, nevertheless, lay awake the third night. The fourth morning I rose at four. This broke up the habit of lying awake at night, and I continued to rise at that hour for sixty years, and taking the year round, I never lay awake a quarter of an hour for a month."

Some clergymen make a great account of "the Fathers" in the church; and perhaps a doctor may cite the authority of "the Fathers" in reference to hygiene. There might be more profit in such authority, if the Fathers in Physics did not, like the Fathers in Theology, give us such wide discrepancy in their canons. Thus Codagan recommends not to lie in bed more than seven hours in summer and eight in winter. Willish, in his Lectures on Diet and Regimen, advises "to go to bed at eight o'clock in winter, and to rise at three or four o'clock in the morning. This plan has been adopted in some of the European universities.

Too much sleep is injurious. This is always very pernicious to a clergyman, as it debilitates the body, and renders the mind sluggish and dull,—two evils which the ministry of our day are but ill-prepared to bear. By it, the senses are blunted, and both mind and body disqualified for action. It causes apoplexy, dropsy, lethargy, in a word, *the* many ills which accompany "stalled theology." It renders "the legate of the skies" too much like Cowper's "Alderman of Cripplegate, who first invented elbow-chairs." It was for this reason, I suppose, that Galen called sleep *the father of death*, and says, when carried to excess, nothing is more pernicious.

The *nervous* disorder, which is but another name for half "the ills that flesh is heir to," often arises from what Wesley called "*soaking*" too long in bed.

We would not intimate that these evils are all found among the clergy. This would be injustice to others, and too much credit to them. Valangan relates the case of a young man, who, in consequence of too much sleep, and too little exercise, died of an apoplectic fit at the age of twenty-three. Boerhaave mentions the case of a physician, who, by too much sleep, lost his intellect, and perished in a hospital. We suppose this must have been one of the too many doctors, who either do not understand their profession, or do not practise in correspondence with their prescriptions for their patients. As Sir Philip Sidney calls sleep "the poor man's wealth," so we may add, it is *every* man's health; and, above all, the student's life.

A medical writer of some eminence furnishes the following interesting particulars respecting sleep:

Some boys slept from fatigue on board of Nelson's ship, at the battle of the Nile. Among the impressive incidents of Sir John Moore's disastrous retreat to Corunna, in Spain, not the least striking is the recorded fact that many of his soldiers steadily pursued their march while fast asleep. Burdach, however, affirms that this is not uncommon among soldiers. Franklin slept nearly an hour swimming on his back. An acquaintance of Dr. D., travelling with a party in North Carolina, being greatly fatigued, was observed to be sound asleep in his saddle. His horse, being a better walker, went far in advance of the rest. On crossing a hill, they found him on the ground, snoring quietly. His horse had fallen, as was evident from his broken knees, and had thrown his rider on his head on a hard surface, without waking him.

Animals of the lower orders obey peculiar laws in

regard to sleep. Fish are said to sleep soundly; and we are told by Aristotle that the tench may be taken in this state, if approached cautiously. Many birds and beasts of prey take their repose in the day-time. When kept in captivity, this habit undergoes a change, which makes us doubt whether it was not the result of necessity, which demanded that they should take advantage of the darkness, silence, and the unguarded state of their victims. In the menagerie at Paris, even the hyena sleeps at night, and is awake by day. They all, however, seek, as favoring the purpose, a certain degree of seclusion and shade, with the exception of the lion, who, Burdach informs us, sleeps at noonday, in the open plain,—and the eagle and condor will poise themselves on the most elevated pinnacle of rock, in the clear blue atmosphere and dazzling sunlight. Birds, however, are furnished with a winking membrane, generally, to shelter the eye from light. Fish prefer to retire to sleep under the shadow of a rock, or a woody bank. Of domestic animals, the horse seems to require least sleep, and that he usually takes in the erect posture.

Birds that roost in a sitting posture are furnished with a well-adapted mechanism, which keeps them firmly supported without voluntary or conscious action. The tendon of the claws is so arranged as to be tightened by their weight when the thighs are bent, thus contracting closely, and grasping the bough or perch. In certain other animals which sleep erect, the articulations of the foot and knee are described by Dumeril as resembling the spring of a pocket-knife, which opens the instrument, and serves to keep the blade in a line with the handle.

Upon no one thing is the enjoyment of life, both as regards body and mind, more dependent, than upon sound sleep.

CHAPTER XIV.

The Ear—Importance of Hearing—Curious Formation of the Ear—Transmission of Sound—Difference of the External Ear in Man and other Animals—Deafness Hereditary—Propagation of Sound—Injury from tinkering the Ear—Hearing by the Teeth.

THE sense of hearing has been said to be next in importance to that of vision. This, undoubtedly, is the case, whether we regard it either as the source of enjoyment, or of utility in our intercourse with mankind. Through this medium we receive, or perceive sounds; and we all know how pleasant and useful sounds may be. Light and hearing are called by Plato, "the senses of the soul;" implying that the other special senses were but those of the body.

The ear is one of the most complicated organs in the human body. Its whole apparatus is complex and wonderful. I shall not attempt to give a minute description of its anatomy, though I will refer to some of its principal parts.

The auricle, pinna, or external ear, visible to the eye, is a cartilaginous substance, so formed as to catch sounds and convey them to the internal ear through a bony material. This aperture is open on the outside, and closed at the inner end by a membrane, called the *tympanum*, which is stretched across it like the head of a drum.

The wisdom of the great Architect may be seen, not only in the adaptation of the ear to catch sounds; but, also, in the sounds themselves, and in the way in which they are propagated. Sound passes in the same manner that light does, in rays, from the body by which it is caused. If it strikes against any body, it is *reflected*, by the same laws. Light is said to be *reflected*, when it is turned back. *Sound*, when turned back, is called an *echo*. As light excites the eye, so sound excites the ear. If we strike an elastic body, that strikes the air, and produces vibrations of the air resembling *waves*. When these vibrations, or waves, reach the auditory nerve, the mind takes cognizance of sound. But *how*, we know not.

The *foramen*, or passage into the ear, is *crooked*, and contains a sticky, bitter wax, which keeps the parts soft, and prevents insects from entering the ear, as they neither like its taste, nor the obstruction it presents to their passage.

In this opening, there are four small bones, articulated, or joined to each other, so as to conduct the sounds across the drum-head to the internal ear. As a hard substance is a better conductor of sound than a soft one, we see how much better these bones answer their designed purpose, than any connection made of flesh could do.

In the internal ear, the nerve of hearing is spread out, and its filaments or little branches float in a liquid. Now, this passage from the outside of the head into the drum of the ear, and a passage up from the back of the mouth to the same membrane, make the sound, as you may see in the case of the drum. How very curious this is!

I was once called many miles to see a man who had been deaf in one ear for five years. On examining the ear, it was found to be filled up with wax, and, as it was removed gradually, and he was spoken to, he said he heard better. When it was all removed, and the passage thoroughly syringed out with warm soap and water, the hearing was perfectly restored. When the drum of the ear has been perforated, or had an opening made through it by disease, or from some other cause, the hearing has been very much improved by the skilful application of *glycerine* upon a small piece of cotton.

The particular function, or use, of some parts of the ear is not known. It has already been said that the use of the external ear is to collect sounds and convey them into the ear. In some animals this part of the ear is movable. In beasts of prey, it is inclined forwards. In timid animals, as in the case of the hare and rabbit, it is directed backwards. It is slightly movable in the human species, and hence Virgil speaks of ears *erect*, when listening in the sacking of Troy. Solid substances, as well as air, will conduct sounds. If you tap on one end of a stick of timber, and put your ear close to the stick at the other end, the sound will be distinctly heard. When bathing, there are some very curious phenomena observed by listening to sounds *under water*.

Natural philosophers and physiologists have had much discussion about the theory of hearing; and, there are some points connected with this special sense which are not yet settled. The ear is adapted to catching sounds and conveying them; but, it is the mind, or the brain in connection with the mind, that really gives hearing.

Education may do much to promote or advance the sense of hearing. This is seen in the wild man of the forest, or the red men of this country. They will hear sounds which are inaudible to us. The blind compensate their loss of sight in some degree by cultivating their sense of hearing. Hence it is, that we have so many blind persons that are good musicians.

Perhaps, the defects of no other organ of the body are so often hereditarily transmitted to offspring as those of hearing. We very seldom find a musical ear in a family, unless one of the parents, at least, was musical;

and, it is very generally found that deafness goes down from generation to generation in some families. Where this is the case, little can be expected from medical aid. Inflammation of the ear, or of the parts of the head contiguous to it, often produces deafness. The hearing is often impaired by a cold in the head, or by stopping up the passage from the mouth to the ear by an inflamed throat. Typhus and typhoid fevers generally impair the hearing during their continuance. The deafness of old persons is generally incurable, as we have no remedy for old age.

It is an old proverb that the ears should never be picked, except by the elbows. Much injury is often done by thrusting pin-heads and other instruments into the ears. Sound is produced by whatever excites the auditory nerve, whether it be mechanical, chemical, electrical, or by impressions originating from within the brain from disease. Those originating within the brain have been called the *subjective* sensations of sound; and they sometimes amount to a species of hallucination: as when persons have imagined that they have heard peculiar sounds of musical instruments, or harsh voices, or angels' songs. In air, sound travels 1125 feet in a second;—in water, 4708 feet in a second. Thus, water is a much better conductor of sound than air. It has already been said, solid bodies are better conductors than fluids. Two sounds may be made at the same time, and both reach the ear, but at a different time, one coming through iron or gold, the other through air. *Conducted* vibrations are those by which we hear. They are the only sounds that can properly be said to be propagated. A vacuum will not conduct sound.

Perhaps, there has been no one particular in which people have been so much cheated out of their money, and received so much injury from itinerating quacks, as in the management of their ears. It is a reproach, even to surgery, that so little benefit is conferred by the best practitioners in their efforts to remedy deafness. What, then, shall be said of those who advertise and promise to relieve patients of this misfortune who have no knowledge of the anatomy of the delicate apparatus of the ear, and no skill in remedying defects in bearing? All we can say to console such patients is, if they employ ignorant mountebanks, they must take the consequences.

The *Watchman and Observer*, Va., gives the following curious fact, which is worthy of consideration:

"HEARING WITH THE TEETH.—Many years ago, an old subscriber who was entirely deaf, called at our office; and with the help of a slate, which he always carried with him, we were enabled to converse with each other. In the course of our interview, he remarked that for many years he had not been able to hear the loudest thunder; but added that, to his great surprise, a few evenings before, he was at the house of a friend, and was seated by the side of a piano, his elbow resting upon it, and his teeth upon his thumb, when he heard distinctly the tune which the daughter of his friend happened to be playing. Again and again he tried the experiment, and he could always hear when the connection was kept up, but could hear nothing whatever when it was broken, either by the removal of his elbow from the piano, or by placing his thumb upon any other portion of his face. From the character of our informant, we have never heard a doubt as to the truth of his narrative — and we give it now chiefly as a suggestion, whether some simple instrument cannot be framed, by means of which deaf persons may be enabled to hear with their teeth."

CHAPTER XV.

The Eye—Beauty—Design—Education of—Rules for Preserving the Sight—Effects of Darkness — Spectacles — Importance of Vision — Waywardness of the Blind—Bad effect of Tobacco on the Eye—Of Reading in Cars — Of Quack Oculists.

WE have read of a philosopher who, when asked for proof of the existence of a Deity, picked up a straw, and began to demonstrate from it the existence of a Great First Cause. But, if the existence of a Supreme Being can be inferred from a straw, how much more conclusive must be the proof, in the design manifested in the human eye? Paley well said, "were there no example of contrivance in the world, except the eye, *it* would be sufficient to establish the fact that an intelligent creative Power existed. No human art, or ingenuity, can produce anything equal in beauty and perfection to the eye."

In treating of the subject of vision, one feels compelled to exclaim, in terms of the highest admiration, of the superior beauty and wonderful contrivance of the inimitable organ — the eye. It is the most beautiful, as well as the most important of all the organs of sense. It is the great medium between the mind and external objects. It has been appropriately called the *window* of the soul. We could never gain so perfect a knowledge in any other way of many objects as by once *seeing* them. It is the source of a large part of the enjoyment of life.

It will not be necessary in speaking of the healthy eye, or of the means used to *preserve* the sight, that the anatomy or physiology of this organ should be minutely described. It is the property of all our special senses that they are capable of being educated. The education of the eye is of vast importance. In the management of infants, attention should always be given to the eye. A full blaze of light should never be allowed to break upon the eyes of an infant; nor, indeed, upon the eyes of any person.

Infants have no knowledge of distance; and hence, they always attempt to grasp every object which they see. The knowledge of distance is wholly a matter of education.

Proper training may do much to remedy *near-sightedness*. The object to be seen should be kept at as great a distance as possible, and still be within the range of distinct vision. It should be daily removed to a little greater distance, as the eye is educated to see farther. In this way, by habit merely, vision will be gradually lengthened.

The eye may be educated to see objects at a far

greater distance than it naturally can. The sailor will see objects when the student cannot. This long sight of the sailor has been gained by the habit of looking at a great distance; and this short sight of the student acquired by conning over his books. Among the Jews, who regulated their time by moons, certain men were appointed to give notice of the first appearance of the new moon; and, it is said, these watchmen would discover the hair-like crescent a day before others could see it. Persons have been known who could see the moons of Jupiter with the naked eye.

The eye may be trained so as to measure distances about as correctly as though it were done by rule. Persons, who use lines, or ruled paper, to write on, will not write a straight line without; but, by habit, they will soon learn to do without these unnecessary guides.

The eye may be educated so as to judge correctly of height or depth, form or size. There is a great difference in persons in *observing* objects. We might see a dozen persons in a room, and go away and not be able to tell how a single one was dressed, while an observer of fashion could describe minutely the dress of every one of them. The eye (like any other organ of the body) requires to be used, that it may be usable. It should be employed for a time, and then rested. If the eye is not called into active use, its functions soon cease to be discharged, and its power of vision becomes enfeebled. Many persons who have had bad eyes in their youth, have found them much improved in middle age. In general this improvement may be ascribed to their knowing much better how to use them. The following rules may be useful to all who will practise them, both in strengthening and preserving the eye:

Good eyes depend, principally, upon the measure, the time, and the kind of labor we exact from them. We may either weaken or preserve them. It is not injurious to the eye to look upon small objects, at a proper distance, if we do not move it too quickly, nor fix it too long upon one point. Reading constantly and quickly enfeebles the eye more than writing, because in the former, we move it more frequently than in the latter. Hence, it is less injurious to read and write alternately, than to read constantly. It is very necessary to have from our window a distant view, because the fatigued eye rests with pleasure and advantage on distant objects. The eye is often injured by looking at one object for a long time through a magnifying glass, such as the telescope. The same injurious effect is produced by looking for a long time, through a microscope. Those who are much employed with these instruments should always choose the morning hours, and fair days, for their observations, and temper the too dazzling sunlight by proper screens. No microscope should be used which does not give to the object the necessary clearness. A lens which magnifies very much injures the eye. Lenses with a small focal distance are more injurious than those whose focus is greater. We should never close one eye, while observing with the other. It is better to change, or look for a time with one, and then with the other eye, keeping both open at the same time.

It is as injurious to the eye to work with too bright sun-light, as it is to read in the twilight, or with too little light in a dark winter's day. We have all felt the inconvenience of reading in too bright a light, or in a green-house.

The study of a scholar should not admit too much light, and it should be so constructed that the light should fall moderately upon the writing desk.

The eye cannot be very much fatigued without being injured. It is always better to rise and work early in the morning, than to sit up late at night, because the first part of the night is best for rest. Sleep is then more refreshing, and we are much more apt to get it, than when the brain and the eyes have both become fatigued by late study.

We should never undertake work which fatigues the eye, immediately upon rising from bed. The long repose and darkness of the night have made the eye very susceptible, and even slight application weakens it.

Nothing tends more to strengthen the eyes than to wash them thoroughly, upon rising, with cold water. But there are cases in which warm water is preferable. After ablution, a walk of a mile or two, allowing them to rest on distant objects, will aid much in strengthening them. Every student, for the good of his eyes, as well as for other considerations, should avoid whatever may cause a strong tendency of blood to the head. Heating liquors and indigestible food, especially at night, should always be shunned.

Darkness, constant darkness, is ruinous to the eye. Persons who live almost constantly in dark caves, or mines, or who have been long confined in dungeons, are unable to see objects distinctly, excepting in a dark shade, or in the twilight. So, also, those who are exposed to bright fires are very apt to become blind, or to have cataracts. All brilliantly illuminated apartments are prejudicial to the eyes.

The fashion of wearing glasses for short-sightedness is very injurious to the sight. Not half so many persons are short-sighted, as generally imagine themselves to be. That person only is really short-sighted, who cannot recognize the features of a man, three steps from him, and who cannot read a tolerably large print, at the distance of a span. When convex spectacles are really necessary, the glasses should be arranged for each eye, in particular; as it is rare for one eye to have the same power of vision with the other. Convex spectacles are necessary only when we are unable to recognize *near* objects. Spectacles of *green* glass ought to be used never. When we were young, we were *green* enough to use green glasses for many years. At that period, we visited the father of President Wayland, of Brown University, at Saratoga Springs. The old gentleman was a pure-blooded Englishman, and one of the best gardeners in the country,— not that this was his profession, for he was a worthy and exemplary minister of the Baptist denomination. He worked every morning in his fine garden, and the writer with him, with his green glasses on. One morning the old gentleman said: "It seems to me, all our young men are growing blind." Why so, sir? we inquired. "Because so many of them wear glasses," said he. We replied, we had been advised to wear them on account of weak eyes. "For that very reason," said he, "I advise you to leave them off." Soon after, we laid them aside; and there they have laid; in all their greenness, for more than twice the period that old Troy was besieged.

Vision is a subject of momentous importance to a professional man. Without eyes, it is very difficult for him to work. He can accomplish but little. In making this remark, we are fully aware, that it has been said (and perhaps truly), that Milton never could have written his "Paradise Lost," if he had not been blind; and with equal truth, may it be added, he could never have written *such* a "Paradise Lost," as he has, if he had not once seen. We are also aware that President Dwight could dictate to two amanuenses at the same time, and that in this way a large part of his Divinity-Discourses were prepared for the press. If all this were so — and we would not vouch for its truth — we would add, we have but few Miltons, or President Dwights. They form the exceptions, not the rules. We are also aware that the blind are now taught to read, and do many wonderful things. But they are generally an indolent and "perverse generation." In justification of this remark, we may be allowed to relate the following story: Some time since, we visited an old friend and class-mate, Dr. M., who is a very large man, and has charge of a public institution for paupers. Among the anecdotes which he related, was this: "I was more perplexed to know what to do with three or four blind men, than with all the others under my care. At length, it occurred to me that I would set them to sawing wood, directing some men, who had eyes, to put the wood in order for being sawed. They had been at work but a few minutes, when, having occasion to pass near them, I heard one of the blind men say to the man who had eyes, 'Is the pig doctor about here?' 'Why?' asked the man with eyes. ''Case, if he ben't we'll take a smoke,' said the blind man."

The proper management of the eyes, especially to a student, is an affair of no trivial moment. If his eyes be ruined, all his other acquisitions must be, comparatively, of but little value. The clergy of this country some time since were called to realize this, in one, who for many years stood prominent among them, and who has written an eloquent and extensive commentary upon the sacred Scriptures. By an abuse, or rather misuse of his eyes, he was wholly laid aside from the pastoral office, and from the employment of his pen. Such occurrences are comparatively rare. But cases, in which the duties of students are but imperfectly performed, on account of an improper use of the eyes, are very common.

A frequent cause of partial or total amaurosis, or loss of sight, is snuffing powdered tobacco, often mingled with other vile stuff, up the nose. If the nose had been designed for a dust-hole of this kind, judging from the fitness of means to ends in the rest of the body, it would have been anatomically constructed with the bottom side up; as, by such a change, it would answer this purpose much better.

Dr. Lacock, of York, at a late meeting of the British Medical Association, communicated some very interesting matters upon the use of tobacco. Omitting in this place, as irrelevant to the present subject, its injurious effects upon the lungs, brain, and whole nervous system, when chewed or smoked, we will quote the following, as causing disease in the eyes, or loss of vision. "It (excessive snuffing) causes falling off of the hair, sloughing of the eye-lids, and blindness." Many cases of blindness, caused by snuffing, are related in the medical books, to which we might refer, were it deemed necessary.

Scarcely any practice has a more deleterious effect upon the eyes, than reading in the cars, when riding on a railroad. The jar of the vehicle, by the wheels, the noise of the moving machine, and more especially the sudden transition of light and darkness, seriously affect the organs of vision. It may seem to some, quite too much time to lose, without reading, when journeying from one place to another by railroad; and this temptation to read is enhanced, usually, by the example of the multitude. Almost every one, at such a time, has a newspaper or book in his hand, which he is engaged in perusing, and we know that evil example is quite too often followed. Now we assert — and the assertion is not made without some data and too much sad experience — that the time thus occupied, had better be lost, if lost it must be, without reading, than employed in this way.

Upon the perfection of the optical instrument, the eye, the most important inlet of knowledge, the most valuable medium of our communication with surrounding persons and objects; and a prime contributor to the full enjoyment of our other senses; or, of the wisdom and skill of the Great Architect exhibited in its construction, we may say that blindness is one of the greatest misfortunes which can befall a human being. With all the alleviations which circumstances the most favorable can afford, there is scarcely any affliction, short of death, more trying than blindness. The great English bard, already named, frequently alluded to his loss of vision, in tones of anguish and despondency, as though some great recent misfortune had overtaken him; and if, in a mind highly gifted as his, and furnished with such inexhaustible stores of knowledge, it was so irreconcilable an event, we may imagine somewhat of the magnitude of this loss, in others whose minds are less cultivated and refined. It has always been a matter of surprise to us, that people who have eyes, take so little care of them, and misuse and abuse them, as they often do. But this is almost always the case where health is concerned. It is the last thing to which a well man will give his attention. He will blunder on, unrestrained by remonstrances and cautions, till the calamity overtakes him; and then, no pains are too great, no expense too unbounded, and no potion too bitter, to regain what is now lost. This has been a principal reason why we have thought it important to dwell so long upon the preservation of health. No maxim can be more true than this,— "an ounce of prevention is worth a pound of cure."

Many eyes have been ruined by the prescription and dabbling of itinerant, ignorant oculists. We know a man, whose eyes were bad, but who lost what little sight he had by having them tinkered by such a quack, and who paid the mountebank fifty dollars for tinkering them. It was the case with John Quincy Adams, that he never had cause for wearing spectacles, and report said, the reason of this was, by a process of *rubbing* them *towards* the nose, he kept up the roundness of the pupil, as it is in youth. The person here alluded to, paid the fifty dollars for this *privilege of rubbing his eyes.*

CHAPTER XVI.

Amusements—Man superior to other Animals—The Hand—Speech—Laughter—Fun—Individuality of Countenance—Reading Countenances on the Street—Enjoyments from the Imagination—Natural and Artificial Appetites—The true province of Body and Mind—Skating—Ball—Billiards—Bagatelle.

WE have already referred to recreation and relaxation from study as necessary to the health and enjoyment of professional and literary men, and stated the manner in which Cicero and Sir Isaac Newton relaxed their minds from their arduous mental efforts. But, in writing a book on human enjoyment, when, as in this age, so many professional and studious persons are losing their health, becoming melancholy and insane, some more extended remarks upon amusements and recreation seem necessary; we have, therefore, concluded to devote a chapter to this subject. The trite, but graphic aphorism,

<blockquote>
All work and no play
Makes Jack a dull boy,"
</blockquote>

applies equally to children of a "larger growth." As it is never healthy to live always upon one kind of food, so, men require some change in their pursuits. As the anatomy of man indicates that he was made to walk upon two legs instead of four, so, there are other characteristics connected with his physical and mental being, which equally demonstrate that he was made for enjoyment and amusement. Frederick the Great, one of the most observing of men, said: "Man seems to have been designed for a postillion."

While man and other animals have many things in common, it can be clearly seen, from their nature, that the enjoyments of the former were designed to be of a superior character, and more substantial than those of the latter. Take, for instance, the *hands* of man. Nowhere will you find the hand, but in the human race. Some resemblance to it may be found in the lower animals; but nowhere among them can you find a hand. Cicero describes the manifold utility of our hands as above all price. Cuvier says: "That which constitutes the *hand*, so called, is the faculty of opposing the thumb to the fingers, so as to seize the most minute objects— a faculty which is carried to the highest degree of perfection in man, in whom the whole anterior extremity (forward or front part) is free, and can be employed in prehension." Hence, we have *hand*-writing, *hand*-manufacture, *hand*-work.

Now, the hands afford one of the grandest sources of amusement, and tend greatly to the enjoyment of life. Who has not witnessed this in children, as they make their stone-money, cob-houses, and mud-walls? How many parents have contributed, not to the enjoyment of their own families only, but to the whole community, by their *handy*-work! How thankful should we be for hands!

Speech is another great source of amusement, and contributes much to the enjoyment of life. It is not our design to repeat here what has already been said about the human voice; but rather to refer to this gift as a promoter of the enjoyment of life. How much are innocent amusements and the happiness of life dependent upon a kind word, a witty reply, or a beautiful expression from the lips of a friend or a companion! Who will not be grateful for the gift of speech?

Laughter, also, is a great promoter of the enjoyment of life. Health is often greatly benefited by laughter. It is not only an exhilarating, but a healthy exercise. "Laugh and grow fat," is an old adage, that contains very much truth; for, persons who laugh much will be found almost invariably to be fat.

It has been said, "man is the only animal that laughs." It rather seems to us, however, that there is something very nearly allied to laughter in some other animals. The ape seems to laugh, and the dog likewise; but, it is only when they are pleased. Some never consider laughter, nor, indeed, any other amusement, as allowable. But, as the Creator has made man capable of laughter, and as he will laugh, we say, let him do it. Solomon was as wise when he said, "There is a time to laugh," as when he said, "There is a time to weep."

Though "the loud laugh" may sometimes "bespeak the vacant mind," yet, it is believed, if some persons laughed more, both they, and others around them, would enjoy life much better than they now do.

Laughter promotes digestion, sharpens wit, quickens the mental faculties, and increases the enjoyment of life.

Nearly allied to this is *fun*. Now, that there is much evil in what is sometimes called *fun*, will not be denied; and still, there may be innocent fun. Children enjoy it, and who are not children in many respects? Indeed, animals seem to enjoy life better when funny, and why should not man? We find the following in a work entitled the "Passions of Animals:"

"Small birds chase each other about in play; but perhaps the conduct of the crane and trumpeter is the most extraordinary. The latter stands on one leg, hops about in the most eccentric manner, and throws somersets. The Americans call it the mad bird, on account of these singularities. Water-birds, such as ducks and geese, dive after each other, and clear the surface of the water with outstretched neck and flapping wings, throwing abundant spray around. Deer often engage in sham battle or trial of strength, by twisting their horns together and pushing for the mastery.

"All animals pretending violence in their play, stop short of exercising it; the dog takes the greatest precaution not to injure by his bite; and the ourang outang, in wrestling with his keeper, pretends to throw him, and makes feints of biting him. Some animals carry out in their play the semblance of catching their prey; young cats, for instance, leap after every small and moving object, even to the leaves strewed by the autumn wind; they crouch and steal forward ready for the spring, the body quivering, and the tail vibrating with emotion, they bound on the moving leaf, and again spring forward to another. Bengger saw young jaguars and cougars playing with round substances, like kittens. Birds of the magpie kind are the analogues of monkeys — full of mischief, play, and mimicry. There is a story of a tame magpie, that was seen busily employed in a garden gathering pebbles, and with much solemnity and a studied air buried them in a hole made to receive a post. After dropping each stone, it cried "currack!" triumphantly, and set off for another. On examining the spot, a poor toad was found in this hole, which the magpie was stoning for his amusement."

It is true, man has nobler enjoyments than those of laughter and fun, but this by no means proves that these may not in their proper places contribute to his enjoyment.

In a former chapter, we spoke of the human countenance as conveying expression, and gave Dr. Blair's remarks on its beauty. But, in conveying enjoyment, it may well be referred to once more. Who does not find enjoyment in gazing upon an intellectual countenance? Nay, more, who is not pleased with a beautiful countenance? The countenance distinguishes man from all other animals. A dog or an ox, if struck, may turn upon us a speaking *look;* but it is not *the* look of the human countenance. Almost the whole of the enjoyment of the artist is found in delineating the human countenance and in conveying its expression to others. Who has not found enjoyment in walking up and down Washington Street, in Boston, Broadway, in New York, and Chestnut Street, in Philadelphia, reading human countenances? For one, I confess, I have found infinitely more pleasure in the countenances (and instruction too) than in scrutinizing all the rich dresses which are employed as street-brooms, and all the jewels and diamonds that sparkle upon the ladies of Fashion.

Much of the utility of life, also, as well as its enjoyment, is derived from the human countenance. Survey the ten thousand millions of the human race. Every-one's face is his own. No two are exactly alike. Suppose they were, what inconvenience would result!

Suppose you could not recognize one friend from another, or a friend from an enemy, the expression of Cowper would, indeed, be verified:

"Friendship, in truth, is but a name."

Were it not for these distinguishing characteristics of the countenance, all business, and all family relations would be destroyed. You would not know your own wife or daughter, nor your partner in business from others. What confusion!

All the enjoyments of friendship, of relations, of business, are dependent upon this *individual* mark of identification in the human countenance. How grateful should we be for such a discriminating mark!

We have already spoken of the vagaries and misery arising from a diseased and distempered imagination, and shown them to be numerous and weighty. It now remains that we advert to the enjoyment and pleasures of a well-directed imagination. There are many "Pleasures of the Imagination." Were the imagination to be left where it was in a former chapter, you might infer that it is capable of producing only evil in leading to such results of unhappiness, as have already been named. This is not the fact. It was given to man for enjoyment, and it affords many pleasures.

Our senses are sources of enjoyment; but they are not the only sources that we have. Those of the mind are of a higher and nobler character: and of these mental powers, the imagination is one.

It is indeed true that in an evil hour, after having received, or supposing we had received an affront, the imagination may draw together all the moon-spots of the offender, and figure out others yet in the dark, till it forms a perfect night-piece, and makes its possessor very miserable, and leads to results already named. But there may be, and often is, an off-set to this. It may, and often does, afford much enjoyment. It can crowd together all the light parts, and bring all the rays of its object into one bright and burning focus; and under this burning-glass of the imagination, every dark spot is consumed, and a radiance bright as the noontide sunshine is produced. This is true enjoyment from the imagination, and when we have this enjoyment from inspecting the condition of others and surveying our own, we realize wherein consists much of the true happiness of life. Sum up, then, the virtues and blessings that you have from your families, relatives, and friends. This is one way to enjoy life. It is true mental hygiene.

Even our *appetites* are sources of enjoyment. The appetites of hunger and thirst, if allowed to run to excess, are painful. Nevertheless, they are blessings. What is their design? Manifestly, to awaken us to activity, — to induce us to take food and drink, — in a word, to sustain life. These appetites, in their gratification, do even more than this. They promote social enjoyment, and civilization. Who can estimate what an influence has been exerted upon human enjoyment by the daily gatherings of families around the social board at the hour of meals! By the appetites, we mean those that are natural, not those which are artificial. Those appetites which demand luxurious food, alcohol and tobacco, are all artificial — all acquired; and all at war with nature. Take that of tobacco; — at its first approach, every human organ loathes it. Man is always rendered miserable by unlawful indulgence. Hence, while our natural appetites are all blessings, when they are unduly cherished or indulged, they become sources of misery: and, though there often is some enjoyment in artificial appetites, yet, generally, they prove destructive of human happiness. The history of all nations is replete with warnings against lascivious indulgences; and sacred history but re-echoes the admonitions of profane, as, in the ruin of Sodom, it informs us that "pride, fulness of bread, and abundance of idleness," proved its destruction. Babylon, Alexandria, and Rome, all sunk under the overwhelming sensuality into which their ungoverned appetites and unbridled passions led them. The great question now pending as to the perpetuity of our nation; as to the success or failure of a Republican government, is, whether we will obey nature's laws; or, by the indulgence of our appetites and passions, be drawn into the same vortex that has swallowed up the happiness and glory of other nations. Men utterly mistake the compound nature of their being, when they allow the mind to lead the body into forbidden indulgences; or, the body the mind. While the true relation between body and mind is understood and pursued, the best good of both will be secured; but, when this is not done, *neither* can be happy. When the mind resorts to the body for *its* enjoyments, the consequences are disastrous beyond description. Then, all the senses are taxed to their utmost capacity. They are compelled to give all that can possibly be extorted from them: and soon, both body and mind are overwhelmed and crushed. Human enjoyment is destroyed. Human happiness is gone. Then may be found the dimmed eye, the palsied hands, the shaking, tottering knees, and the general paralysis and destruction of all the bodily energies and powers, and the mind itself, like the beleaguered castle, when its lord is vanquished, sinks into irretrievable ruin.

We spoke of amusements. Some of them may here be named.

Skating, in its season, is one of the best and most healthy.

Playing ball is an amusement in which I used to take great enjoyment.

Billiards is a very innocent in-door amusement and recreation.

Bagatelle is a similar amusement, and promotive of health — a true hygiene for body and mind. The following from *Praed* gives the idea

> "I saw one day, near Paphos' bowers,
>   In a glass — sweet Fancy's own —
> A boy lie down among the flowers
>   That circled Beauty's throne.
> Poor youth! it moved my pity quite,
>   He looked so very sad; —
> Apollo said "his head was light,"
>   But Pallas called him "mad."
> A little sylphid, hiding near,
>   Flew out from some blue-bells,
> And whispered in the pale youth's ear,
>   Pray, try our Bagatelles!
>
> You've pondered o'er those musty books
>   Till half your locks are grey; —
> You've dimmed your eyes, you've spoiled your locks,
>   You've worn yourself away!
> Leave Wisdom's leaden page awhile,
>   And take your lute again,
> And Beauty's eyes shall round you smile,
>   And Love's repay the strain;
> Leave politics to dull M. P.'s,
>   Philosophy to cells, —
> Good youth! — you'll ne'er succeed in these —
>   So — try our Bagatelles!
>
> We've cures in these enchanted bowers
>   For every sort of ill, —
> *Our* only medicines are flowers,
>   Sweet flowers that never kill!
> Our leeches, too, are wondrous wise
>   In mixing simples up, —

We've frozen dew-drops from the skies
   For the fevered lover's cup;
We've moonbeams gathered on the hills,
   And star-drops in the dells;
And we never send you in our bills —
   Pray, try our Bagatelles!

And youths from every coast and clime
   Come here to seek advice,
And maids who have mis-spent their time
   Are kept preserved — in ice!
Bright fountains in our garden play,
   And each has magic in it, —
We cure blue devils every day,
   Blue stockings every minute:
And heart-aches when they're worst, and when
   No other medicine tells,
In maids or matrons, youths or men,
   Yield to our — Bagatelles!

Last week a statesman came, whose eyes
   Scarce knew what sweet repose is,
We gave one draught of Beauty's sighs, —
   Look there — how calm he dozes! —
A lawyer called the week before,
   Who talked of naught but Blackstone;
We took him to our sylphid store,
   And a pair of wings we waxed on;
And if you'll look in yonder grove, —
   Just by that grot of shells, —
You'll find him making shocking love,
   And talking — Bagatelles!"

The sick youth raised his drooping head
   As the sylphid ceased to speak, —
"Hush, hush," she cried, "you must to bed,
   And be quiet for a week!"
And soon a muse with rainbow wings,
   And looks of laughing joy,

> Came with a lute of silver strings,
>   And she sat beside the boy;
> And when I saw them last, they lay
>   Far up those flowery dells,
> And the boy was growing glad and gay
>   As she sung him — Bagatelles!

Ten-pins, as it used to be called, is a healthy amusement.

Anything out in the air is better than the crowded house away from the sun and the cheering breeze.

There are several innocent and amusing *Games* which employ the mind, though they do not exercise the bodily organs.

The grand point is, however, to get amusement for the mind, and, at the same time, exercise for the body.

CHAPTER XVII.

The Passions Defined — Effect on the System—Love Letters—Nelson's — Napoleon's — Difference between Man and Woman a chief source of Happiness — Love — Choice of a Wife — Importance of Good Health in a Wife — Paul a Widower — Sir James Mackintosh's Wife.

"'Tis the great art of Life to manage well
 The restless mind."

THIS motto is taken from Dr. Armstrong's "Art of Preserving Health." Armstrong was one of the most eminent physicians of his day, and though not renowned for *poetical* talents, yet he said, or sung many wholesome truths.

By "the passions," I mean to include everything, from the slightest emotion, up to those paroxysms of love and rage which sometimes agitate the frame. These have been quaintly, but not inaptly termed "*fulmina perturbationem.*" Burton called them "the thunder and lightning of perturbation, which causeth such violent and speedy altercations in this our microcosm, and many times subverts the good estate and temperature of it." These various emotions are to the mind, what food and drink are to the body. They stimulate, they depress, they tranquillize, and they ruffle the soul. But, what is more to our present purpose, they produce similar effects upon the body. The vascular and nervous systems are perpetually under the influence of the emotions and passions. Witness the tremors and palpitations excited by the postman's rap, when we are expecting intelligence from absent friends involving matters of grave mōment. See that shaking hand while breaking the seal of an important letter!

The effect of the emotions and passions upon the circulation was early observed. Witness the detection of Antiochus's passion for Stratonice, by the pulse. Let the sense of *shame* cross the sensitive imagination, and, in an instant, the capillaries of the cheek are gorged with blood, looking as though it would burst through the skin. Change the emotion to *fear;* and quick as thought, the lily usurps the rose,—the face is bloodless.

History abounds with instances where life and death have been in the power of the passions. Thus, we are told of "a Roman lady who fell suddenly dead of joy upon meeting her son, whom she supposed had fallen in one of the battles of Hannibal;" and of a Jew, who came safely by night over a dangerous place: but, on viewing the perilous situation he had been in, the next morning, he fell down dead. A child has been known to die on seeing a corpse taken from a grave.

The phenomena of love are very curious. Naturalists have painted two young persons in love, as representing the best specimen of the enjoyment of human life; and, it must be confessed, such a picture is often the perfection of life's happiness. While this is the case in true love, it is still true that the class of compositions called "Love Letters," are often mere fiction, and replete with folly. We have the tender epistles of Henry VIII., Anne Boleyn, Princess Elizabeth, Lord Grey and Lady Henrietta Berkeley, Lady Mary Wortley Montagu, Pope, Dean Swift, Laurence Sterne, Lord Nelson, Napoleon, Heloise and Abelard, and many others; and while there are some very fine and truly touching scenes in them, it is, nevertheless, true that they abound in folly, and exhibit but little of the true enjoyment of life.

In the letters addressed by Lord Nelson to Lady Hamilton, that hero's "guardian angel," we find the most attractive and interesting of all this class of epistolary writing. They breathe forth this tender passion in the sweetest language, and one is forced to regret that such tender effusions were not addressed to a worthier object.

Napoleon, in his tender epistles to Josephine, stands next on the list for writing the best "love letters." That wonderful man, amid scenes of carnage, could withdraw himself from the horrors that surrounded him, and pen such tender epistles to his beloved Josephine, as make us smile and rejoice to find the hero outshone in the husband. As soon as the battle was gained, and victory perched on his banners, he congratulates the sharer of his joys by a missive, in which he sends a kiss even to his wife's lap-dog. Who can but admire to read such love! But its *end* spoiled the chief enjoyment.

When feeble men, of feeble mental calibre, have exhibited such want of brain, as to show, by their epistles, that they could never love any one less important than a Diana, it excites our risibles, and we almost wish they had kept their love letters, not "nine years," but ninety times nine.

It is believed much of man's enjoyment springs from his knowledge, and his adapting himself to the character of woman. She is much more diverse from him than he imagines; and this opposition is the source of the soft, harmonious charm that forms the enjoyment of life. The peculiar constitution of woman consists in her elevation and dependence, wonderfully combined — elevated, by beauty, poesy, quick perception, almost amounting to divination — dependent by her very nature, and held in servitude by weakness and suffering. The true ideas on this subject are so much better expressed than the writer could do it, by one in the "National English Magazine," that he here gives the quotation:

"She does nothing like us men. She thinks, speaks, acts differently. Her tastes differ from our tastes. Her blood does not follow the course of ours; nor does she breathe as we breathe. Nature has arranged that woman's respiration should be effected mainly by the four upper ribs. She does not eat like us; neither so much, nor of the same dishes. Why? Above all, for the reason that she does not digest like us; at every moment her digestion is troubled by the excitability of her emotions. These internal differences are outwardly translated by another, even more striking still. Woman has a language of her own. Insects and fishes remain ever mute. The bird sings; he would like to articulate. Man has a distinct language, precise and luminous speech, the clearness of the word. But woman, besides the word of man and the song of the bird, possesses a completely magical language, with which she intersperses the word or the song; it is the sigh, the impassioned breath. Incalculable power! Scarcely is it felt, when the heart is overcome by it. Her bosom heaves, she cannot speak, and we are already persuaded, gained over to all she chooses to command. What language of man will influence like woman's silence?

"Woman loves, and suffers; she requires the support of a loving hand. This is what, more than anything else, has strengthened love among the human race, has given fixity to union. It has been often said, that it was the weakness of the infant which, by prolonging the cares of education, originally created family. True, the child retains the mother; but the man is attached to his domestic hearth by the mother herself, by his affection for the wife, and by the happiness which he feels in protecting her. Superior and inferior to man, humiliated by the heavy hand of nature, but at the same time inspired by visions, presentiments, and intuitions of a higher order than man can ever experience, she has fascinated him, innocently bewitched him, for ever. And man has remained enchanted by the spell. That is what society is. Women are said to be capricious. Nothing is more false than that. Quite the contrary; they are regular and submissive to the power of nature. They are barometric, if you like; sensitive of weather, times, and season; but not capricious. Of themselves, and when themselves, they are good-natured, gentle, and affectionate toward the man on whom they lean. Their ill humors, their little fits of anger, are almost always the effects of suffering. He must be a great booby who would dwell on such involuntary faults as those. He ought, at such times, to be all the more forbearing, and to show greater attention and sympathy."

Man's dependence upon woman for happiness is much more than is usually supposed; and, were it not for the too useless system of education which prevails at present, he would be still more dependent upon her. The number of useless, idle young women is greatly on the increase in most of our large cities, and their routine of life seems to be filled up in lounging, or sleeping through the morning; promenading with dresses sweeping the streets in the afternoons, and attending frivolous amusements during their evenings. If this course is not preparing the way for miserable lives to themselves and miserable families, then, indeed, the duties of life must be greatly changed. If taught no domestic duties, woe to the young men who become their unfortunate husbands. What kind of wives and mothers will they be? But, as we have heretofore illustrated by cases of the clergy, we will still pursue the same plan.

As clergymen are supposed to be, and as they really should be, removed from the passions of fear, anger, hatred, jealousy, "*et id omne genus,*" which are called *dire;* and, as we do not wish to prescribe without a cause, we will pass them by, and take one for our consideration, which is lawful; yea, even necessary for them to cherish. It is *love.* As a bishop *must* be the husband of one wife, and as every good man should *love* his wife, we say this is a passion which he *must* cherish.

Love is a cordial drop which Heaven has cast into the bitter cup of life, not excluded from that of the clergy, for both Peter and Paul had wives: yet love, that sweetens our sorrows and doubles our joys, destroys, and ever has destroyed more victims than the conqueror's sword.

It has been said (though we do not vouch for the truth of the assertion), that "ministers are the greatest fools in love." Whether this be true or not, it must be granted that they often marry very unwisely, and one of the legitimate fruits of such indiscreet connections is often loss of health and happiness.

Often young men, designing to enter the ministry, during their early studies allow themselves to become attached to a young lady, and attach her affections to them. Their minds are constantly expanding, and tastes continually changing; and, while this is the case with them, the minds of the young ladies remain nearly stationary. The consequence is, that when the young clergyman is about to enter upon the duties of his profession, he finds there is a vast difference between their intellectual culture. He is now introduced into society; perhaps settles in some popular parish, and has a wide circle out of which to choose a companion. In these circumstances, he is strongly tempted to break off his early engagement. But this he cannot do with honor, to say nothing of religion. While he is thus strongly tempted to play upon the young lady what some have called, "a minister's trick," he must not allow himself to do it. If he does, he must expect bitter repentance. We knew a case of this kind. The engagement was broken off most dishonorably "to the cloth." But the wife, which he afterwards chose, proved not only "a thorn in his flesh," but, also, like "a messenger of Satan," to fetter his soul. Better, far better, unless the contract can be dissolved "by mutual consent," make the best of a bad bargain.

Sometimes a young minister, after having kept himself aloof from female society till he enters upon his profession, allows himself to fall in love with the first pretty face he meets, irrespective of her mental, moral, or physical qualifications to be the wife of "a Bishop." Perhaps she makes no pretensions to piety. We have heard of an orthodox clergyman, who became attached to a young lady of a Unitarian family, residing in the same town in which he was settled. When he asked the consent of her father, he replied: "I should not think my daughter would make a good wife for a *pious* minister. She has been brought up in a *fashionable* way, and has been educated to attend parties, balls and theatres. It strikes me that these would not be suitable accomplishments for the wife of a very *pious divine*, and an example to the flock." They were, however, married.

Sometimes, she has not the health, or the constitution to fill the place, bear the trials and sustain the duties devolving upon the wife of a bishop. Now, however incumbent it be, for a clergyman to marry such a lady, after he has become engaged to her, it certainly does not savor of wisdom to make choice at the outset of a nursling. The minister generally has too hard a task, and quite too severe a warfare to attempt to carry a sick wife with him; we mean, to *commence* the work with such an one. He had better allow such to be provided for by those who can better own horses, hire nurses, and fee doctors. But if her health fails *after* they are married, he is bound, by every sense of duty, to render her as comfortable as he can, and to bear his affliction with Christian fortitude.

Is it asked, What has this to do with clerical health, or the enjoyment of life? Let us see. Does it make no difference with his labors, trials and afflictions, if he has one who can "help" him bear them, or, one whose influence is always like a weight to drag him down? Suppose, for instance, he marries a debilitated, nervous, waspish woman, who has always had her own way in her father's house, and who expects and means to be the same in that of her husband, and in his parish. Would it not be likely to make some difference with his health and happiness, if, on her account, he found himself compelled to change his residence every year; and if, instead of "building her house," like Solomon's "wise woman," and managing her children and her domestic affairs properly, he was compelled to nurse the children and be his own housekeeper?

Socrates might choose Xantippe because she would teach him to exercise patience and the more rigid virtues; and Billy Gray, or a Girard, might choose a feeble and indigent wife, and both, from good motives: the former, that he might be made better in spirit, and the two latter because they could better provide for such than others. But a clergyman had better demur in such a case, till he *becomes* a Socrates, or a Girard.

If we wished to be facetious, we might give some specimens of imprudent clerical unions, but the subject is too serious, and we should never sport with human infirmity. "Passions are the elements of life;" not to be annihilated, but governed; and, if they get the reins, like Phœbus driving the chariot of the sun, they soon set the soul on fire and dig an early grave for the body.

Marriage was ordained of God, and instituted in Paradise, and the first miracle of Jesus was to do honor to a wedding. The celibate, or bachelor, has been said to live like a fly in the heart of an apple, dwelling in perpetual sweetness, but sits alone, and dies in single desolation. Marriage is a school of virtue, and it is doubtful whether "a bishop" who has not "one wife," and who does not "govern his own house well, having his children in subjection," can govern the house of God, or be a fitting example to the flock of Christ.

It is clearly a scriptural duty for "a bishop" to marry. Many have erroneously supposed that the Apostle Paul intended to discountenance this idea, when he said, "It is good for a man not to touch a woman;" and, also, when he says "to the unmarried, it is good for them if they abide even as I." But they do not consider that Paul, at the time he wrote this, was a widower. Ignatius states this fact, in his Epistle to Philadelphia, and Clemens says the same in the third book of his Ecclesiastical History. Eusebius, also, mentions the same fact. As there is no command that a bishop should marry *twice*, and as Paul had once been married, he was at liberty afterwards to remain single.

If a clergyman selects a wife, who has the *pride* of *property*, or *birth* and *family*, or, who possesses *a temperament* very different from his own, she will be one among a thousand, if she does not render him unhappy; and, eventually, destroy his usefulness and his health.

Happy the clergyman, who can say, as did Sir James Mackintosh of his deceased wife: "She was a woman, who by tender management of my weaknesses, gradually corrected the most vicious of them. She gently reclaimed me from dissipation;—to her, I owe whatever I am,—whatever I shall be."

CHAPTER XVIII.

Ventilation — Effect of Air on the Blood — Scrofula — Impure Air in Church — Beds — Food, Animal and Vegetable — Hot Bread and Butter — Fruit — Homœopathic Diet — Bad Cooking — Quantity of Food in Winter and Summer for the Laboring and the Sedentary.

MANY books have been written, and numerous lectures given upon ventilation; and yet, perhaps, there is no subject, so vitally connected with health and happiness, which is even at the present time so little understood. Probably, the writer has visited as many public institutions and schools as any teacher or physician of the present age, and he feels compelled to say, in this last half of the nineteenth century, that few, very few of the large number visited, are by any manner of means properly ventilated. Even a large proportion of the " chimneys," as expressed by that eccentric man, David Crockett, " smoke at the wrong end." Indeed, until recently, no man could be found who would build a chimney and guarantee that it should " carry smoke;" and even now, we do not know of one who will do it, unless under the Patent secured by Mr. Joseph Leeds, of Philadelphia. The wildest and most absurd ideas, even now, prevail upon the subject of ventilation. Still, there is an inquiry going on, which will not rest, till this art shall accomplish what is absolutely necessary to the health and true enjoyment of life. Heaven speed the day when *all* buildings shall be ventilated, so as to aid in the promotion of health, happiness, and longevity!

Air.—No person can enjoy health, for any length of time, who breathes a vitiated atmosphere. "The blood is the life," and the blood will become corrupt, when impure air is breathed. There are other things that may render the blood impure, but this is one. By the constitution of our nature, the blood is brought to the lungs, to be purified, that it may again go on its course with alacrity, strengthening, invigorating, and restoring all the various parts of the body. The blood from the lungs is carried through the whole body by the arteries. In a red, leaping, bounding current, it pours along, dividing and subdividing, till it forms the *capillary* circulation, in the skin; where the little hair-like tubes are so thick, that not the point of the smallest needle can be inserted without wounding some of them, and causing them to bleed. From these little vessels it is carried into the veins, after it has done all it can to promote the growth, or restore the waste of the body. Every portion of the system, even to the finger nails, is made by the blood. When it enters the veins, it returns sluggishly to the lungs. It is then *black*, and charged with pernicious matter, and goes to be aerified, or, as it is called, *arterialized* in the lungs. If, when it arrives there, pure air is admitted into the lungs, the blood again changes to a *bright red* color. A noxious gas, called *carbonic acid,* is thrown off, and the blood goes on its course, again to renew and set in motion the whole machine.

Now, if the air admitted into the lungs is vicious, that is, deprived of its oxygen, which sustains the vital principle, the body must suffer. Suppose, now, that we put a person into one of the little, narrow, ill-ventilated rooms in one of our very contracted streets or lanes,— what is the consequence? He becomes pale and lank; his skin is yellow; — a dingy, dirty, nasty color covers his countenance; his appetite fails, and he looks just like multitudes whom you may see any day in such places. It cannot be otherwise. He must have air.

One would suppose enough had been said on this subject, within a few years past; and yet, I have no doubt, that hundreds and thousands die annually for the want of good, wholesome air. If you wish to test this question, look at the children in the country, and in the city. The contrast is vast; except, perhaps, among a few families in the country who try to make a *city* there, by living in a confined atmosphere. Not long since, I was spending a Sabbath a few miles from the city. An elderly gentleman, from the city, drove up with his little grand-daughter, about eight or nine years of age. She was one of the frailest, feeblest little creatures that I ever saw. She appeared *so bloodless* that I was led to make inquiry after her mode of living. "Oh," said her grandpapa, "her *mother* takes excellent care of her; but she fears, sometimes, that she shall never raise the poor little thing. She scarcely ever lets her go out of the room."

Thus, the secret was out in a moment. The poor child needed the atmosphere, which God made for her, and made her to breathe. Now, look at a child who has the country air,—he is strong, his muscles are hard, he looks as though the blood would come through the skin. He is all life and activity; he knows not what lassitude and ill health mean.

You will scarcely drink after another person from the same glass, and yet, you will breathe over, and over, the same air, charged with all the filth and poison of a hundred human bodies around you. You cannot bear to touch a *dead* body, because it is so poisonous and polluting, but you can take right into your lungs, and consequently into your body, your system, those poisonous particles and noxious exhalations, which the bodies around you have refused, and which have been cast into the atmosphere, by their lungs, because the health of their bodies required them to be thrown off. If the "timorously nice creatures who can scarcely set foot upon the ground," who are so delicate that they run distracted at the crawling of a worm, flying of a bug, or squeaking of a mouse, could *see* what they breathe, at the midnight carousal, the very polite ball, and the sweet theatre, they would never be caught in such company again. Nay, if they could *see* what they breathe in their own dwellings, after the doors and windows have been closed a little while, they would soon keep open houses. More sickness is caused by vitiated air than can well be imagined.

It is one of the most prominent causes of scrofula, which is but another name for half the diseases that attack the human body. It vitiates and destroys the whole fountain of life, the blood.

In the sick-room it often augments the disease, or renders it incurable. If the physician comes in and opens a window, or a door stands ajar for a moment, the good nurse, or the tender mother, or the kind wife, or the loving sister, will fly up and close it, as though the life of the sick were at stake. All this is well-meant kindness, but really cruel. If you would have health, breathe fresh air; throw open your windows every morning, and often during the day; leave off your mufflers from the chin. For twenty years, I was accustomed to go out never without an extra handkerchief tied closely around the mouth, and for nearly that period have left it off; I have had fewer colds and suffered far less from changes of climate than previously. Let air into your bed-rooms; you cannot have too much of it, provided it does not blow directly upon you.

Many are injured by vitiated air in their studies. These are often small, and when the door and windows are closed, the atmosphere soon becomes loaded with noxious vapors. The student is intent upon his subject; he scarcely knows whether he breathes or not, much less does he think of *what* he breathes. Many, also, are seriously injured by the manner of heating their studies. All closed stoves should be avoided. The good, old-fashioned, open, large chimney, with a fire-place sufficiently capacious to receive the wood with but little chopping, is much preferable to the stoves and grates, and whole paraphernalia of modern fuel-saving inventions (except the one named on page 283), which have racked the brains and tortured the intellects of many laymen and some clergymen.

Then, men often, while buried in study, allow too sudden and too great a change in the air of the study. If the fire is too large, they do not know it, and if they discovered themselves in a free perspiration, would be as likely to call the servant to move back the chimney, as Sir Isaac Newton is reported to have done, as to think of the possibility of moving back the chair. Then the other extreme is much more likely to happen, and the fire go out, and the room become so cold that he gets a severe chill before he knows whether the room is warm or cold. Many have thus laid the foundation for a fever. Often the minister suffers by preaching in an ill-ventilated church. Few clergymen there are who cannot call to mind times when they have preached under great oppression. They have felt themselves to be in a torpid state, more like sleeping than speaking. They have almost gasped for breath. The reason or cause of all this they have not known at the time, but have at length perceived that they have been preaching in a nearly exhausted air-pump. The house had been closed since the last Sabbath. Not a window had been raised, nor a door opened, but for the ingress or egress of the people. Of what air there was, the minister had the worst of it, especially if he was compelled to ascend one of those pulpits which seem designed to raise him as far towards

> "That heaven to which he points
> And leads the way,"

as was at all practicable. The rarified air ascending, he had to take its most deleterious effluvia. Many a minister, too, has laid the foundation of ill health by preaching in a house without a fire, between winter and summer. The sun had begun to return from the chambers of the South, and it was sufficiently warm while walking in the open air; the sagacious sexton, therefore, concluded it would be warm enough in the house, and was pleased to be relieved of the trouble of kindling a fire. Far better would it be, in such cases, to imitate the "Celestials," who put on an extra garment when within doors. The case of the lawyer in a crowded court-room is often worse than that of the minister.

Beds.— Never have a *feather* bed about your premises. They are greasy, dirty, unwholesome things. In many rooms where I have been shut up, when visiting, or travelling, it was poisonous to remain. The way, too, in which many manage them, is to be abominated. They creep out of them in the morning, make them up steaming hot, shut the doors and windows, and leave all till bed-time. Then the scene is acted over again, and the poor feathers almost *scream* out as loudly as the goose did when they were plucked from her. It is difficult to say which is the bigger *goose*, the one that furnished the feathers, or he who feloniously plucked them off for a bed. There are many materials which make much more healthful beds than feathers; such as husks of corn, straw, hair, springs, &c., &c. *Cotton* is about as bad as feathers. In most persons, it creates a heat which resembles ants running over the body, or what physicians more politely call a sense of *formication*. Hard beds are much to be preferred, and that for more reasons than can be here stated. If you would not be sick, then look to your beds, as well as to the air you breathe.

Food.—Many volumes have been written upon diet, and while some recommend naught but bran bread, others would surfeit you with luxuries. Either extreme should be avoided, and you will need to be careful that while you shun Scylla, you do not fall into Charybdis. Plain, wholesome food, and a sufficiency of it, is the best course to pursue. Food taken three times a day, is often enough, and nothing but liquids should be taken between meals. By luncheons and *tit-bits* the whole digestive arrangement is broken up; and, if such a course is persisted in, digestion is permanently deranged. No person can have good health long who eats every two or three hours in the day. As to vegetable and animal food, you may eat either, if you can use them with moderation. Of meats, the lighter kinds are generally the most healthful, such as mutton, lamb, veal, young beef, venison. Old, tough, hard beef, and all kinds of pork, should never be eaten, nor any animal that has been stalled or confined. The idea of shutting up a hog in a close pen, and feeding him upon poisonous, dirty slops and offal, and then *eating him,* "shocks all common sense." It is enough to make a man sick to think of it. If you would preserve health, never touch the abominable thing. It is, however, more to the *confinement* of the animal which renders him unhealthy, that we would object, than to the quality of his food, though something is dependent upon that. To fatten a goose, and make its liver peculiarly palatable to epicures, it is recommended to tie its legs and wings, put it in the chimney corner, and cram it with Indian meal. The liver of the animal thus fattened, very much resembles a pathological or diseased specimen; and it is not much different with a hog, as he is usually fattened.

Many kinds of birds are wholesome food, but all carnivorous fowls should be avoided. Such food is very pernicious. Man is so nearly an omnivorous animal, that he needs to regulate his appetite, if he would preserve his health. Animal food, when well digested, is the most nourishing; but no person should live on that alone. A free use of animal food alone destroys the energy of man, and renders him dull and heavy. If you are of a plethoric or full habit, and wish to preserve your health, you must use animal food very sparingly. It produces more blood than vegetables, and stimulates the system to a far greater extent. Hence the circulation of the blood is much augmented by it. Persons who use much animal food, are also much more subject to inflammatory diseases than those who make use of a mixed diet. Persons who live too much on animal food, acquire a putrid *diathesis*, or tendency to putridity.

Excess of animal food has, also, a bad effect upon the mind, rendering persons peevish, fretful, and highly irritable; and the mind, again, reacts upon the body, and thus produces disease. I would not advise you to weigh or measure your food, or seek for great nicety between the proportions of animal and vegetable. Persons who do this are generally restless enough to injure their health. The quantity of food, and the proportion between animal and vegetable, depend very much upon the climate, or the season, and other circumstances, much more being necessary in cold, than in warm weather.

Good bread is essential to the preservation of health. It is, indeed, *the staff of life.* Bread should be made of good wheat unbolted, or rye and Indian meal. No fine flour should be eaten by a person in health. One grand design to be answered by bread, in the animal economy, is to fill up the stomach, as food will digest much more readily in the human stomach of a healthy person, when it is well filled, than when a very small quantity, or rather very nourishing, or hearty food is taken alone. When the alimentary canal is gently filled up, the mass carries the nutritious juices along, so that they are much better prepared to be acted upon by the lacteal absorbents (little vessels which take up the nourishment and convey it into the blood). Bread contains nourishment, but it is, nearly, equally useful for its bulk. The closest and richest food will not nourish a person, unless the alimentary canal is properly filled. Butter alone will not support animal life. The experiment has been tried upon a dog, by feeding him with rich broth, but it failed to support his life. If you would preserve health and enjoy life, you must learn to unite nutritious food with a proper quantity of light or farinaceous materials.

Mixed bread is generally preferable to that which is made from one kind of grain. Bread well fermented, is light, pleasant to the taste, and easily solved by the gastric juice. One prominent cause of indigestion, or dyspepsia, so prevalent in this country, is the general use of fine, hot bread. To increase the evil, not unfrequently it is not sufficiently baked. The most injurious food that can be taken into the human stomach is this fine, hot, half-baked bread. Rarely do we see, in these degenerate days, those large, well-kneaded, and well-baked brown loaves of our grand-mothers. Good, mealy *potatoes* are a wholesome article of diet. But those raised for a few years past have mostly been of a bad kind, and, if eaten, very injurious. The cause of the potato-rot, we shall not attempt to assign, as we are not writing for the premium. *Butter*, and all oily substances, should be used but sparingly, and not at all when rancid. An erroneous opinion generally prevails as to the use of *fruits*. They are thought to be unwholesome. This is not the case when they are fully ripe and fresh, and eaten at a proper time. This should always be at the time of an ordinary meal. Those fruits which have been long kept, or which have begun to decay, are unfit to be eaten.

Broths and soups are hard to digest, and should be used very sparingly. The reason is, the watery or liquid parts are immediately taken up by the absorbent vessels of the stomach, and the animal portion is left—as a solid substance which has not been properly mixed with saliva, having been unchewed—to be digested by the stomach and other viscera. Whatever may be said of the Homœopathic treatment in other respects, all must acknowledge that their system of *dietetics* is an excellent one. We are all in the habit of eating a thousand indigestible things which lay the foundation for disease. But the limits of this chapter will not allow me farther to particularize.

The system of *cookery*, now pursued, is well calculated to create disease. No person, who wishes to preserve good health, should follow it. The using of so much *grease* in cooking is a very pernicious custom, and all things fried in it are unwholesome. They tend to injure the organs of digestion and induce debility.

As to *drinks*, pure, soft water is infinitely the best. Black tea may be taken in moderation, but coffee, cocoa, and green tea, all produce diseases. They are much better calculated for *medicines*, than for common drinks.

Why do we require more food in winter than in summer? Because we breathe faster. We consume more oxygen. We require more food in winter, for the very same reason that we require more fire, and because a large fire requires more fuel than a small one. There is more heat to be supplied; the furnace of the lungs burns up oxygen faster, the colder the climate. For the same reason, the laborer requires more food than the student. The former breathes faster, and thus consumes more air, and needs more fuel, than the latter. For the same reason, children require food oftener, and more in quantity, than adults. They respire more frequently, and the *waste* must be more than supplied, or there can be no growth of the body. For the same reason, birds require more food, in proportion to their weight, than serpents. The former respire twice, or thrice, as much air, as the latter. For the same reason, hibernating animals require no food during their hibernation. They scarcely breathe at all, or but once in a minute or two. And for a similar reason, many corpulent men should often fast. They would breathe oftener, breathe easier, and live longer. For the same reason, the Esquimaux and Laplander require grease, while the inhabitants of tropical climates abhor it. Thus these different races live so differently. The one wraps himself in his greasy skin, and swallows grease, as meat and drink; the other abominates it in all its forms, and feasts on fruit. And thus each looks forward to his own favorite heaven; the one, where he shall dwell amidst beds of roses, breathe their fragrance, and feast on oranges, pomegranates, and sweet raisins; the other, where he shall never be cold for want of his favorite food, but be able to feed on lard, and quaff full bowls swimming to the brim with the grease of the sea-otter, train-oil, and whale-blubber.

Sometime since I was requested, by letter, to prescribe for the weak eyes and general debility of a clergyman, at a distance. One of his brother ministers, from the neighborhood, who happened to be in at the time of receiving the letter, remarked, "You can never cure Brother ——— unless you can put him on short allowance, and make him give up nut-cakes, mince-pie, pound-cake, and confectionery." The exhibition of creative designing wisdom in the digestive apparatus should forever preclude men from abusing it.

CHAPTER XIX.

Biblical Rules relating to Health — Bible designed for all — Blood the Life — Hygiene of the Bible — Bread — Fish — Shell-fish — Swine's Flesh — Mosaic Ritual of Health, founded in Nature — Daniel and his Companions — Prescribed Care for the Sick — Cleanliness — Hebrew Law of Marriage — Hereditary Diseases — The proper use of Stimulants.

IT is admitted that the Bible was not given for the exclusive purpose of teaching how to preserve, or recover lost health. Still, it is believed that no man has read this book understandingly, who has not discovered much in it which relates to both these particulars. The science of *Hygiene* is clearly taught in the Scriptures. It is to be remembered that the Bible was not composed in a single age, nor by any one man. The period from the time Moses wrote the first book till the Apostle John wrote the last, was about sixteen hundred years. It was designed, not for one particular age or nation, but for all nations, throughout all time. Its instructions, therefore, are general, rather than particular, and designed for all, rather than the few. What, then, does the Bible say about the *preservation* of health, &c.? Surely every man should know this. As the *blood* is more important than any other portion of the animal economy (if one part can be considered more important than another), let us see what is said of this vital fluid. Immediately after the flood, God said to Noah, "The life of the flesh is the blood," and he was forbidden to eat the blood, *because* it *was* "the life of the flesh." The same was repeated again and again, in the statutes given to Israel. " Ye shall eat no manner of blood, whether it be of fowl or of beast. Whatsoever soul it be that eateth any manner of blood, even that soul shall be cut off from his people." Though the reason, originally assigned, why they were not to eat the blood, is not repeated in all these cases, yet, undoubtedly, it remained the same as when given to Noah. The truth of this declaration, to wit, that "the life of all flesh is the blood, was alternately believed and denied from the days of Noah till about the year 1770, when *Dr. John Hunter* established it (as one would suppose) beyond all controversy. It has already been stated that every part of the body is made from the blood, and this of itself would seem to establish its vitality. This command to eat no blood, shows what regard was had originally to the preservation of health.

The prescribed treatment for recent *mothers* among the Hebrews, shows, also, the same fact; and the excuse rendered by the Hebrew midwives to the officers of Egypt for not obeying the cruel mandate, to "slay all the male children," shows that the hygienic rules of the Hebrews were highly beneficial to these mothers. There was an idea communicated in this excuse of "*Shiphrah* and *Puah*," that "the Hebrew women were not as the Egyptian women," in the hour of their trial, which speaks volumes in favor of the Mosaic regulations for the promotion of health.

The Mosaic treatment prescribed for mothers, after confinement, is worthy the attention of the physicians of our times; and, if the same regulations were enforced now, it is believed we should be greatly relieved from those fearful ravages of puerperal fever, which often make sad havoc among mothers. By an observance of similar rules, the greatest affliction might have been averted from many families, and reproach from many physicians.

The *dietetics* of the Bible are worthy our attention. The bread of the Hebrews was of much better quality than is usually found in our day, being neither spoiled by being *too fine*, nor soured with *leaven*.

Those *fish* which were possessed of fins and scales only were to be eaten. Carnivorous quadrupeds and birds were prohibited. Of those which lived upon *vegetables*, the camel, the cony, the hare, and the swine, were forbidden. Shell-fish were also prohibited. It is known that these latter have a strong tendency to produce cutaneous diseases. Some physicians **now** prohibit them, especially in persons subject to diseases of the skin. Though many devour shell-fish voraciously, yet they are a very questionable article of diet; especially, as they are usually taken with but little mastication, and but a small share of vegetable food. But even if they were wholesome among *us*, they might well be interdicted among a people in a country where the leprosy prevailed. Besides, shell-fish have been found to be poisonous from the substances on which they have fed. Some have supposed that *salt rheum*, and other cutaneous diseases, have originated from a diet consisting mostly of shell-fish.

As it respects those *birds* and *beasts* which feed on carrion, it is well known that they are prone to hydrophobia. But if there were no danger on this ground, their flesh is so disgusting that this alone would be a sufficient reason why it should be rejected. The flesh of the *swine* is a questionable article of diet. It has been a very general opinion of medical men, that their flesh is apt to produce scrofula.

There is generally some foundation for old maxims; and it is well known that scrofula takes its name from a Latin word which means a swine. Many diseases have, unquestionably, been produced by what is called "measled pork." Somebody has to eat this pork. Rarely is the carcass of a "measled" hog destroyed. In a warm climate, the grease of the hog cannot be tolerated as an article of diet. The food of the hog is of the most loathsome materials; frequently, from offal, poultices, and filth of every kind. Those who advocate the necessity of hogs acting as scavengers of the city, do not consider that they may be recommending the re-hashing of garbage for their own stomachs. It has been said that one great object of the Puritans coming to New England, was to establish a religious commonwealth, as nearly upon a model of that of the Jews, as the difference of circumstances would admit. To say nothing of other innovations among the first settlers, forbidden food was presented at almost every meal;— pork with beans, pork in gravy, pork with fish, pork with chicken, and, it is said, though I do not vouch for its truth, "pork with molasses."

It is believed that these prohibitions of Moses to the people of Israel have substantial reasons in nature. The Bible forbids the eating of that which "dies of itself, or is torn of beasts." This is but the dictate of common sense. That which "dies of itself" must be diseased. That "which is torn of beasts" may be infected with poison or hydrophobia. The diseases of animals have often been communicated to man. Persons have died by wounds received while dissecting diseased animals. The *cow-pox*, though harmless, proves that disease may be taken from an animal; and, if a harmless disease may be thus communicated, a deadly one may be.

From these remarks may be inferred the importance of avoiding those kinds of food prohibited by the statutes of Moses. If the Hebrews kept all these statutes they were to be blessed, and no small part of this blessing consisted in the *act of keeping them;* while, by disobeying, they were sure to find among them "consumption, and burning ague, which should consume the eyes and cause sorrow of heart." Did any nation ever have more of these plagues than ours? Was "consumption" ever more prevalent than among us?

If the meat which is sold in our city were butchered upon the principle which we have seen laid down in the Bible, of not "eating blood," it would be much more healthful than it is at present. It is said, the manner in which the Jews kill their meat divests it in the shortest possible time of almost every drop of blood. The throat is cut so quickly, and thoroughly, at a single blow, and the animal placed in such position, that the blood spouts out so as to drain the flesh almost in a moment.

It is generally admitted that too much *animal* food is taken for the health of our community. Such was, undoubtedly, the case in the luxurious court of Nebuchadnezzar. The Jews there had been brought up in a different system, and were fully satisfied that that kind of living, partaking profusely of the king's meat and wine, was not the best way to promote health. They, therefore, made this request to the king, or rather to his officers — " Certain of the seed royal, from the land of Judea" were there; among them were Daniel and his companions. " He purposed in his heart that he would not defile himself with the king's meat, nor with the wine which he drank." His request to be fed on *pulse*, with its success, is well known. "At the end of the ten days — the time allotted for the experiment — they were fairer and fatter, than those who drank of the king's wine and ate of his meat."

Though this may not prove that we should never partake of animal food, yet it does prove that the diet which these Hebrews preferred, was better calculated to promote flesh and beauty, than a course of "meat and wine." It shows, then, all that we have referred to it to show, namely, that their course of diet was a good one, and superior to that of the king of Babylon. " Hast thou found honey ? — eat so much as is sufficient for thee, lest thou be filled therewith and vomit it." Here we are taught the importance of *temperance* in eating. *Honey* is taken for all eatables, and, being *sweet*, it is supposed one would be inclined to eat that to excess, as much, at least, as any one thing. Therefore, in giving us a caution in eating this, it is sufficient for all times and kinds of eating.

Are we satiated with an excess of aliment ? — the Bible points to a remedy : " The full soul loatheth an honey-comb, but to the hungry soul, every bitter thing is sweet." This, as every physician can testify, is the best remedy for an overburdened stomach. Who does not know that "*hunger* is the best sauce?" Thus the Bible teaches a good system of hygiene and human happiness. Indeed, the true enjoyment of life will be found in obeying this Book.

Nor is this book wanting in prescribing for the sick. Thus, in the case of young Timothy, worn down with the exhaustion and mental anxiety, so inseparably connected with the duty of the ministry, we find the great Apostle, who had seriously "charged" him in many things pertaining to the duties of his office, prescribing a *stimulating* course: "Drink no longer water, but use a little wine for thy stomach's sake and thine often infirmities." Timothy must have been a remarkably *temperate* young man, who would not take even *wine*, in sickness, until he received the direction of Father Paul.

The *cleanliness* demanded in the Bible shows that this book is calculated to promote health. Hydropathy, ablutions, the use of water in almost all forms, are not simply recommended, but *required*. They were enjoined as religious rites, and a part of the common hospitality bestowed upon strangers. Even the priests (clean as they were), when consecrated to the sacred office, were to be "*washed with water.*" Abraham provided it for the angels who visited him. The great Head of the church *"washed his disciples' feet."* No devout Hebrew would eat without the previous application of water. Every Jewish place of worship had ample provision for "washings." If we, Gentiles, came nearer to these Jewish customs, we might be quite as healthy. In contagious diseases, the Hebrews were commanded *to separate the sick from the healthy.* This was especially the case with those infected with the *leprosy.* A person laboring under this disease was to dwell without the camp of Israel, and must be marked as a *diseased* man by a covering upon his upper lip; and, when he saw any one approaching, even before he came within the polluted atmosphere, he was to cry *"Unclean, unclean,"* which was equivalent to *"Stand off,* for death is here." Nor was the *diagnosis* of this disease to be left with the patient himself, or to any self-constituted umpire, but to the regularly commissioned *priests,* who were, also, the regular *physicians.*

The Hebrew law of marriage between persons of certain degrees of consanguinity was of vast moment in promoting health of body and vigor of mind. This Mosaic law, if enforced among us, would be of vital importance to our community. Says a most respectable physician of our own time: "Idiocy, deafness, blindness, and other imperfect development of the offspring, are results which we frequently witness from intermarriages between relatives. Congenital blindness is often the effect of marrying *cousins*. In one family, from this cause, three children have been known suffering under this misfortune. Almost every physician has witnessed instances of this kind. *Dr. Wallace*, of New York, says: "In the New York Institution for the Deaf and Dumb, there are several pupils who owe deafness to the relationship of their parents."

This subject has not received that attention which its importance demands, either from physicians or theologians. If that portion of the Presbyterian Church which suspended one of their clergymen for marrying a sister of his deceased wife, had turned their attention to, and directed their efforts to prevent, intermarriages between *blood* relations, they would have been much more worthily employed, and rendered better service to their generation. There seems to be an allusion to *hereditary* diseases in the following passage: "I, the Lord thy God, am a jealous God, visiting the iniquity of the fathers upon the children unto the third and fourth generation of them that hate me, and showing mercy unto thousands of them that love me and keep my commandments. Take heed, in the plague of leprosy that thou observe diligently, and do according to all that the priests, the Levites, shall teach you; as I commanded them, so ye shall observe to do." The law of leprosy, here referred to, had been made known, and in connection, with the promises of reward to the obedient and punishment to the disobedient. Thus, we see how strictly the Mosaic institutions were guarded. Half the diseases of life are hereditary; insanity, gout, epilepsy, scrofula are among them. Let physicians and clergymen do their duty to the community, and there would be a vast improvement in the health and happiness of coming generations.

The Bible prescribes the proper use of alcohol: "Give strong drink to him that is ready to perish, and wine to him that is of a heavy heart." Every physician, at all skilled in his art, understands this. He administers his *stimulants*, his cordials, even rum, brandy, and wine, when Nature flags. Thus, he jogs her vitals and rouses up her sleeping energies, until the powers of the run-down machine acquire their accustomed play.

In fine, the Bible inculcates more tending to preserve and give health, than one half the numberless "Practices of Medicine," and three-fourths of the sermons and "Bodies of Divinity," ever written or spoken.

CHAPTER XX.

Longevity — Instances of Longevity among Philosophers, Physicians, and Clergymen — Greatest among active men, Farmers, Soldiers, Hunters — Religion, a Companion of Longevity — The body must die, the spirit live.

MANY men have lived to old age; and, upon examining their history and mode of life, we find that exercise, activity, study, contentment, and regular habits, apparently contributed much to their longevity.

Solon, one of the wisest men among the Greeks, lived to the age of eighty years. Epimenides, of Crete, lived to the age of one hundred and fifty-seven years. Anacreon, the poet, mirthful and jovial, died at the age of eighty. Sophocles and Pindar at the same age. Georgius, who spent much of his time instructing the young, died at the age of one hundred and eight years. The temperate and modest Isocrates, at ninety-eight Democritus, a great naturalist, good-tempered and serene, at one hundred and nine. Diogenes, frugal, but slovenly, at ninety. Zeno, the founder of the Stoics, at one hundred. Plato, a genius of the rarest kind, a lover of rest and meditation, at eighty-one.

Instances of longevity were also numerous among

the Romans, both male and female. M. Valerius, a man popular and fortunate, lived more than a hundred years. Orbilius, a soldier and a teacher, also over one hundred. Fabius, one of the slowest of men, ninety. Cato, a friend to rural life, and an enemy to physicians, ninety. Terentia, the wife of Cicero, one hundred and three. Livia, the wife of Augustus, passionate, but fortunate, ninety.

Several of the Roman actresses lived to a great age. Luceja performed a century, and appeared on the stage in her one hundred and twelfth year. Galeria Copiola made her first appearance, as an actress, at the age of ninety. She appeared again, to honor the triumph of Pompey; and again under Augustus; but *acting* has become a very different affair from what it was anciently. What actress in modern times ever becomes old? Acting and its modern attendants consume life more rapidly than any other occupation.

Pliny, the secretary of the Emperor Vespasian, has given us, from a perfectly reliable source, the census taken in the seventy-sixth year of the Christian era, the following list of persons then living in that part of Italy lying between the Apennines and the Po: one hundred and twenty-four men, one hundred or more years of age; fifty-four of one hundred; fifty-seven, one hundred and ten; two, one hundred and twenty-five; four, one hundred and thirty; four, one hundred and thirty-five; two, one hundred and thirty-seven; three, one hundred and forty. There were in Parma three men who were one hundred and twenty, and two, one hundred and thirty; in Placentia, one of one hundred and thirty; at Faventia, a woman one hundred and thirty-two; in Vellejacium, a small town near Placentia, ten, one hundred and ten, and four, one hundred and twenty.

As evidence that mere study, at proper times, and under judicious regulations, is not injurious to health or longevity, we may remark that the students of nature have, generally, lived long. The Stoics and Pythagoreans were of this kind. Several of these lived to the age of a hundred years; among whom were Spollonius and Xenophilus.

Among the moderns this class of philosophers have been long-lived. Bacon was seventy-eight; Newton, eighty-four; Euler, seventy-seven; Kant, eighty; Fontanelle, ninety-nine.

Many schoolmasters have been remarkable for longevity. Poets and artists, however, have not been noted for long life. Fancy and imagination consume life much more rapidly than calm, contemplative study.

The most remarkable instances of longevity are found among gardeners, farmers, soldiers, sailors, and such as lead peaceable lives in the open air. In such employment Henry Jenkins lived to the age of one hundred and sixty-nine years; Thomas Parr to one hundred and fifty-two; and his great-grandson to one hundred and three; a Dane named Drakenburg, one hundred and forty-four; Stender, one hundred and three; Mittelstedt, one hundred and twelve; Kuper, one hundred and twelve; Helen Gray, one hundred and five; Glenn, one hundred and fourteen; Anthony Lenish, one hundred and eleven. All these were active or laboring men. Most of them were from the poorer classes of society, and obliged to labor for a living. Physicians, as a class, are shorter lived than any other professional men.

The life of man now, is what it was in the days of David; and we learn from the above, that *the age of the world,* since the flood, has made no perceptible difference in the length of man's life. Men may now live, through the care of a good Providence and temperate habits, to the age which they attained in the days of Abraham. Cold countries are, perhaps, more favorable to longevity than warm ones; but in almost all the varieties of climate, some have attained to a very advanced age. There is ample reason to put forth efforts for a long life. Providence smiles upon all who obey his laws; and hence, those who live most in accordance with the simplicity of nature, generally attain to longevity.

Clergymen, notwithstanding the great amount of

labor imposed upon them, and the inequality of it, can attain to the good old age of our fathers. They have ample encouragement to obey all the laws of their being, and as watchmen, they cannot but be neglectful of duty, unless they so live as not to "die before their time," or to destroy their happiness.

Religion ought to be a companion of longevity. It was designed to calm the troubled sea of human life, and to prepare man for a peaceful exit from this to a holier and happier world. On the Apostle of the Gentiles it produced this tranquillizing effect, by teaching him, "in whatever state he was, therein to be content." It is to be lamented that it should ever be converted into an engine of wretchedness and suffering. This is not the characteristic effect of true devotion. Panaticism and enthusiasm have no more relation to true religion than base coin to the genuine. It is only the abuse of Christianity that tends to the destruction of the human fabric. This abuse has sometimes proved dire indeed. But true piety calms all the passions, moderates the desires, checks fanatical notions, and, bringing the whole man in subjection to the laws of evangelical temperance, prepares him for a long and a happy life.

Clergymen now have much more to do than the Fathers had. They must engage in all that pertains to life. Of this we have seen some specimens, when speaking of their connection with their parishes, in a former chapter. Then, once settled, it was for life, for "better, for worse," the knot was tied. They lived more then in the open air — they were accustomed to take long journeys on foot and on horseback.

"The sofa then was not;"

nor easy carriages, nor railroad-cars. Their food was coarser and more conducive to health. They rose earlier and retired earlier. Their mental perplexities were far less than at present. They expected their counsel would be followed, and their expectations were not disappointed. Their parishioners sought to make them happy, rather than miserable. They never attempted, in the midst of their days and of their usefulness, to thrust in a *colleague* upon them. What would *Dr. Emmons* have said, if the people of *Franklin* had proposed to him, when fifty years old, to have a *colleague?* Methinks I see the flash of his keen eye, and hear the withering sarcasm, as when he was wont to criticize a young and self-sufficient brother, or to rebuke a "busy body in other men's matters." But how many, even before fifty winters have passed over them, have been compelled either to relinquish *one half* to a colleague, far less competent and efficient than themselves, or the *whole* to a fastidious and *ear-itching* people!

No wonder ministers at present do not live so long as their fathers did! There are ample reasons to every reflecting mind. A change must come over both clergymen and parishes, and they must go back to the good and stable customs of the Fathers, in New England, or forward to the system of thorough *itinerancy*.

Having said thus much of the body, of the best management of its passions, and of the means to be used under the physical government of God for its longevity, we may close this sketch by remarking that, the body is not our most noble part. It is wonderful, as the workmanship of God; but the *soul* is, after all, the tenant. The body should never be allowed to clog and impede the progress of the mind. As God is the head of the universe, and "man the head of the woman," so intelligence, reason, conscience, are the head of the body, and designed to preserve, ennoble, purify, and, through Divine grace, elevate it to a resemblance to the glorified body of the Redeemer.

While, therefore, we would make the most of the body, never allowing its powers to stagnate, or be abused; while we would ever recognize its skilful workmanship, and "human form Divine," and inculcate the best means to give to it longevity, we would desire to feel that it is "of the earth, earthy," and must soon return to its original dust. With these views, we would enjoin upon all the vast importance of cultivating those higher intellectual and moral powers which ally man to beings of superior endowments—and to Him who has exalted our nature above all created beings by taking it upon himself.

Let all, then, remember that the present life of the oldest man is but as a grain to the globe in comparison of the endurance of his being, and of the ever-increasing function and progress which await him who makes the most of both body and spirit. The cultivation of these nobler faculties will tend greatly to advance the joys of life.

CHAPTER XXI.

Sympathy in the Human Body — Spare Diet — Cornaro — Brandy and Rheumatism — Cases in Point.

EVERY well-informed physician knows that what are called *masked diseases* are numerous. Even patients, themselves, become familiar with such cases, after a little experience. They know that certain diseases, or disturbances of the *stomach,* produce pain, or vertigo of the head. Sometimes, also, there is no pain, nor any perceptible sensation of annoyance in the stomach, and we should not even dream that this organ was implicated in the least; and yet, the whole difficulty is to be found, or is really, *there.* To such an extent does this masking of disease prevail, that, in the language of the celebrated John Hunter, "the organ secondarily affected (in this case the head) sometimes seems to suffer more than the organ to which the disturbance had first been directed."

Now, this sympathy, which exists between the stomach and the head, is but one case of the many which occur in the animal economy. The want of that due regard which should be paid to this sympathetic action between various organs of the body, often misleads even the medical practitioner; much more, the uninitiated in medical science. As a consequence of not comprehending the extent of this sympathetic action, the whole disturbance, or disease, is referred to the organ symptomatically affected, and the remedies are, consequently, addressed to an organ which is not diseased, and both disease and unhappiness are augmented.

A *lung* may be affected, and the cause may not be in the chest; or, the brain may seem really diseased, and yet, the whole difficulty may arise from disordered digestion. There may be no signs in the organ first affected, and hence we often have to seek for the disease or disturbance elsewhere than where the *symptoms* are.

The organs of digestion are usually very much oppressed. As a general thing, all *sedentary* persons take more food than nature requires, and they often take such a quality, as well as quantity, as is indigestible. Oppression, lassitude, hypochondria, headache, and a thousand real, or imaginary diseases, are the consequence; and, at the same time, any and every cause is assigned but the true one; and every remedy is resorted to, but the right one.

Take any sedentary man who is in the habit of eating three full meals each day, and diminish the quantity of his food one-half, or cut off his *suppers* merely, and he will be a great gainer. From being nervous, peevish, irritable, and listless, he will become calm, patient, and active.

One of the remarkable cases of this effect of a diminished diet, we have in the case of Cornaro, the noble Venetian. But let any one of nervous habit, or in the least disposed to indigestion, live in a very simple manner, say on bread and water, or gruel — he will find a very sensible diminution of nervous irritability, and often, in a short time, those clouds of gloom and dark forebodings of the future, which had hung around him, will be dispersed, and he will appear cheerful and happy. Let not this remedy appear so simple that the restless, nervous invalid shall be disposed to treat it as Naaman did that of the prophet; if he does, we may well say to him as the servant of the Syrian general to his master, if we had prescribed "some great thing," wouldst thou not have done it? How much more when we say, abstain only, and be well!

The object of these remarks is to direct attention to the digestive organs, and to convince him whose health begins to be impaired, that the seat of the difficulty is much more frequently *there* than he has been wont to suppose, and that his enjoyment depends on his stomach.

A clergyman called on a physician for advice respecting a troublesome inflammation of the eye. After a careful examination into his habits and manner of living, and the character of the disease, he was advised to change some of them, and especially to curtail his diet. Not thinking much of such a simple prescription, he went to another physician, who directed him to apply lotions to the eyes and nostrums to the stomach. After teasing the organs of vision with collyria, and the alimentary canal with physic, for a considerable time, and bleeding his purse sufficiently to *feel* it, and getting no better, he at length concluded he would try the first-named prescription. Soon, his eyes recovered their accustomed health. Like the "tenth cleansed leper," he "returned" to thank him who had recommended what was so simple, and yet so effectual. "But who would have thought," said he, "that inflammation of the eye would have been caused by what a man put into his stomach?" This unfolds exactly what we mean by these remarks. Disease, or abnormal action in the extremities, or the most distant organ, may be caused by irritation, or disease of the stomach. Every well-informed physician knows that a twinge of the gout may be, and often is, caused by putting improper food, or stimulants, into the stomach. This troublesome complaint usually arises from abusing the stomach. In the same manner rheumatic affections are caused. Nothing is more common than for *lumbago*, or *sciatica*, to arise from the use of *brandy*. A physician was called to see a patient suffering with this disease. Upon inquiring into his habits, it was found he was in the daily use of brandy. He was advised to leave it off. He did so, and had no return of the disease for five years. He then commenced the use of brandy again. In a short time, the rheumatism returned. It is a well-established fact among medical men, that brandy will cause rheumatism.

But the chief point now under consideration, is the action of the irritated or burdened stomach, and, indeed, the whole digestive apparatus upon the system, producing, by sympathy, through the medium of the nerves, disease in even the most remote parts of the body. These, it is well known, are very common cases, and many clergymen, and other sedentary men, are subject to disease arising from this cause, while they are ignorant of its origin. A hint to the wise is sufficient; and it is, If you would enjoy health, *be abstemious in diet*.

The writer has now under medical treatment a clergyman for disease of the throat and liver, which, he believes, originated in too sedentary habits, and taking too much food, and at improper hours, and of a too stimulating kind. He has, also, an *epileptic* patient whose disease arose, unquestionably, from the same causes. The remark upon "*late suppers*" is of vast importance. It would be far better to take *no supper* than a hearty one, at a late hour.

Most of these statements have been proved both by personal experience, and in medical practice. As illustrations of the sympathetic influence between one portion of the body and another, the following cases may be adduced: A child, six years old, was struck by lightning in one foot, no other part of the body being injured so far as could be discovered. The shoe upon the foot was burned, and the foot itself considerably injured. When fourteen years old, this girl became subject to epileptiform convulsions, which disappeared upon remedies addressed to the injured foot, thus proving that the whole system had become affected by the injury to the foot, though this had healed and appeared perfectly well, and none of the family suspected that the epilepsy resulted from this cause. Another girl had her hand caught in the machinery of a factory, and thereby severely injured. It, however, healed kindly. But three years after the accident, she grew extremely nervous, and finally became subject to spasms and convulsions, all of which disappeared upon opening an issue, or producing irritation in the hand which was originally injured. A familiar illustration of this same character is frequently met with in children who have convulsions, simply from the irritation of the gums in *teething*.

CHAPTER XXII.

Tobacco — Neatness a Gain — The Deacon and the Merchant — Tobacco ruins Health; defiles everything — Its Expense — The Theological Student.

IT is not our object to inquire *when,* or *where* tobacco originated, or was first used, or what amount is raised in, or exported from, the United States. These inquiries may all be pertinent to the historian, the merchant, politician, or political economist. Nor, is it our purpose to speak of its praise, or dispraise, from the time that "king James's counterblast" was blown, down to that of a Southern physician, who has recently come to the rescue in behalf of this "weed."

Our only business with it is, as to its use by clergymen, and other students, and its effects upon their health.

It was well said by Whitefield, that "a clergyman should always be neat." But who ever heard of a tobacco-chewer, or smoker, being neat? On the contrary, who does not know that they, and all that appertains to them, are the essence of filth? Look at the mouth of the smoker or chewer. Who can describe its impurity, its *nastiness?*

A deacon from the country, a professedly good man, and one, too, who gave many "alms," and "built" many "a synagogue," once called upon a wealthy gentleman, in Boston, to beg something for the erection of a church, to which the deacon himself had already contributed "somewhat." The gentleman being engaged for a few minutes, when the deacon entered the counting-room, asked him to take a seat. The deacon abhorred intemperance, but was an excessive tobacco-chewer. In a few moments the gentleman was at liberty, and the deacon presented his request for aid. The gentleman, looking him full in the face, said: "Sir, I have but one rule about such matters, and that is, never to give anything, however good the object may be, when the petitioner is an *intemperate* man." The deacon, not a little excited, replied: "I'm not an *intemperate* man." "You're *not*, are you!" said the merchant, with an air which showed that he knew what he said, and meant not to be diverted, in this case, from his usual course. The deacon reddened, and with vehemence exclaimed: "I tell you, I'm *not* an intemperate man." "*Look at the fire-place*," was the reply of the gentleman. During the few minutes our applicant sat there, he had covered it all over with *tobacco-juice*.

The writer had this story from the gentleman himself, who added, "the deacon left off chewing tobacco from that time."

The reader will pardon this digression, for though

this rencounter was not with a clergyman, yet it was nigh unto it, as it was with a *deacon*. Especially, may we be excused for this wandering from our text, when it shall appear that the same gentleman met with much better success with the deacon, than he did with the clergy, in the following attempt: He, about the same period, having prepared some *resolutions*, condemning the use of tobacco, visited the "Pastoral Association" of congregational ministers, to get the "pastors" to adopt them. He received a hearing — laid the matter fairly before that venerable body — spoke of the great evil attending its use, &c. But, did the ministers adopt the *resolutions?* Or, did they, like the deacon, cease to use the nauseous drug? Neither, by no manner of means. Some of them treated the subject *ludicrously*. One, who then held a commanding position, as chairman of the committee to report upon it, said, this was one of the points in which he "condemned himself in that thing which he allowed."

"The Pastoral Association" of Massachusetts ought to have set a better example.

I have submitted this to the gentleman, who says it is a correct statement. But yesterday, a clergyman called on me for medical advice. He thought he had some symptoms indicating paralysis; and so he had. In describing his case, he said he had, some time since, given up chewing tobacco, and had been using camomile flowers as a substitute. He had had an excellent appetite; and, as he was not aware that his food injured him, he had fully indulged it. Undoubtedly, he had taken too much food; and so he was told.

I mention this case to show how desirable would be the change, in those clergymen, and all others who use tobacco, and who are weak, emaciated, and have but little relish for food.

A number of such I have known, who, upon relinquishing the use of this poisonous narcotic, have found appetite return, with an increase of flesh, and renewed vigor.

Is it not strange that clergymen, — men of sense, as they are generally supposed to be, — men of education and politeness, as they certainly should be; men who are both expected to be, and who ought to be, examples to the flock of Christ, and witnesses for Him in the world; men, whose influence runs through all the woof and web of society, — is it not superlatively strange, that *such* men will defile their own mouths, destroy their teeth, nauseate their stomachs, emaciate their bodies, and in all manner of ways impair their health,— yea, more, soil their neighbors' furniture, and the house of God, and disgust two-thirds of the community, by using this noxious drug, either by chewing or smoking it?

One would suppose that a plant so disgusting that

no living animal will eat it, save the "tobacco-worm" and a species of filthy "goat," would, above all other luxuries, be abominated by Christian ministers!

But, if that which makes a healthy man sick, and is so offensive to others that they can scarcely tolerate it, or those who use it, must be the companion of the public mouth of God to the people in the sanctuary, and the spiritual adviser in their parlors, then, we say, give us back the "Counterblast of king James," and the *penalties* to his laws. Yes, give us back the laws of our "Pilgrim Fathers," and of their immediate descendants, made and enforced, in the early settlement of this country, against such transgressions. Candidly, who would not suppose that its unpleasant smell, its acrid, burning taste, its extreme nauseousness, its vertigo, its cold, death-like sweat, its general prostration of the whole animal man, together with its defiling, polluting effect upon its votary, would be enough, and more than enough, to deter any herald of salvation from touching the unclean thing!

Many clergymen complain that their salaries are small; and it is, unquestionably, but too true. Their salaries *are* small — often too small to afford a comfortable living. But how many clergymen, in America, who have but small salaries, afford the *luxury* of tobacco! Is this right, or just, or honorable to the cloth? Does it not too much resemble a poor man who begs himself, and who sends around his children to beg, and who can scarcely get bread for them, and yet keeps half a dozen great, hungry, lazy dogs, every one of which eats as much as a child?

A student, designing to become a clergyman, once called on me for medical advice. He was young, pale, emaciated, nervous, timorous. It was evident there was a *cause* for such appearance. After several questions, tending to disclose his habits, he was asked if he used tobacco. He answered in the affirmative. How much? he was asked, and in what way? He replied, *Considerable*, and both by chewing and smoking. It was ascertained that he did one, or the other, all the time. He was advised to leave off the use of it. He did so, and recovered his health, without a grain of medicine.

There might be much more said upon this subject, but, as "a word to the wise is sufficient," we shall enlarge no further, save only to add, much of the enjoyment of life is destroyed by the use of tobacco.

CHAPTER XXIII.

Extract from an English writer—Health promoted by Conversation—English Dinners productive of Health—"Take me on Leather"—Clergymen should understand something about the Business of Life—Example of Paul; of the Great Teacher—A Successful Minister.

An English writer declares the fact—that the women of our day do not "converse so much, nor so well, as their grandmothers and mothers," and then attributes it to the multiplicity of studies, and the evening confinement to books and school companions. He says:

"It should be as much a matter of duty and of conscience to insist on out-door exercise, and in-door social recreation, as upon any of the regular exercises of the school-room. School studies should be confined absolutely to school hours. To allow them to encroach upon the later hours of the day, and upon the graceful household duties, and recreations, which either are, or ought to be, provided for every girl at home; in other words, to subordinate the home training to school training, or to intermit the former in favor of the latter, is a most palpable and ruinous mistake. It is bad even in an intellectual point of view.

"To say nothing of other disadvantages, it deprives girls of the best opportunities they can ever have of learning that most feminine, most beautiful, most useful of all accomplishments—the noble art of conversation. For conversation is an art, as well as gift. It is learned best by familiar intercourse between young and old, in the leisure unreserve of the evening social circle. But when young girls are banished from this circle, by the pressure of school tasks, talking only with their schoolmates till they 'come out' into society, but monopolized entirely by young persons of their own age, they easily learn to mistake chatter for conversation, and 'small talk' becomes for life their only medium of exchange. Hence, with all the intellectual training of the day, there never was a greater dearth of intellectual conversation."

The health of a clergyman is greatly promoted by free conversation with his people. By free conversation is not meant descending to any thing low, or degrading, in word or manner. Some clergymen seem to stand so much upon their dignity, that they seldom or never converse with the mass of their people. This has a pernicious effect upon them, and also upon their parishioners. Some appear to lack the power of making any conversation, and can never speak but with the measured stiffness with which they are accustomed to address their people from the pulpit. This is unfortunate, both for them and for their people.

Social converse greatly promotes health. Even the long sessions of our fathers, in England, at the dinner-table, filled up, as it usually is, with enlivening conversation, promotes digestion and increases health. In this, Americans, and some American clergymen even, are often very deficient.

Others will *make* conversation upon almost any subject. Talk they will, and talk you must. The following illustrates this point: Rev. B. T. Lacy, of Virginia, was one day riding in a stage-coach with a man who seemed utterly averse to conversation. Every conceivable means was adopted to interest and draw out the taciturn stage traveller, but in vain. At last, the man, evidently observing the aim of his companion, spoke out with some abruptness. "*Take me on leather, and then I can talk with you.*" Mr. L. happening to be posted up, to some extent, on the subject suggested, complied with the request, and the result was a very interesting and profitable conversation between the minister and the "tanner."

That minister, or any other professional gentleman, who, when he finds a man that will not converse on theological subjects, can speak about "leather:" agriculture, the arts, education, or any of the ordinary substantial topics of conversation, will be likely to do more good in the end, and draw in more persons to hear the gospel, than he who never converses upon any of these last-named topics; and he will better promote his own health, and the happiness of all concerned, by the latter course.

Pastoral conversation, at a proper time, and in a proper place, is a religious duty, and of the first importance. But, even the truly pious wish to see their pastor, as a man, a sympathizing friend, as well as in the character of an official minister of the gospel. That minister, in this latter half of the nineteenth century, who confines his studies wholly to theological subjects, and his conversation to the *sole* topic of religion, will find himself greatly in arrears in taking that position which he ought to assume, and is expected to fulfil, in the great educational and philanthropic movements of the day. He will also find his opportunities for personally addressing the unconverted and irreligious greatly curtailed by such a course. It is only by the minister's appearing, as an intelligent and well-informed man, that he can win the respect of the man of the world. Let a pastor be well versed in the general topics and science of the day, and he will not be obnoxious to the trite and common expressions, often familiar to the men of the world, such as, "He preaches fine sermons, but he lacks common-sense;" "He is a man of great learning, but he knows nothing of the world;" "He is a mere child in matters of every-day life." Who does not know, such expressions are often made, and that they have an influence adverse to the minister's usefulness; especially, among those who most need religion? Just in proportion as such ideas gain currency in a community, does the minister's influence among worldly-minded and intelligent men diminish.

> "Would I describe a preacher such as Paul,
> Paul should himself direct me,"

in his practice, as well as his teaching. If Paul had not shown himself learned, in his defence before Agrippa, Festus would never have said that "much learning had made him mad." If he could not have *conversed* on tent-making, he would probably never have wrought at that occupation in Corinth. If he had possessed none other than theological knowledge, would he have confounded the philosophic Epicureans and Stoics whom he encountered at Athens, by proving from certain of their own poets that men are "the offspring of God?" Had he been conversant with the prophets of the Old Testament only, would he ever have proved, from one of their own, that the "Cretans were always liars, evil beasts, slow bellies?" Wherever you find him itinerating through the whole then known world, his knowledge of the philosophy of men and things stands out pre-eminently; and, in its proper place, he makes it *tell* upon his hearers, in the great mission of his life, that of preaching the gospel to the Gentiles.

It was thus he labored, by all means, that he might save men, and while able in the Scriptures, exemplary in conduct, and kind in spirit, showed by his daily intercourse that, he was well informed on matters of business and social interest, mingling with the people in all their lawful undertakings. In this he only imitated his Divine Master.

All this tended to promote bodily health and human happiness.

Pastors not only often lose their influence over their parishioners, by failing to cherish and cultivate those amenities and courtesies of common life which all should practise, but they utterly fail to ingratiate themselves into the favor and friendship of others around them; and, consequently, they do not draw in the multitude, that might be induced to attend upon their public ministrations, if they pursued a different course. The clerical recluse is but poorly qualified to gain the hearts of an unbelieving community. They see him only in the pulpit. They hear him only upon solemn subjects, and behold him only with a sedate, or possibly, frowning countenance, and associate him with what is unpleasant and irksome, having no tendency to promote innocent social enjoyment and health. Let him come into their families and stores, and business matters, and show them that he has a heart to feel, and a mind to comprehend, and a tongue to express, his views and feelings upon every-day life, and a new phase will come over the people who formerly stood aloof from all his instructions.

Such was the procedure of our Great Teacher. He

cast about him for familiar illustrations, and gathered them from the every-day avocations of life; from the characteristic traits of humanity, the lilies of the field, the birds of the air, the fisherman's net. Though he had all power, yet no man ever associated more than he did with the poor, the sick, the hungry, and the wicked, to do them all good.

There is something in this associating with men in their various attitudes and conditions, in this mingling in these innocent social pleasures, which wonderfully promotes elasticity of spirit, enjoyment of mind, and vigor of body. While he who rarely leaves his study, but to perform his public services, will grow faint in spirit and weak in body; the clergyman who associates with his people in a kind, friendly manner, rejoicing with those who rejoice, and mourning with those who mourn, will renew his vigor, instead of becoming more and more debilitated.

One of the best pastors I ever knew was always among his people; he "knew the state of his flock," was ever ready to converse, was admired and loved by all. His church was ever full, and receiving additions almost constantly. It was the wonder of many how his ministry came to be so successful. It was not by his pulpit services, but rather by his daily converse with the people in their home avocations. In visiting and conversing with them, he preserved his health and found true enjoyment.

CHAPTER XXIV.

Historical Sketch of the Union of Theology and Medicine—The Jewish Priests made Doctors—Luke and the Apostles follow the example of Christ, their Master—Medical Books written by Clergymen before the sailing of the "Mayflower"—Clerical Missionary Physicians—John Wesley's Primitive Physic.

SEVERAL causes have already been named which have had their influence upon the health of the clergy in these modern days. It remains now to mention one more, and this is a present want of that medical, physiological and hygienic knowledge, which the fathers in the ministry possessed, and which laid the foundation of their long-continued and vigorous health.

This idea may never have occurred to our modern clergy, as a fact, and, as possibly some may be led to doubt the truth of the statement, it may not be amiss to offer some data upon which it is founded.

Commencing then, where, above all others, clergymen ought to begin, at the pure fount of Inspiration, let the Jewish Lawgiver first be selected. We are informed that "Moses was learned in all the wisdom of Egypt." And what *was* "all the wisdom of Egypt?" We are assured of one branch of it, to wit, that "the physicians," whom Joseph ordered to embalm Jacob, his father, and who afterwards embalmed Joseph himself, were skilled in this art beyond all their fraternity in modern times. Was not Moses, himself, then, skilled in the learning of the Egyptian physicians? And, might not this skill, well applied, have been a reason why, at the "age of 120 years, his eye was not dim, nor his natural force abated?" But we are not left to a mere inference to arrive at this fact. Clemens Alexandrinus expressly asserts, "that Moses was taught Arithmetic, Geometry, *Physic*, Music and Hieroglyphics," to which Philo adds, "Astronomy."

But even if inspired "Stephen" had not said, he was "learned in all the wisdom of the Egyptians," and the "fathers" had not borne their testimony to his having studied "*physic*," no one could read the hygienic rules which he prescribed for the Israelites, and witness with what consummate wisdom he made the "Priests," physicians, and laid it upon them, as a part of their official duty, to *diagnosticate* disease,—to say, what was curable and what incurable, and to separate those who could not be relieved from those who could, and from the healthy, generally, without believing that he was learned in the medical science of Egypt. If it be said that, he ordained "these statutes," because they were of *Divine* appointment, then the argument for the union of the priest's and physician's office, in the same class of men, is the more powerful and conclusive, as coming directly from heaven. It would not be at all singular, if the *heathen*, who represent the healing art as coming directly from the gods, by making Æsculapius, the son of Apollo, their god of medicine, derived this knowledge from the fact of Moses, the Lawgiver of God, constituting the priests, the physicians of those early days; especially, when we consider that a large part of their mythology was originally drawn from Bible-facts. They *believed* their physicians sprung from the gods; we *know* God made the Jewish priests the physicians of their day.

Come we forward to the New Testament dispensation:—we find Christ himself, the great Physician, "healing all manner of sicknesses and diseases among the people," and when he commissioned his Apostles, and sent them out to preach, he included in that commission the following, "as ye go, heal the sick."

The Apostle Paul calls "Luke the beloved physician," and though Luke was not an Apostle, yet he was an evangelist, and the writer of the Gospel bearing his name, and of "the Acts of the Apostles."

Paul was brought up at the feet of a Doctor of the Jewish law, and we have as much evidence that he was an M. D. as a D. D. But whether he were either, or neither, we know that he prescribed " wine for Timothy for his often infirmities."

Leaving the age of the Apostles, and coming down to the earlier centuries of the Christian Church, we find a large proportion of the clergy skilled in the healing art; and, it may be safely asserted, that a majority of the medical works published in Christian lands, from the days of the Apostles down to the sailing of the "Mayflower," from Delft Haven, freighted with the Pilgrims, were written by Presbyters, Ecclesiastics, or Clergymen. As this assertion may seem to need proof, a few examples will be here adduced.

Gregory Abulfaragius was a physician, and ordained bishop of Guba, also, Bishop of Lacabena and Aleppo. He died in his sixtieth year, 1284, and his memory, says his biographer, was deservedly honored with the highest encomium, which his nation could bestow.

Claude Achillini, grand-nephew of Alexander, was distinguished for his knowledge of medicine, theology, and jurisprudence.

Lewis Atterbury, LL. D., Chaplain to the Lord Mayor, one of the Chaplains of Princess Anne, was also a physician. His biographer says, "his charitable disposition was strongly displayed in his studying physic for the benefit of the poor, at Highgate, and distributing advice and drugs gratis."

Walter Baley, Fellow and Proctor of New College, Oxford, divided his attention equally between physic and divinity.

Herman Boerhaave, one of the most eminent physicians of the 16th century, was the son of a clergyman, and first educated to the profession of his father, and it was not till after his father's death, that he studied medicine. His productions are standard works down to the present day.

John Bond, born in the 15th century, an eminent "*commentator*," was also an eminent "*physician*."

John Boyss, one of the translators of the Bible under James I., and one of the six who revised the whole translation, the son of a clergyman, was learned in both medicine and theology, and succeeded his father as rector of West Stowe.

Samuel Bradford, Bishop of Carlisle and of Rochester, was also a physician.

Dr. George Cheyne, one of the most eminent physicians that ever lived, and whose medical works have been held in high estimation for nearly two hundred years, was first educated as a clergyman.

Christopher Codrington, educated at Christ church, Oxford, in 1689, Fellow of All Saints, and almost the only man who manifested a true missionary spirit, of his day, and made large appropriations to propagate the Gospel in foreign parts, was equally learned and skilled in theology and physic.

John Lugo, a Jesuit, a Cardinal, and a popular professor of theology for twenty years, at Rome, and, strange as it may seem, an excellent man, in 1650, first introduced the general use of bark into France, whence it received the name of *Jesuit* bark.

Charles Webster, M. D., his biographer says, was a learned physician, educated at St. Andrews, where he also studied divinity. He practised medicine, and lectured on chemistry and materia medica at Edinburgh, and was minister of the Scottish Episcopal congregation at Carubber's-close, and afterwards at St. Peter's chapel, Boxborough place. He lived many years highly respected, and did much good.

George Leopold Cuvier, a peer of France, was educated a Lutheran clergyman, and amidst all the honors of the greatest naturalist, and while professor of Comparative Anatomy at *Jardin des Plantes*, and when the Papacy ruled in France, was a director of Protestant worship. One of his eulogists says of him: "The Christian part of his countrymen rejoiced to see in the labors which constituted his fame, none of those elements of fragility which mark the conclusions of science when opposed to the word of God."

Now, in view of these data, I wish to ask, may it not be reasonably inferred, that one cause of *failure of health*, among clergymen of our day, may be found in the fact, that they have not generally cultivated physiological and medical knowledge, and used hygienic measures, in their own persons, and searched out remedies for disease, as the "Fathers" did? And would it not be a part of wisdom to return to these good customs of the "Fathers," and reunite what men have in a great measure divorced, since the Great Head of the Church joined them together, namely, medicine and theology— or, in other words, seeking the health of body and soul?

This question is asked, because some in our day, among both clergymen and physicians, seem to take it for granted, that there is something wrong, or out of order, or tending to remove the "ancient landmarks," and disturb the old foundations, in a man's being both a clergyman and a physician. At the same time, they admit the wisdom of the "American Board of Commissioners for Foreign Missions," in requiring their missionaries to obtain all the medical knowledge they can, as better qualifying themselves for their duty; and that such men as *Doctors Parker* and *Grant* did more good than they otherwise would, by their knowledge and practice of medicine, while they preached the Gospel. But this, they say, is necessary, and will *do* among the *heathen*. But, pray tell us, why it will not do here? The recent letter of the Rev. Dr. Anderson, the oldest Secretary of the American Board, for a "*Missionary Physician*," stating that "it seems scarcely possible to prosecute much longer the mission among the Nestorians of Koordistan," and also the "*Madura* Mission," unless such men can be sent out, is demonstration of the truth of these remarks.

Rev. Mr. Lindley, of the Zulu Mission says:—"A woman named *Somemay*, the first convert, the widow of a chief, was bitten by a poisonous snake." Mr. Lindley was called on for medicine.

John Wesley, the founder of Methodism (and no man ever preached more than he did), like his Master, took peculiar interest in restoring health to the sick, and has left us, among his various works, one entitled, "Primitive Physic, or an Easy and Natural Method of Curing most Diseases." I have now in my possession a copy of the "Twenty-third edition" of this work, "Revised and Corrected, and republished at Philadelphia, 1793." In the preface, which was written by Mr. Wesley, dated London, June 11th, 1747, there are many valuable remarks, bearing the image and superscription of that wonderful man, and which are well worthy of the perusal of clergymen of our day. The republication, in this country, is directed " to the members of the Methodist Episcopal Church," by the authority of Thomas Coke and Francis Asbury, Bishops of that church. They say, "*Friends and brethren*, the grand interest of your *souls* will ever lie near our hearts; but we cannot be unmindful of your *bodies;* we present to you now, the '*Primitive Physic*,' published by our much honored friend, *John Wesley*. We lay the publication before you, and earnestly recommend it to you."

CHAPTER XXV.

Health of Clergymen's Wives — The Health of a Clergyman's Wife depends much on her Husband — More Clergymen's Wives die than Clergymen — Anxiety, Care, and Cruel Treatment on the part of Parishioners, often a cause — Reflections on this great evil — Want of proper Education a cause — Conclusion with an Eastern Tale.

PERHAPS I cannot close these sketches with a more appropriate topic than the one which stands at the head of this chapter.

It has been said that a clergyman's health depends very much upon his wife. But it may now be remarked that this is one of those rules, which, in common phraseology, may be said "to work both ways." If the health of a minister depends much upon his wife, so does the health of a clergyman's wife depend much upon her husband.

It has been found, upon calculation, that there are many more widowers than widows, in ministers' families. Indeed, so remarkable is this fact, that it has been often made a theme of conversation; and, not long since, one of our religious journals contained a very appropriate article upon this subject.

We all know the fact, and can call to mind, among our acquaintance, many clergymen who have had two, three, and four wives. Such events occurring ordinarily, or what may be called frequently, must depend upon some adequate cause. If (as has been heretofore shown), the anxiety, trials, poverty, ill treatment from parishioners and frequent change of residence are among the chief causes of the failure of clerical health; and, if, the health of clergymen's wives is oftener impaired than their own, and two to one of the wives die in proportion to their husbands, then, it seems to be appropriate to inquire for the causes. Are they to be found in the greater cares, sorrows and trials of the wife, over and above those of her husband? Painful as is this admission, it is believed that the question must be answered in the affirmative; and, if this be so, the sooner it is known to all young ladies, who are candidates for marriage, the better for them, that they may govern themselves accordingly; for, although the Jewish proverb, to wit, that "a young woman," who was a daughter of Abraham, and well taught, and behaved herself becomingly, "was worthy to marry a priest," was complimentary, yet, if the penalty must be so great, as almost certain loss of health, and a premature death, not every one would feel called upon to perform so severe a penance; especially, while self-preservation remains the first law of nature, and, certainly, is not incompatible with the law of God.

It is true, *some* must assume these extra responsibilities and dangers; or the Protestant clergy must remain, like the Papal, in a state of celibacy.

I do not remember ever to have heard this argument urged by the Papists against matrimony, amongst their priesthood; but, still, I cannot but believe it to be a more valid one, than any which they are accustomed to employ.

If it be said, the duty of a clergyman's wife is only that of every other good wife to her husband, — She is married to the minister only, and *she* is not installed over the parish, but her husband, &c.,—in reply, it may be said, All this is literally true, but practically false: for, she is considered, equally with her husband, the property of the parish. She is expected not only to preside over all of his domestic concerns — to visit all the families of the parish — to be the leader at all the "female prayer meetings," and "Mothers' Associations," and the President, Treasurer, or Directress-general of all the "Ladies' Benevolent and Beneficent Societies;" but, also, to be the model for all other females, in dress, demeanor, and economy—to be at the bed of all who are afflicted with sickness — to attend every marriage and every funeral — in a word, to be omnipresent, at home and abroad, in private and in public.

No woman, unless she be made of iron, or of India-rubber, can accomplish all this.

Woman has her sphere, and in it, she is all-powerful; but it is not as a public functionary. At home, in her appropriate place, and her divinely appointed place, she exercises a sweet control over her husband, children, and domestics, which perfumes the whole atmosphere with the fragrance of her graces. There, she is the " wise woman, seeking flax and wool, and working willingly with her hands, so that she is not afraid of the snow, for all her household are clothed with scarlet." There, she dwells in peace, and shines in modesty. There, she rules her household well, having her children in perfect subjection. This is *the* place for woman's influence.

But when she is withdrawn from this, her legitimate sphere, and forced into public notoriety, whether it be in the form of " Women's Rights" measures, technically so called, or to attend "Anti-Slavery Conventions," or to speak at public religious assemblies, she loses her womanly characteristics, and becomes either the Virago, or the Amazon, or loses her health from a sense of modesty and the deprivation of all that characterizes the true woman. In any, and all of these movements, and in whatever goes to unsex her, or strip her of her instinctive modesty, there is such violence done to her nature, that she never, or rarely, recovers from it.

And even if this were not the case, she could never attend to her domestic affairs, as a woman of discretion ought, and, at the same time, manage those of a convention, church, or parish. This would be a harder task than Pharaoh laid upon the Israelites. Yet this, in the main, is what every parish expects of the minister's wife. This demand is unwise, unjust, and consequently wicked. Hence, I have often thought of the following sentence, which I once heard a clergyman use in an address to a parish, upon the initiation of a pastor. "Remember," said he, "that you settle this *man*, as your minister, not his *wife*." Whether this people remembered it or not, I am not apprised. But it may be stated as a general fact, that few parishes do.

It is no marvel that clergymen's wives " break down " (as the expression is), when it is considered how much they are compelled to do. Usually they have as many children as other women; and, generally, they entertain as many " strangers " as others do. Imagine the minister in his study, where he must not be disturbed. The "help," if she has "help," which many have not, and can but ill afford, is busy in the kitchen. The good woman is in the " nursery," with three or four children, all of whom demand a mother's constant care. The door-bell rings, and Mrs. H——, the deacon's wife, and Miss H——, the deacon's daughter, enter. The " maid of all work " has run to the door, and ushered them into "the sitting-room," and then informed her mistress. But **how** can she leave her children, when one is but half dressed, and another is sick, and a third is crying for this or that? Then she must "change her dress," as she cannot appear before Mrs. H. and her daughter, occupying the station which she does, and they do, in the church and parish, in her nursery apparel. The dress is changed in a hurry — the children still crying, and she meets her company, with her nerves all excited, and her heart palpitating.

The ordinary compliments are passed, and Mrs. H—— says: "I called early this morning to inquire about the new private school, which has just been opened in the village, as I understood you thought of sending your eldest daughter. I concluded, upon consulting with the deacon, that if you knew enough about the school to send your daughter, you could inform me what I had better do about sending H——. I was sorry to trouble you about it, but I felt as though I could not send her, until I knew your mind about the matter." In fine, the teacher is sufficiently recommended, and Mrs. H—— concludes she will send H—— to the school.

They have just arrived at the door to leave, when Esquire T. walks up, and enters. He says: "I called to see Mr. M—— a moment, about the *wood*, of which he spoke to me. I suppose he is in his study at this hour, and does not wish to be disturbed. Perhaps you would do just as well, ma'am. I was going to ask whether you would have it *half* pine, or not? *I* burn more pine than hard wood."

The lady replies: "I heard my husband say, he preferred the *hard* wood, as it lasts so much longer." The wood question is soon settled, and Esquire T. is about leaving, when up comes a young man, a stranger, with rosy cheeks, and beard upon the upper lip, and with many bows and scrapes, and a good degree of confidence, enters, and introduces himself as Mr. ———, a *music*-teacher from the city.

Addressing himself to Mrs. M. as the lady of the house, whom he could not well mistake (as he heard Esquire T. pronounce her name when he departed, saying "good morning"): "I was informed by Mrs. G., one of your people, that she thought your two daughters ought to take *music* lessons, as they were old enough, and the minister's children, above all others, ought to learn *music*, as it is so important that *they* should be able to sing; and, as we pay him a good salary,— six hundred dollars a year,— he can certainly well afford to give them such an education as should be an example to his people." Mrs. M. concludes, very much to the disappointment of the music-master, that she will not have her daughters take lessons yet, as they are young, and she does not feel that she can afford it; and the city music-teacher leaves.

But as he withdraws, she says to herself, What

could Mrs. G. mean by speaking so, about our salary? Does she not know that we cannot live upon six hundred dollars, and never have lived upon it? She must know it.

The children (in the plight in which Mrs. M. left them, when the first callers came), had now remained so, for an hour or more; and, just as she was approaching the nursery to look after them, Betty appeared, with anxious countenance, and inquired, "What were we to do about *dinner?* The market-man had not come, and they were to have company to dine." "Oh! dear!" exclaimed Mrs. M., "what more can I do?" At this crisis, the door-bell rang again, and Miss P——, the dress-maker, made her appearance. Betty ushered her into the "sitting-room," when she commenced as follows: "Mrs. B., the landlord's wife, at the hotel, was very much pleased with Mrs. M.'s new dress, last Sabbath, and she (the dress-maker) was going to the city with her, to get just such an one. *Where* did she get it? and what was the *price?* Did she get it *cut* in the city? Was it a *Paris* pattern? She never *did* see a dress so beautiful, and fit so well!"

Betty hastened to the nursery to inform her mistress, and to request her immediate presence, as the dress-maker was in a hurry; for they had been delayed so long already, that the cars would start and leave them.

But Mrs. M. had found the children in such condition that she could not leave them immediately; so, as the dress-maker could not wait, she had to leave without the necessary information.

When Miss P. communicated her ill-success to the landlord's wife, the latter was quite discomposed. Her visit to the city would be of no use, as she might hunt from street to street, and store to store, and spend the whole day without at last finding the one where Mrs. M. bought her dress; and if she found it, of what use would it be, unless she could know where it was cut? She did wish their minister's wife could leave her children a minute. They were no better than other people's children, if they were the minister's, though their mother thought they were. She hasn't a spark of politeness about her, if she is the minister's wife. She don't know what good manners are; if she did, she wouldn't treat her in this way, when her husband paid ten dollars a year towards the minister's support. It was astonishing how ungrateful some creatures were. Her husband should leave that meeting, that he should. She'd let the parson know that."

All this was soon carried to the ears of Mrs. M. and her husband, by Miss Spinster, who boarded at the hotel, and who was a very good friend of the minister and his wife. "I am *so* good a friend to you," said she, "that I can't hear such things said about our minister's wife without telling you on't. Some people keep everything from the minister till all the parish get against him, and then he has to leave, and makes a great stir, and we're all broke up, and have to get a new minister. But that was never *my* way. I don't think it's *Christian*. When I hear anything against my minister or his wife, I always come right straight off and tell him on't: and I think, if everybody'd do so, it would save a great deal of trouble: because, you know, he ought to know what the people say about him, and who are his friends, and who are his enemies.

"But the landlord's wife is dreadfully put out: and there's another thing, now I'm here, which I 'spose I ought to tell you. My Aunt Q——, you know, she's an old lady, and been a leading member in the church a great many years, long before you came here, and she's got money, and paid ever so much to help the parish along. She says 'she's very sorry you offended the landlord's wife so, for though she's heard that he didn't keep a very orderly house, and sold liquor, and had dancing parties, and other company from the city, yet he helped support you; and we can't afford to lose any more from the parish now, since so many have gone away of late.' She says 'she don't think you meant to offend Mrs. B., but you didn't consider how hard it comes upon a few of us who have to bear "'the heat and burden'" of supporting you. It didn't used to be so, when our last minister was here (dear man), and his wife too! What a woman she was! She loved everybody, and visited the poor as well as the rich. But they got kind of discouraged, and a richer society gave him a call, and so he left us; and my aunt says, 'we never got along so well since; and she don't know what we're coming to now, if the landlord won't pay any more.'

"Besides, my aunt, (she's had to pay so much here a great while, that she keeps the run of things pretty well,) says, 'she's heard of two or three families, down to t'other end of the parish, which are going to leave because you don't visit 'em more. They never see you only at church, on Sundays, no more than though you wasn't our minister; and they say, they should think Mrs. M. might call once in a while, if you can't.'"

Thus, Miss Spinster run on, till the company came, (a neighboring clergyman and his wife and daughter,) and then staid to dine.

It was Friday, and the Preparatory Lecture came in the afternoon, and the visiting clerical brother was to preach it, as used to be the general practice in olden time in the State of "steady habits."

Mrs. M., poor woman, though she had not had a moment's rest, prepared herself to attend the lecture, as well as she could, which was, however, but thinly attended by the church.

The poor pastor's health, and, especially, that of his

wife, began to fail: and when, at night, they came to retire, she could suppress her sorrow no longer. Nature was overpowered — the drops of this last day's trial had caused the cup to overflow — the heart was breaking, and she burst forth in a flood of tears.

When nature was a little relieved by the breaking up of this fountain of scalding tears, Mrs. M. said: "Oh! dear husband, what shall we do? I have labored and suffered, and tried to do the best I could, till I feel as though I can do no more. I have neglected my children, neglected my household affairs, and neglected you, all to try to perform my duty to this people, to do them good."

In a few days, Mrs. M. was taken sick. It was not sickness of the body only, but that, also, of "a wounded spirit," which none can bear. It was a low, lingering fever, with delirium, such as attends extreme exertion and overaction of both mind and body. It was her *last* sickness, — that, by which, she was taken home to her Father's house above. It was death from a *broken heart!* — death from a fastidious, ungrateful, wicked people. And when the day of final reckoning comes, on whose heads will the blood of this poor, innocent, devoted, but unfortunate wife and mother, fall?

How often do parishes, members of churches, and sisters even, in such churches, by their exactions plat crowns of thorns for those dear pastors' wives, who have labored to the utmost of their strength, for their good! When the history of these cases shall be written out, and the sufferings of pastors' wives shall be made known, the world will be astounded, and there will be no occasion to ask, *why* so many wives of clergymen have gone down to an early and premature grave.

The labors devolving upon these ladies are altogether too arduous; the expectations too great from them; and, when it is impossible to answer these unreasonable demands, the fault-finders are outrageously cruel. The task imposed upon females among savage tribes is less burdensome, less exhausting to body and mind, than that laid upon clergymen's wives in our civilized and nominal Christian society, inasmuch as among the former, it is but the drudgery of the body, to which they were early accustomed, while among us, it is a perpetual strain upon both body and mind.

As the requirements and expectations of parishes now are — under the many foolish, absurd, luxurious customs of society, as now existing — her services, of both body and mind, of soul and spirit, would task to the uttermost the strength of a giant and the powers of an angel. To attempt to meet these unrighteous demands can be compared to no service, but that of the poor horse in the tread-mill, to grind, and grind, and know no end till death. If the minister, in view of his own arduous duties, is compelled to exclaim, "Who is sufficient for these things?" well may she, in view of hers, as she bears at home and abroad "a wounded spirit," till the silver cord of life is about being loosed, cry out, "These are the wounds which I received among my professed friends—these, the reward of my fidelity, my Christian efforts to do them good!"

It is these little annoyances, these perpetually repeated trials, driving the life-blood of the vital spirits to the citadel, which destroy the happiness and cause many a minister's wife to droop and die in early life.

Another cause of this great and early mortality (and which might have been named first,) is, the physical training of the girls who become these clergymen's wives. Instead of being trained to endurance, most of them are mere hot-house plants, stimulated by artificial means into a premature development of both corporeal and mental powers: whose self-denial has never been called into requisition — whose every wish was gratified by fond parents, while they remained at home — whose warm affection, when they entered into the family-relation, never anticipated the crushing sorrow which soon overtook them. This was the bitter root which rendered the burden of their sorrows so intolerable.

Would parents, instead of training their daughters to be indolent — to get a little smattering of French and Latin—a little music—to embroider a little muslin—to take an airing in an easy carriage—to rise at nine in the morning,—loll about till mid-day, make fashionable calls until five in the afternoon—to flirt and coquette till midnight—instead of these, and hundreds of other such like follies, would they teach their daughters to be economical, industrious, early risers, to exercise in doors and out of doors; to bear disappointments—to understand that life is not all sunshine, and, above all, that it is through great tribulation that any are to enter into the kingdom of heaven, they would bear the toils of real life with stronger fortitude, and more seldom fall a prey to such diseases as now frequently put a period to their lives. This picture may appear to be overdrawn to those who live in a city; but, it is believed, it will not be so considered by those who dwell in the country.

It has been our object to illustrate the condition of all classes in this book, by following up the subject from one profession. That profession has been the clergy. The reason has already been stated, to wit, the unbounded influence of the clerical profession.

We are now done, and the book is committed to the public. May it do good. If so, the end had in view by the writer will be answered.

As an appropriate conclusion, comprehending the sources of the happiness of life, we conclude with the following Eastern Summary of enjoyment:

"Dabschelim, King of the Indies, possessed a library so large, that it required a hundred Brahmins to revise and keep it in order, and a thousand dromedaries to carry the books. As he had no intention to read all it contained, he commanded his Brahmins to make extracts from it, for his use, of whatever they judged most valuable, in every branch of literature. These doctors immediately undertook to form such an abridgment; and after twenty years' labor, composed from their several collections a small Encyclopædia, consisting of twelve thousand volumes, which thirty camels could scarcely carry. They had the honor to present this to the King, but were astonished to hear him say, "That he would not read a work that was a load for thirty camels." They then reduced their extracts, so that they might be carried by fifteen; afterwards, by ten; and then by four; and then by two dromedaries. At last, no more books were left than were sufficient to load a mule of ordinary strength. Unfortunately, Dabschelim had grown old, while his library was abridging, and did not expect to live long enough to read to the end this master-piece of learning. The sage Pilpai, his vizier, therefore, thus addressed him:

"Though I have had an imperfect knowledge of the library of your sublime Majesty, yet I can make a kind of analysis of what it contains — very short, but extremely useful. You may read it in a minute; yet it will afford you sufficient matter for meditation during your whole life."

At the same time, the vizier took the leaf of a palm-tree, and wrote on it, with a pencil of gold, the four following maxims:

"1st. In the greater part of science, there is only this single word, *perhaps;* in all history, but these phrases: —They were born; they were watched; and they died.

"2d. Take pleasure in nothing which is not commendable; and do everything which you take a pleasure in. *Think* nothing but what is true; and do not utter all you think.

"3d. Oh! ye Kings! subdue your passions; reign over yourselves, and you will consider the government of the world only as recreation.

"4th. Oh, ye Kings! Oh, ye Nations! listen to a truth ye can never hear too often, and which sophists pretend to doubt. There is no happiness without virtue, and no virtue without the fear of God."

THE END.

תמ 6-3 77

RETURN TO: **CIRCULATION DEPARTMENT**
198 Main Stacks

ALL BOOKS MAY BE RECALLED AFTER 7 DAYS.
Renewals and Recharges may be made 4 days prior to the due
Books may be renewed by calling 642-3405.

FORM NO. DD6 UNIVERSITY OF CALIFORNIA, BERK
50M 5-02 Berkeley, California 94720–6